In our Hispanic culture, we are known for placing great value on faith, hard work and family. But Hispanics, just like men and women in every other culture, are usually uncertain on how to be successful in the most important human relationship. I recommend *Marriage on the Rock* to everyone who wishes to improve marital communication and who would like to meet the needs (even sexual needs) of his or her spouse. It has been said that marriage can be either a little heaven or a lot of hell on Earth. Thank you, Reverend Jimmy and Karen Evans, for writing a book that not only gives us wise and inspired advice but leads us to the Rock—*La Roca, Jesucristo*—who truly wants us all to have not just a little joy in marriage but also marital bliss!

DR. JUAN HERNÁNDEZ
Author, *The New American Pioneers*
Former Cabinet Member under Mexican President Vicente Fox

Marriage on the Rock is at the top of my recommendation list for every person I meet. Whether married, divorced or single, its personal, practical, humorous and scriptural approach is a must-read. As a pastor, *Marriage on the Rock* is one of my most valuable resources. Jimmy and Karen Evans have been called by God to change the tide of divorce in America. Their non-condemning, non-conforming, compassionate and caring message is exactly what our sin-sick society needs. In my opinion, Jimmy Evans is the best there is on the subject of marriage and family.

ROBERT MORRIS
Senior Pastor, Gateway Church
Author, *The Power of Your Words, Dream to Destiny* and *The Blessed Life*

Marriage on the Rock gives plain and tested ways in which simple obedience to biblical teachings, in dependence on the presence of Christ in life, can resolve the entire range of difficulties that plague marriage today. The secret of the advice given is that it really does bring husbands and wives into harmony with the realistic action of God in their hearts and lives. It tells them how to find the kingdom of God right where they are.

DALLAS WILLARD
Professor of Philosophy, University of Southern California
Speaker and Author

MARRIAGE
ON THE
ROCK

JIMMY & KAREN EVANS

Regal

From Gospel Light
Ventura, California, U.S.A.

PUBLISHED BY REGAL BOOKS
FROM GOSPEL LIGHT
VENTURA, CALIFORNIA, U.S.A.
PRINTED IN THE U.S.A.

Regal Books is a ministry of Gospel Light, a Christian publisher dedicated to serving the local church. We believe God's vision for Gospel Light is to provide church leaders with biblical, user-friendly materials that will help them evangelize, disciple and minister to children, youth and families.

It is our prayer that this Regal book will help you discover biblical truth for your own life and help you meet the needs of others. May God richly bless you.

For a free catalog of resources from Regal Books/Gospel Light, please call your Christian supplier or contact us at 1-800-4-GOSPEL or www.regalbooks.com.

Library of Congress Cataloging-in-Publication Data
Evans, Jimmy.
    Marriage on the rock / Jimmy and Karen Evans.
        p. cm.
    ISBN 0-8307-4291-3 (hard cover) — ISBN 0-8307-4292-1 (international trade paper)
    1. Marriage—Religious aspects—Christianity. I. Evans, Karen, 1954- II. Title.
    BV835.E88 2007
    248.8'44—dc22
                                                                        2006039489

1 2 3 4 5 6 7 8 9 10 / 10 09 08 07

Rights for publishing this book in other languages are contracted by Gospel Light Worldwide, the international nonprofit ministry of Gospel Light. Gospel Light Worldwide also provides publishing and technical assistance to international publishers dedicated to producing Sunday School and Vacation Bible School curricula and books in the languages of the world. For additional information, visit www.gospellightworldwide.org; write to Gospel Light Worldwide, P.O. Box 3875, Ventura, CA 93006; or send an e-mail to info@gospellightworldwide.org.

P.O. Box 59888
Dallas, Texas 75229

Phone: 972-953-0500
Fax: 972-953-0384

or visit our website at www.marriagetoday.org

DEDICATION

To our grandchildren—Elle, Abby and Baby Evans—
you bring abundant joy to our lives. We pray blessings on you and
your future families. We also pray that the seed we sow today
through this book and our ministry to marriages will be
harvested by you and your generation.

CONTENTS

SECTION I:

THE MOST IMPORTANT ISSUE
IN MARRIAGE

SECTION II:

THE FOUR FOUNDATIONAL
LAWS OF MARRIAGE

SECTION III:

HOW TO BUILD YOUR
DREAM MARRIAGE

SECTION IV:
FIVE ESSENTIAL SKILLS FOR
MAXIMUM PLEASURE

APPRECIATION

Our special thanks go to the following people:

To our parents, M. L. and Mary Evans and Bud and Jane Smith. Thank you for your love and faithfulness to us and to each other. Your encouragement and support through the years means the world to us. We appreciate the heritage you have worked hard to provide for us and for your grandchildren. You've been wonderful role models and we are very grateful to you.

To the greatest elders, staff and congregation in the world for supporting us and allowing us the time and resources to write this book and to be released to fulfill our ministry to marriages. We are so grateful for the love and support we continually receive from all of you at Trinity Fellowship Church in Amarillo, Texas.

To the board of MarriageToday™—you amaze us with your dedication, love and support. Thank you for your encouragement, prayers and generosity all of these years.

Also, we couldn't forget to recognize the staff at MarriageToday™. You are such a gifted and dedicated group. You are God's gift to us.

Special thanks to our son, Brenton, and the leadership team. You are the backbone of MarriageToday™ and do such a great job. To our assistant, Donna Griffin, thanks for your dedication and hard work for many years. We also want to give special thanks to Bill Greig III, Kim Bangs and the wonderful team at Regal Publishing. You are a joy to work with. Thanks for believing in us.

INTRODUCTION

I (Jimmy) had been sitting behind her all year in sophomore biology class, thinking how pretty she was and wondering if she would go out with me. Finally, late in May, I worked up the courage to ask her to a Three Dog Night concert. Although I had been planning for more than a month, I waited fearfully until the morning of the concert to call her for a date. In spite of my late call, Karen accepted and the rest is history.

After three years of intense and, at times, troubled dating, we were married. At 19 years of age, neither of us had the slightest idea of the skills it takes to succeed in marriage. However, we knew we loved one another and were determined to make a life together. Little did we know the dangers before us.

The first several years could be best described as two parched people trying to satisfy their thirsts in a desert. As most couples do, we married one another because we each believed the other could meet our needs and fulfill our desires. Our courtship had not been perfect, yet we believed that any problems we experienced could be solved if only we were married. So we jumped from the proverbial frying pan into the fire and tied the knot.

As a result of poor premarital preparation, after several years of collective ignorance and immaturity, we found ourselves out of love. Every year, we had fought with increasing frequency and intensity, becoming number and more disillusioned with each quarrel. However, the darkest moments began when we both became convinced we had made a mistake. If only we had chosen the *right* persons to marry, we would not have all of these problems—or so we thought.

I would like to say that our story is about what happened in our lives before we became Christians. Unfortunately, both of us were committed Christians, but we had not been taught how to function in the most important human relationship on Earth. We were victims of a society that requires years of preparation for almost any significant career endeavor but requires no real preparation for one of the most crucial undertakings in life: marriage.

We attended church each Sunday. We believed wholeheartedly in the Bible. Yet we were racing toward marital ruin. The final hurdle in our downward slide came one evening when we were having the same old fight about unmet needs and pet frustrations for what seemed the five-hundredth time.

Karen repeatedly accused me of not loving her as much as I loved my job or golf and of not meeting *her* needs.

Finally, angry, hurt and defensive, I jumped to my feet, pointed a shaking finger toward our bedroom, and shouted, "Go pack your bags, and get out of this house and out of my life!"

As Karen ran out of the room sobbing, I sat down in my chair and stared at the blank television screen as if nothing had happened and as if I could not care less if something had happened. In reality, my heart was being torn in two. I didn't want her to leave, but I did not believe I could take any more of the strife and contention if she stayed. That was one of the lowest points of my life and, without a doubt, the lowest point in our marriage.

While I recovered from the fight in the living room and contemplated my options, Karen cried in the bedroom. She felt the same as I did. She cared deeply for me and cherished many of the memories of our lives together, yet she had lost respect and much of her affection for me.

I began to rehearse what I would do and what she probably would do if we broke up. The more I thought about it, the more I hurt. I didn't want to lose her, but I didn't know how to keep her. Fortunately, two things happened that would be instrumental to the healing and restoration of our marriage:

I broke. For the first time ever, I realized that I was wrong and could see how bad of a husband I was. It was like scales fell from my eyes and I could see myself as I really was—a very selfish and dominant man.

Also, for the first time, I humbled myself and confessed my weakness and need for God's help.

For years, I had been unwilling to accept responsibility for any of the problems with our marriage. When Karen and I fought, I always found a way to make it look as if it were her fault. But that evening, I was overwhelmed with the reality that I didn't know *how* to be a husband. This realization was a stark contrast to the overbearing arrogance and chauvinism that had characterized my life up to this moment.

As the truth concerning our problems began to sink into my heart, I was reminded of a Scripture concerning the Holy Spirit that I had read just that morning:

> But the Counselor, the Holy Spirit, whom the Father will send in my name, will teach you all things and will remind you of everything I have said to you (John 14:26, *NIV*).

As clearly as my own shortcomings were being exposed that evening, the Lord spoke to my heart that He was the solution. Through the Lord bringing this verse to my mind, I began to realize that He was present in my life to teach me *all things*.

Those two words, *all things*, kept echoing through my mind until they finally sunk in. If the Holy Spirit was sent to teach me *all things*, then He could teach me how to be a husband!

So, first of all, I understood the reality that He was with me to help me. Then, second, I asked Him to teach me. By faith, I asked the Holy Spirit to help me be the husband I needed to be. Alone in the living room, I got out of my chair and fell to my knees.

"Holy Spirit," I whispered, choked with emotion, "Jesus said He sent You to teach His followers all things. I am asking You to show me how to be a husband, because I don't know how, and no one has ever taught me. Please help me to learn to love Karen as I should. I am so sorry for all of the things I have done to damage our marriage and her. Please forgive me, and help me. In Jesus' name, amen."

As I got up and sat down again in my chair, I knew something was happening within me. It was not some hyper-spiritual or "spooky" experience. Nevertheless, something was happening inside me. I was not only recognizing how wrong I had been in our marriage but, also, I was willing to admit it. That was a miracle!

God began a work that night of bringing truth and humility into my heart, preparing me to learn what He was about to teach me.

The contents of this book are a result of what God has shown Karen and me about marriage. In this spiritual-education process, God healed our marriage and gave us a love for one another far beyond any we had ever known or imagined. Today, after more than 33 years of marriage, not only are we deeply in love, but we also understand how to stay in love. We have learned how to meet one another's needs as we walk through life's seasons and challenges.

In what seems just as much of a miracle, I am now senior pastor of an interdenominational church with more than 8,000 members. I began ministering at Trinity Fellowship Church in Amarillo, Texas, in 1983 as a marriage counselor. Since then, through personal counseling, marriage seminars, books, audio and video resources, and our national television ministry, Karen and I have had the privilege of helping many individuals and couples succeed in marriage.

We are dedicated to helping people build strong and healthy marriages. Together, we host a nationally broadcast television program called *MarriageToday*™. We also founded a national marriage ministry based in Dallas, Texas, that bears that same name. God has not only blessed our marriage, but He also has blessed us with the opportunity to share with many others the wonderful truths we have learned and experienced.

This book is offered as a tool to help and encourage you in marriage. We pray that you will be blessed by what you read and that whether you are married, separated, divorced, widowed or single, you will find God's perfect will for your life and be able to enjoy His will in a secure and satisfying relationship.

To help you enjoy this book and receive its message, we have chosen to write in a casual, personal and reader-involved style. We pray the truths delivered through these stories and experiences will empower your spirit, encourage your heart, and enlighten your mind.

Jimmy Evans

* * *

Jimmy's description of our courtship and marriage is pretty accurate—he's just kind in the fact that he focused on his shortcomings and not mine. I (Karen) had my share of problems, just as he did. As much as he was dominant and chauvinistic, I was insecure and manipulative. If he pushed, I reacted—often quietly, but nevertheless just as strongly and just as damagingly. I was mentally so twisted—so insecure. I didn't believe Jimmy really loved me and I certainly couldn't believe God did. I was unlovable and unworthy of anything better in my life.

The night our world came crashing down around us, I ran to our room and flung myself on our bed. My heart was broken. Jimmy didn't want me or our marriage anymore (or so I thought), and my life was over. Little did I know that as I was pouring my broken heart out to God, He was dealing with Jimmy in the other room.

I had asked God for years to change Jimmy. There were so many things I had loved about him, but not the arguing—not the accusations—not the put-downs. The feelings of love and affection I had once had for him were dead—killed by the anger, resentment and overwhelming hurt that I had endured for years.

When Jimmy came and apologized to me, after telling me to leave, that was the first time he had apologized in the seven years we had been together. I was surprised but very skeptical that any real change had taken place in his heart.

As the days and weeks began to go by, I could see a change in Jimmy. He was softer and kinder to me and he wasn't hurling angry or hurtful words toward me anymore. Little by little, the affection and the love began to stir in both of our hearts. God was doing a miracle and we were falling in love again.

Every day I would get up early and spend time with the Lord. As I read the Bible, God was showing me through the Word how much He loves me and how He sees me. Believe me—He saw me very differently than I saw myself. The unworthiness and insecurities that I felt began to melt away. God was healing my heart and my mind.

My issues were different from Jimmy's, but the same Holy Spirit was healing us both and setting us both free. That was almost 30 years ago and now when I think back on it, it's hard to believe how we both used to be. We are so in love—so proud and respectful of each other—so thankful that we stayed together and worked through the tough times.

I still have my quiet time every morning. We wouldn't be where we are today if we didn't each make that a priority. That time with the Holy Spirit every morning—that's where the real power comes from and Jimmy and I both know that.

You might feel that your situation is too far gone—that there's no love left and no desire to be together. We understand that, because we were there. But trust me—God can do the impossible. If you yield to Him and let Him be the third person in your marriage, He will surprise you and will do more than you ever thought possible. That is our prayer for you as you read this book.

Karen Evans

SECTION I

THE MOST IMPORTANT ISSUE IN MARRIAGE

FINDING THE ROCK

For they drank from the spiritual rock that accompanied them,
and that rock was Christ.
1 CORINTHIANS 10:4, *NIV*

On the last and greatest day of the Feast, Jesus stood and said
in a loud voice, "If anyone is thirsty, let him come to me and drink.
Whoever believes in me, as the Scripture has said, streams of
living water will flow from within him.
JOHN 7:37-38, *NIV*

Then Jesus declared, "I am the bread of life. He who comes to me will never go
hungry, and he who believes in me will never be thirsty."
JOHN 6:35, *NIV*

The most important Scriptures you will read in this book are those above. At first glance, they may not seem pertinent for a couple searching for answers in their marriage or for a lonely single person seeking that special lifetime relationship; but, actually, they are invaluable for these very people.

The most important information you will ever read in this book—or in any other book—concerning success and fulfillment in marriage is found in this chapter. Sound pretty sure of ourselves, do we? Well, *you* be the judge of whether we're right or wrong. Just do us and yourself a favor: If you don't read anything else or remember anything else in this book, *please* read and remember the information in this chapter.

Let us begin by asking you a question, and we want you to think about your answer and be honest: *Who meets your deepest needs?* In other words, on a daily basis, on whom do you rely the most and to whom do you go first to get your deepest needs met?

Before you answer, let us define "deepest needs" and give you a list of the most common sources for the meeting of those needs. Then it will be easier for you to understand what we want you to see.

Although each person has particular areas of desire or certain preferences that are important to him or her and may not be to someone else, all of us have certain needs in common. Those common needs are your "deepest needs." We're not talking about physical needs, such as food, oxygen or sleep. Rather, we're talking about needs that transcend the physical, going deep into one's heart and soul. Each person's craving for those things is every bit as real as the built-in appetite for food.

The four basic needs that all human beings are instinctively motivated to satisfy all of their lives are:

1. *Acceptance:* knowing you are loved and needed by others
2. *Identity:* knowing you are individually significant and special
3. *Security:* knowing you are well protected and provided for
4. *Purpose:* knowing you have a reason for living. In the case of Christians, this means knowing that God has a special plan for your life.

Whether you have consciously realized it or not, these needs have been motivating you throughout your life. All of us are driven in some significant way to find an avenue in life to satisfy these needs. We are as strongly driven emotionally to satisfy them as we are to find the right food for our stomachs when we are hungry.

These needs are *deep needs, not wants.*

Now, let us give you the list of the most common resources people seek for the fulfillment of their deepest needs, although these are not in the same order for everyone:

1. Yourself
2. Spouses
3. Friends
4. Children

5. Employers and/or work, jobs or careers
6. Churches and pastors
7. Parents
8. God
9. Money/material possessions
10. A combination of two or more of the above

After you have read this list carefully and have thought seriously about these things, try to answer honestly the question we asked earlier.

Who Meets Your Deepest Needs?

In your everyday life, whom or what do you seek first and most to fulfill your needs for acceptance, identity, security and purpose?

You may have realized that the correct answer is something like, "I seek God first and more than anyone else or anything to meet my deepest needs."

The fact is that most people cannot honestly give that answer, and that is the root of their problems.

The reason for this is simple. Most people never come to Jesus to get their deepest needs met, so they never find what they so desperately seek in life or marriage. The Scriptures at the beginning of this chapter tell us that Jesus has the ability to give us spiritual drink and food to satisfy our inner longings. He invites us to come to Him for true fulfillment. He promises us complete satisfaction if we do that.

As a matter of fact, when God created humans in His image, He built in a "Jesus-sized" hole from which all of those deepest needs stem. Because of that, no human being or anything else on Earth can satisfy those needs but Jesus. Those needs were designed to draw you to the One whom God intended to fulfill you as a person.

Unfortunately, most people choose to seek inner satisfaction through a "quicker and surer method." They get married and expect their spouses to do for them what only Jesus can do. Or, perhaps, children have grown up being trained to look to their parents for everything. Sometimes, teenagers—especially girls—deliberately have babies, thinking that then they will have someone to love them. Others move from job to job or place to place, seeking possible fulfillment, but these are only diversions. They never satisfy.

The first thing you need to understand in order for *your* marriage to work is this simple truth: *No* human being can meet your deepest needs. *Only* God can. Of course, if you are operating in God's will, you can find someone who will encourage you, or who will be God's vessel to help you experience love in a real way. However, even the most spiritual person on Earth is very mortal and, therefore, quite limited. When you put too much hope in a person, you always are headed for disappointment and, sometimes, even for disaster!

Many marriages end in disillusionment or, even worse, divorce because the parties involved enter the relationship with unrealistic expectations, not because they are evil or even irresponsible. Each expects the other to meet his or her deepest needs. When they realize this is not happening, the real trouble begins.

Whenever a Christian does not allow God to meet his or her deepest needs, that person automatically transfers the expectation for fulfillment to the closest person or resource, the one in whom the most hope has been placed. For most people, that person is a spouse. When the expectation of having deep needs met is transferred to anyone or anything other than God, three main problems are created:

1. You always will be disappointed with the results, no matter how well things go.

2. You will lack the inner resources you need to love others the way you should and to confront life successfully.

3. You almost always will be hurt and offended eventually by the one in whom you invested all your trust, because that one cannot possibly meet your deepest needs.

Sometimes the reaction to these problems is an underlying frustration that is manageable. More often, it is an outward anger that is destructive. God's Word tells us what we can expect if we fall into the trap of trusting anyone or anything but Him to satisfy those needs He placed within us to point us to Him.

He who trusts in his own heart is a fool (Prov. 28:26).

Cursed is the man who trusts in mankind and makes flesh his strength (Jer. 17:5).

He who trusts in his riches will fall (Prov. 11:28).

Compare those warnings with the promises made to those who trust in God:

Blessed is the man who trusts in the Lord and whose trust is in the Lord. For he will be like a tree planted by the water, that extends its roots by a stream and will not fear when the heat comes; but its leaves will be green, and it will not be anxious in a year of drought nor cease to yield fruit (Jer. 17:7-8).

Those who trust in the Lord are as Mount Zion, which cannot be moved, but abides forever (Ps. 125:1).

He who trusts in the Lord will be exalted (Prov. 29:25).

In distinguishing among trusting in people, things or God to meet our deepest needs, there are some insurmountable differences. The contrasts are very clear and unmistakable.

Results of Trusting People or Things, or God

When you trust in people or things:

- Your inner security is dependent upon someone or something you cannot predict or control and whose resources to meet your needs are limited.

- Your ability to give is dependent upon your ability to get from others.

- Your life is filled with an atmosphere of disappointment and frustration.

- Your unrealistic expectations of others create a negative atmosphere of tension in your relationships, if not a compelling force field of pressure that drives other people away from you.

When you trust in God, these are the results:

- Your inner security and strength are dependent upon Him who is totally faithful and who has unlimited resources.

- Your ability to give flows from an inner resource available to you at all times—the Holy Spirit. When others are not giving to you, still you can love them generously, thus endearing yourself to them and strengthening your relationships.

- Your life will be filled with an atmosphere of blessing, satisfaction and optimism.

- Your *realistic* expectations of others draw you closer together with them as you love and give to them of yourself.

When I (Jimmy) married Karen, I did not realize I was expecting things of her that only God could do for me, but I was doing exactly that. She also expected me to give beyond my ability. The beginning of God's being able to heal our marriage came when we both realized that only Jesus was capable of meeting our deepest needs.

We repented to God and to each other for the sin of rejecting Him as our greatest resource and for placing unrealistic expectations on one another. The result was a transformed marriage generated in the lives of two people plugged into the life-giving power of Jesus.

Throughout our marriage since that crossroads evening, we have found that although the Bible was written years ago, its words are still true, because they were inspired by a living God who does not change. When you come to Jesus for a drink of water or a piece of bread, He truly will satisfy you just as the Bible says. Your entire life will change as a result of trusting Jesus daily to meet all your needs, the small ones as well as the deepest ones.

Jesus loves you, and He is the best friend you will ever have. Even as you read this, He is with you, ready to give eternal spiritual bread and water to satisfy your hungry soul. As you pray and read the Word of God daily, you will experience the reality of His presence in your life.

If you will transfer your expectations to Jesus, you will not be disappointed, because He is faithful. He loves you more than you love yourself or anyone else. He wants to meet your needs more than you want them met. There is not a detail of your life He does not know—yet He still loves you.

For the sake of your life and the lives of those around you, trust Jesus to meet your needs. Only a person who trusts in Jesus to this depth can truly have a successful marriage. Once Jesus is working in your life, then everything else can work. When Jesus is not with you, success is impossible.

Have you become disillusioned with life in general or with your spouse in particular?

Are you regularly disappointed because you don't experience the inner joy and fulfillment you desire?

Have you reached the point where you wonder if your marriage can ever work again?

If you answered yes to any of these questions, you have been looking to someone besides Jesus to meet your deepest needs. When you are ready to admit your mistake and come to Him, He is ready to pour out His love and grace in your life.

The source of fulfillment of our deepest needs is the most important factor in marriage. I hope you have made the decision to let Jesus be *your* Rock and your Source and to allow God to cultivate your heart and build your marriage upon His Word.[1]

Note

1. For more information on how to have a personal relationship with Jesus, refer to Appendix I. For more information on how to have your deepest needs met by the Lord on a daily basis, refer to Appendix II.

THE FOUR FOUNDATIONAL LAWS OF MARRIAGE

THE SECRET OF A SOLID MARRIAGE

The condition of most marriages today is turbulent and storm tossed. While many people desperately want a marriage that works, fewer and fewer of them really believe they can have that. The reports of true marital success are few and far between, while the stories of tragedies are everyday occurrences.

Over a period of time, fear and uncertainty have increased as the casualties of marriage have mounted in this country. The consequence is a society in which more people stay single, more couples try alternatives to marriage, and those who do get married often do so with greater caution.

Of all the societal groups and individuals negatively affected by the failing institution of marriage, none are more traumatized than those people who try it and fail. Regardless of how permissive our culture has become or how common divorce is, the results of a couple splitting up are devastating. The emotional agony, the social stigma, the pain for any children involved, and serious financial loss for both parties are only some of the reasons why millions of people flinch when the subject of marriage arises.

What makes this situation even sadder is the fact that it is completely unnecessary. Yes, you read that sentence right: The disastrous conditions of marriage today are not necessary. Every bad marriage and subsequent divorce could be eliminated and replaced by a solid, satisfying relationship, *if only each couple would follow God's plan for marriage.*

From the beginning of creation, when God made the first couple, Adam and Eve, He had a perfect design for marriage. Unfortunately, many people have not realized this. As a result, they have turned elsewhere for answers. Since God is the Creator of man and the Inventor and

Designer of marriage, only He is qualified to write the "instruction manual"—and so He did.

Genesis, the first book of the Bible, is a record of the events of creation. Once God had created everything relating to the heavens and the earth, He formed man out of the dust of the ground. Once Adam was created and "no helper suitable for him was found" (Gen. 2:18-20), the Bible relates that God caused deep sleep to fall upon him (Gen. 2:21). Out of Adam's side, God took a rib and formed Eve, Adam's wife.

When you think about it carefully, you realize that God's creation of woman was perfect. A loving God in the beautiful Garden of Eden performed divine surgery on man. Out of Adam's rib, God formed His most beautiful work—woman. It is interesting and meaningful that God created Eve from the place closest to Adam's heart, his rib. From the very beginning God had a beautiful and perfect plan for marriage. That plan has never changed.

Regardless of how much or how often the world around us changes, we can take comfort in the fact that God never changes. Hebrews 13:8 says, "Jesus Christ is the same yesterday and today and forever" (*NIV*).

If Jesus never changes, then God and the Holy Spirit never change, because all three are One. God is changeless throughout all eternity. How different this is from the world around us! What people think or believe can change overnight when a news story breaks, a new scientific finding is announced, or a major movie is released.

It is hard to build a solid marriage on a world system as unstable as ours. That is why we should not be building our marriages on the world system in the first place. We must build our marriages on God's Word. Jesus told us clearly what we could expect if we choose to build our lives upon the foundation of His Word.

Therefore everyone who hears these words of mine and puts them into practice is like a wise man who built his house on the rock. The rain came down, the streams rose, and the winds blew and beat against that house; yet it did not fall, because it had its foundation on the rock. But everyone who hears these words of mine and does not put them into practice is like a foolish man who built his house on sand. The rain came down, the streams rose, and the winds blew and beat against that house, and it fell with a great crash (Matt. 7:24-27, *NIV*).

The sound of "crashing" marriages around us does not shout that *marriage does not work* but demonstrates the lack of solid foundations to those marriages. It is no coincidence that today's society, which has rejected the Word of God, has such difficulty with marriage. If we reject God's Word and His plan, we cannot make marriages work, for *marriages only work when we do them God's way.*

If we dedicate ourselves to learning and following God's plan for marriage, we will begin to experience the security and fulfillment we have desired. As Jesus said, the rain is going to come and the wind is going to blow on everyone. However, the promise for those whose lives are built upon the truth of God's Word is stability through life's challenges and changes. His Word is a solid foundation upon which we can build successfully. *That is good news!*

The remaining four chapters of this section deal with one small portion of Scripture from Genesis 2. Although the text is short, its content is monumental. So important are these words concerning marriage that Jesus quoted Genesis 2:24 to the Pharisees who were confronting Him concerning His views on divorce (see Matt. 19:4-6). Also, the apostle Paul quoted Genesis 2:24 in his instructions about marriage to the church at Ephesus (see Eph. 5:31).

God's Foundational Laws for Marriage

Two important things about this passage in Genesis need to be understood. First, Genesis 2:24-25 is the initial record in the Bible revealing God's will for marriage. Second, four foundational laws for marriage are found within those two verses.

There is no way to overemphasize the importance of these laws because each of them is essential to the success of the marriage relationship. To break only one of them can mean serious damage to the marriage relationship, even if it does not lead to divorce. To violate two or more of these laws means certain doom to your hopes for happiness. Read these verses very carefully:

> For this cause a man shall leave his father and his mother, and shall cleave to his wife; and they shall become one flesh. And the man and his wife were both naked and were not ashamed (Gen. 2:24-25).

In spite of our stressing the importance of these two verses, at first glance, we are sure they do not appear as "power-packed" as we have said. However, they are!

When I (Jimmy) first read them, I thought they were a veiled, poetic reference to the spiritual significance of marriage. While that may be partially true, I have found these two short verses to be life-changing and marriage-saving for my wife and me and for thousands of others.

Unfortunately, misunderstanding and underestimation of these Scriptures have left couples throughout the ages needlessly groping for solid truth about marriage, when that truth has been right under their noses.

One hindrance to recognizing Genesis 2:24-25 as God's consummate foundation for marriage is the brevity of this passage. Perhaps if it were longer and more detailed, one would be inclined to take the message more seriously. However, God said everything He needed to say in a few words, and each word is eternal and an essential truth for marriage.

Remember in John 11 the narrative of Jesus raising Lazarus from the dead? He said only three words: "Lazarus, come forth!" But those few words had the power to resurrect a man. Likewise, God's few, well-chosen words for marriage in Genesis 2:24 have the power to transform ruined relationships. I (Jimmy) know because I once was a casualty of ignorance of those words and consequent disobedience to them.

In 1979, I had not only lost hope in my marriage but also in marriage as an institution. Today, I realize the problem was not with God. From the beginning, He has desired and designed for couples to live in fulfilling, pleasurable relationships. To help us do that, He gave in His

Word all of the instruction and wisdom for success.

Read the next four chapters with an open heart, and God will do something in your life by the power of His Word. Ignorance and rejection of God's Word has caused the problem. Appropriately, only God's Word can provide a real solution.

He sent His word and healed them, and delivered them from their destructions (Ps. 107:20).

THE LAW OF PRIORITY

For this cause a man shall leave his father and his mother.
GENESIS 2:24, *NIV*

When God designed the marriage covenant, He did so with the intent that this special commitment between a man and a woman would be more important than any other human relationship. That is the reason God commanded man to leave his father and mother when he became a husband.

Before a person marries, the most important relationship bond is with his or her parents. So God told man to "leave" his parents in order to properly "cleave" to his wife.

The "leaving" does not mean one should abandon or abuse one's parents in order to honor God's requirements for marriage. If that was what God meant in Genesis 2:24, then the Word contradicts itself! In the Old and the New Testaments, the admonition to *honor your father and mother* (see Exod. 20:12; Deut. 5:16; Matt. 15:4; 19:19) is one of the ten commandments.

In fact, in Ephesians 6:2, Paul wrote that this commandment is the first one with a promise: "that it may go well with you and that you may enjoy long life on the earth" (Eph. 6:3, *NIV*).

The word "leave" in Genesis 2:24 is the Hebrew word *azab*, which literally means "to loosen or relinquish."[1] So when God said that a man should *leave* his father and mother when he married, God meant that a man was to *relinquish* the highest position of commitment and devotion previously given to his parents in order to give that position to his wife.

God did not mean a man was to stop *honoring* his parents. That was an admonition to last throughout their lifetimes. However, at the time of his marriage, a man's parents were to be released into a lower-priority position in his life. His wife hereafter was to come first. It is possible to do that and yet honor and respect one's parents, or God would not have said to do it.

Of course, the same instructions apply to the wife.

To put it simply, God designed marriage to operate as the second most important priority in life, coming next to your personal relationship with Him. If we put marriage in any position of priority other than the one God has instituted, the marriage does not work.

If you examine closely the problems and failures of your own marriage or of those around you, it will not take long for you to see that many of those problems and failures are the result of misplaced priorities. In fact, untold millions of couples have ended up in a divorce court because they failed to properly uphold the priority of the marriage covenant. Millions of others live frustrated, strife-filled marriages for the same reason.

To help you understand the importance of rightly prioritizing marriage, let me acquaint you with a term you may not have heard before: *legitimate jealousy*.

Did you know there is a righteous and spiritually legitimate form of jealousy that all of us experience many times during our lives?

An example is this: Imagine walking down the street with your spouse, when suddenly, a stranger walks up and begins to try to seduce your mate and take him or her away from you. How would you feel?

You probably will answer, "Well, I would feel angry and violated and chase that person off!" Of course you would! And the core emotion fueling your response and anger would be jealousy. That same emotional response would occur if someone tried to kidnap your child or steal your furniture. Legitimate jealousy is the righteous emotion that causes us to protect what is rightfully ours.

Webster's Dictionary defines "jealous" as "intolerant of rivalry or unfaithfulness."[2] There is something within us that makes us feel our spouses belong to us before anyone or anything else, except God. So when something threatens that correctly prioritized and pure element of our marriage, we feel legitimate jealousy.

You might ask, "But I thought it was a sin to be jealous. Are you telling me it is all right?" There *are* forms of jealousy that are sinful and destructive, perversions of legitimate jealousy. These come into being when we try to get from someone else something that is not rightfully ours or try in an unrighteous manner to hold on to something that is not ours.

However, in marriage, both spouses have moral obligations to God and to each other to protect their relationship from being violated by people or things of lesser priorities. When time, energy and/or resources that rightfully belong to us are given by our spouse to someone or something else in any consistent or significant way, we will feel violated and experience legitimate jealousy.

God Himself is the best example of this fact of life. In Exodus 34:14, He commanded Israel through Moses, "Do not worship any other god, for the Lord, whose name is Jealous, is a jealous God" (*NIV*).

The first thing we see in that verse is that one of God's names is *Jealous*! The second thing we see is that all jealousy is not wrong, or God would have nothing to do with it, much less call Himself by that name. The third thing we see in that verse is something important about the design of God's relationship with us.

Because God loves us and created us to love Him before anyone or anything else, He becomes jealous when that relationship is threatened. When we turn from Him to follow other gods, He is provoked with legitimate jealousy. Whenever we give time, energy or resources rightfully belonging to Him to a person, project or activity, He is violated.

That is why several times in the Old Testament, God compared Israel and Judah's turning away from Him as their first priority relationship to adultery. That is why Jesus' relationship with the Church is sometimes likened to a bride and bridegroom relationship.

One of the greatest certainties in life is that at some point in marriage, you will feel *legitimate jealousy*. The classic cycle of jealousy begins when a couple is only dating or "in love." During their courtship days, they regularly communicate the importance of their relationship in several ways. They see each other regularly; they sacrifice to meet one another's needs; they defend the relationship against competing demands that might interfere with their ability to relate properly to one another.

Problems Do Not End at the Wedding

All the way to the altar, a couple highly prioritizes their relationship. If there are any problems, they console themselves and each other with the idea that everything will be solved once they are married. During the wedding and honeymoon, they spend a lot of time together and focus attention on one another. For some time afterward, there is the excitement of the new relationship and living situation to keep things going.

Generally, within at least five years, the couple begins to have children. Many couples actually are remarrying, which means children already are involved. However, suppose this is a couple who have no children for about two years. At the point of the change from newlyweds to parents is where the satisfaction with the marriage usually begins to drop significantly—if there have been problems in it.

Often the initial problems are ignored, or masked, by the activity and excitement surrounding a new baby. Nevertheless, it is at this point that any existing problems begin to surface and even magnify.

As the new mother pours herself into caring for the child, the father often becomes more aggressive toward his career. Where once they were prioritizing each other, very subtly now, they begin to allow something else to compete with the time and energy they previously reserved for one another.

For the husband, the temptation is to replace the priorities of marriage with his job, career or interests outside the home. For the wife, the greatest danger to her marriage relationship becomes her children and interests inside the home. Although this classic cycle is changing somewhat as more women pursue careers and work outside the home, the point is the same: To avoid problems, one must not allow anyone or anything to replace the priority of one's spouse.

I (Jimmy) cannot begin to count the number of couples I have counseled whose bottom-line complaints are these:

> "He works all the time, and when he gets home, he is tired and just wants to rest. When he does get time off, he is doing something with his buddies."

"She doesn't even know when I'm home. She is so busy with the kids and the house that anytime I want to get romantic or have her do something with me, she is worn out."

Both spouses are saying to each other, "I'm jealous of what has taken my place in your life, and I feel violated." The wife complains that the energy her husband once gave her is being taken by his job. The husband complains that the attention and affection she once gave him are now being consumed by the children.

Your situation may be different, so in order to understand this concept, substitute whatever are the particular threats to the priority of your marriage: friends, school, parents, a project, a talent, a "busyness" at anything else. However, the point is the same.

If you allow anything or anyone, no matter how good or important, to take the time and energy that rightfully belong to your spouse, you are violating God's design for marriage. Your partner is going to experience legitimate jealousy. If you do not correct the problem, it can seriously damage or even destroy your relationship.

Studies show that, as the average couple gets older and their children grow older, the satisfaction level of the marriage gets lower and lower. The only time this changes significantly is when the children leave home. At that point, the satisfaction of marriage will rise somewhat but still remain lower than when the marriage began.

Unfortunately, the average couple will never again be as happy as in the beginning. That is why such sayings as "The honeymoon is over" have become part of our language. That adage is a way of saying, "The good times of marriage are over, and it is time for you to live in 'reality' and suffer like the rest of us!"

The error in such thinking is the assumption that, because so many people experience this downward trend of lowered satisfaction in their marriages, this is a fact of life, inevitable, and to be expected. But it is not! In fact, God designed marriage to get better every year.

Although most people become *less* happy in their marriages year after year, it is certainly not because God "goofed" when He instituted marriage. It is because we "goof" by failing to follow His plan.

We are an example of a couple who have tried it both ways. For the first five years, as we wrote earlier, we carried out our marriage relationship the wrong way. We were the classic American couple who married because of love but who did not have a clue as to right or wrong attitudes in marriage. The only thing we knew was what came naturally and what we saw everyone else doing.

As usual, what came naturally was ignorance, and everyone else we saw had problems as bad or worse than ours. We made the classic mistakes and were on the brink of divorce after only five years. I (Jimmy) was the classic husband who spent his energies at work, and Karen was the classic wife who spent hers on the children. To make matters worse, when I was not working, I played golf every time I got a chance.

Eventually, every time I walked toward the garage to retrieve my golf clubs, Karen's nostrils would flare. I offered to let her come along and caddy for me, but she refused. I couldn't understand why she was so irrational!

In turn, I was frustrated with her for the little energy she directed toward me, especially when it came to sex.

When I voiced a complaint, she would say, "You don't pay any attention to me all day—until you're ready for bed. Then you start getting really nice because you want sex!"

My blood pressure would jump immediately, and I would respond, "Oh, really! What do you want me to do? Quit my job and never have any fun? Anyway, you are so busy with everything around here, I can't *get* your attention for a minute."

We were caught in the classic vicious cycle. Both of us were doing things that violated the other's marital rights. However, many of those things were reactions and our responses to feeling violated.

For example, because I ignored Karen's needs, she turned her attention more and more toward the children. Likewise, when I came home and got little or no attention, I would watch television or grab my clubs and go play golf. Our relationship became more self-defensive and destructive every year. What made matters worse was the frustrating reality that we couldn't even talk about our problems without getting into a fight.

The night our answers began to come from God was the evening I described in the introduction when I got on my knees and asked Him for help with our marriage. He revealed to me that I had misplaced the priority of my precious wife in my life and that our marriage was in danger as a result.

One of the first things God told me to do for the healing of our marriage was to repent to Karen for the way I had treated her. I didn't hear an audible voice, but I did hear God speak clearly to my heart. There was no mistake: I had put myself, my job and golf above Karen.

After I repented, I went into the bedroom where she was still crying. Because never before had I admitted that I was wrong about anything in our relationship, I am sure she thought I was coming to finish the fight or to make another point in the argument. So she immediately was on guard when I entered the room.

I walked over to the bed where she was lying and knelt down next to her.

"I need to talk to you," I said.

She wiped her swollen eyes with a tissue and asked defensively, "What about?"

"About what I've been doing wrong in our marriage," I replied.

That got her attention instantly!

I told her the Lord had shown me that I had been wrong for not putting her first in my life. I repented of laziness toward the relationship and of selfishness. Then I asked her forgiveness and told her I was hanging up my golf clubs (which I did for several years).

She cried as I repented, and she forgave me. Then she confessed her own shortcomings and sins toward me and repented of her actions and attitudes. Of course, I also forgave her.

Since that night, we have never forgotten the importance of keeping each other first.

I can state without a doubt that every year of our marriage since then has been better than the year before. We are much more in love today, and we know how to love one another better than we did on our honeymoon.

That is how God intended marriage to be.

Love Begins with Priorities

The newly married situation should not be the model. Instead, prospective brides and grooms should observe and learn from veterans who have been married for a long time. Isn't that how it is in other areas of life? The veterans teach the rookies; the older teach the younger; the experienced teach the inexperienced. However, in marriage we have allowed our mistakes to dominate us. As a result, short-lived, ignorant bliss has become the worldwide standard for the newly married. This is tragic, unnecessary and unbiblical.

If we will obey God's command to prioritize our lives to accommodate and keep our marriages higher than anything except our God, marriage will work wonderfully. The misery and hurt in today's world caused by couples' misguided and wrongly prioritized relationships would be removed—if only God's law of priority in Genesis 2:24 were obeyed.

Perhaps you grew up in a value system where work was considered more important than marriage. Or, perhaps, you have always believed that the children in a home are to be valued above the parents' relationship. Perhaps you have never seen marriage work the way we are saying it is supposed to, and you are wondering if it really can.

If you identify with any of the above situations, consider these questions:

1. What do you have when you bring a paycheck home in a marriage where people do not get along? You have a perverted situation where the home is considered a place that supports the job. Instead, it should be the job that supports the home. This confused priority has caused untold damage and divorce.

2. Do you want your children to grow up with the marriage model of unhappy and unfulfilled parents? The most important thing parents can do for their children is love one another and meet one another's needs. Children who

live in the security of a loving home and see a model of marital harmony have a higher percentage of being able to enjoy success in their marriages later in life.

Obviously, our children are more important than almost everything in our lives. However, they are not as important as God or our marriages. In fact, the parents' personal relationships with God and the intimate, fulfilling relationships between spouses are what make the correct foundation for loving and training children. Therefore, when we sacrifice God or marriage for the sake of the children, we do them no favors.

Remember, parents, your children will grow up and leave home one day. What kind of marriage will you be left with when they are gone? Cold and distant, or intimate and fulfilling? And what model for marriage will you have given them as they begin new lives?

Regardless of whether it is for God, for yourself or for your children, you must realize the important role correct priorities play in our lives. After realizing the importance of priorities, we must then commit ourselves to changing those things that keep us from living true to real values, no matter how difficult.

There are three things all of us need to do in establishing and adhering to correct priorities:

1. List the most important priorities in your life in order of importance;
2. Prove those priorities in real ways; and
3. Prepare to protect those priorities the rest of your life.

Most lists should look something like this:

1. God—seeking and serving Him personally
2. Spouse
3. Children (if you have any)
4. Church—seeking and serving God together with His Body
5. Extended family and special friends

6. Work and career
7. Hobbies and other interests

How do you prove those priorities in real ways? Many people say they love God first, but then give very little time and attention to their relationship with Him. Do you really believe God is satisfied or fooled by lip service? Of course not! Jesus said in John 14:15, "If you love me, you will obey what I command" (*NIV*).

If we neglect His commandments and then tell Him how much we love Him, we only fool ourselves. God knows who loves Him as He observes in real terms how we operate in every area of our lives, not just with our tongues or good intentions.

The same principle is true in marriage. Many men ignore their wives' needs, as well as take their wives for granted. At times, when they want sex or want to appease anger on the part of their wives, they might say, "I love you."

Because most men believe what they are saying, they cannot understand why their wives' responses are, "No, you don't! If you really loved me, you would work less and spend more time with me!"

Every man needs to understand that women do not measure love by what they hear. Although it is very important for a man to speak loving and affirming words to his wife often, her ultimate standard of measure for love is, "What will you give up to meet my needs? How important am I to you compared to the other things in your life?"

If a man sacrifices his wants and desires to meet his wife's needs, then she feels loved. If he will not sacrifice for her, all of the words in the world cannot convince her that he really loves her.

Women need to understand the same thing about their husbands. A man will know you love him when you give him the energies and attention he deserves. Your husband feels the same way about your being too tired to give him what he needs as you do about his copping out when your needs are unmet. The answer is putting action to your words.

Although verbalizing love and affirmation for God and for others is important, words will not be necessary to convince people of your love, if you do what is right in prioritizing your life and communicating through actions. If you do not act upon your convictions, words will be of little use.

The third thing I mentioned above was that you must not only set priorities, but you must also prepare to protect them all of your life.

With life's demands constantly bearing down on you, protecting your priorities becomes more of a real challenge and more necessary every day. Once you have decided what your priorities are and have committed to proving them in real ways, the next step is to prepare to protect them from unwanted intrusions.

One way to understand the necessity of protecting priorities is to look at your time and energy as if they were money. Because it is easy to see that money is a limited asset, you can easily understand that you must learn to budget if you want to get the best and most necessary use of your money. If some money is left after the necessities are taken care of, then you can afford some luxuries. Likewise, if you get in a pinch financially, the first thing to do is cut down on the luxuries and other nonessentials.

It is exactly the same with time and energy. It would be foolish to spend all your money on luxuries and nonessentials and leave nothing for the rent or food. When the landlord came to collect, how do you think he would respond to the news that you had spent the rent money on a trip?

Do you think he would accept it if you said, "You know, I don't ever pay you much money, but I really am a good tenant"? Of course he would not!

Time and energy must be budgeted just as you do your money.

What is the first priority you set on the list you made earlier?

If it is God, then God should get the first and the best of your time and energy.

What is your second priority?

"My spouse is second," you say. Then your spouse should always get the next best. Then your children, and right on down the list. If anyone does not get "paid," it should be those at the bottom of the list, not those at the top.

My (Jimmy's) priorities, as God reorganized them, caused me to hang up my golf clubs for three years. That decision is still paying big dividends. After my time and energy spent with God, I "pay" Karen from the best of the time and energy left, which she rightfully deserves as the second most important priority in my life.

If someone or something is going to have to do without my time and energy, it will not be her. As a result, I have a happy wife, and she has a happy husband, because we have learned to love God's way, in His priorities for our lives.

Have you or your spouse been complaining lately about feeling violated by other things or other people invading your marriage?

If either one of you has, then listen carefully to these warning signals. They are being witnessed to you by God to prevent the destruction of a marriage that He designed for enjoyment and blessing. If you will heed the warning signals and fix the problems that are causing your "buzzers" to go off, you will be fulfilled and very glad you took the time and expended the energy to reestablish God's priorities in your lives.

As you commit to establish and protect the proper priorities of your marriage, you will find there are frequent challenges, and also some awesome rewards. You just cannot improve on God's design. He made marriage something sacred and beautiful, and it will stay that way if we do not try to change it.

But seek first His kingdom and His righteousness; and all these things shall be added to you (Matt. 6:33).

Notes
   1. James Strong, *Hebrew-Chaldee Dictionary, Strong's Exhaustive Concordance of the Bible* (Iowa Falls, IA: Riverside Book and Bible House), Hebrew #5800.
   2. *Webster's Ninth New Collegiate Dictionary* (Springfield, MA: Merriam-Webster, 1986), p. 647.

THE LAW OF PURSUIT

And shall cleave to his wife . . .

GENESIS 2:24

Hundreds of times, I (Jimmy) have sat in my office with unhappy couples and heard one or both of them say something like this: "I just don't love him (her) anymore. I guess we must have made a mistake when we got married!"

When I hear those words, I can sympathize, because those were the exact sentiments Karen and I expressed to each other before the final crisis that occurred five years into our marriage. Today, it is hard for Karen and me to comprehend how we ever could have felt that way, because we so deeply respect each other and are so much in love.

However, we can both remember what it was like to experience the emotional numbness and disillusionment that led us to say those terrible words to one another. We also know clearly the steps we took to remedy the situation. Those same steps taught us how to achieve and preserve strong and healthy feelings for one another, as well as how to keep the romantic edge on our relationship.

To understand how you can stay deeply and romantically in love for all of your married life or, for some, how to restore that love you have lost for your spouse, turn once again to Genesis 2:24-25. As we wrote before, those verses are God's definitive words setting the foundational laws of marriage into effect.

After He commanded us to *leave* (relinquish or loosen the bonds of) our parents, thus setting a standard for proper priorities in marriage, He said these words: "And a man shall cleave unto his wife" (Gen. 2:24, *KJV*).

Just as it was important to understand the literal meaning of the Hebrew word translated "leave," it is necessary to understand the literal meaning of the Hebrew word translated "cleave."

When I (Jimmy) first saw the word, I immediately thought of a meat cleaver chopping something into two pieces—as do most people who first read the word "cleave."

I thought to myself, "Yep! That fits with my experience in marriage so far!"

Fortunately for all of us, however, the Hebrew word translated "cleave" does not mean "to cut, or to separate." It means the opposite: "to pursue with great energy and to cling to something zealously."[1]

So when God told man to cleave unto his wife, He was commanding him to zealously pursue her and energetically cling to her for the rest of his life.

From the very beginning, God has known the secret of staying in love—*work!* Marriage only works when you work at it. The push that causes a marriage to begin a downward slide is not work, but the lack of it. Taking one another for granted and trying to coast through life on the sled of past memories and events creates an inertia that causes a slide backward.

When I tell a couple they must work at their marriage for their marriage to work, I am aware that I am challenging one of the deepest romantic misconceptions. Whether we express it or not, most of us believe that if we marry the right person, we should not have to work at the relationship to stay in love. It should just happen.

We think that, day after day, we should be able to wake up, look at our spouses and say, "Hallelujah." So we long to find our Mr. or Miss Right with whom to ride into the sunset and live happily all our lives. After all, that is the way it is in the movies.

Most of us will have to admit that we have been deeply affected by an incorrect and deceptive view of love and marriage. The fallen world has bombarded us with its concepts of how to make love and be in love. But have you ever noticed how miserable and unsuccessful those who sell and demonstrate the deceitful ways of love are in their own personal relationships?

Hollywood, the place where most romantic deception begins today, is ravaged with divorce, venereal disease, infidelity, and homosexuality. If anyone has the authority to tell us what love is—it certainly is not the world.

When people tell me they are out of love or do not want to go on in their marriage, I ask this question: "Do you resent having to work at your relationship with your spouse?"

After a few minutes of denial, usually a person will say something like, "Yeah, well, I'm sure I haven't been doing as well as I should have for some time. But now I don't even feel like trying!"

To help you understand where many marriages break down, think back to the first date with your spouse. How hard did you work at impressing your date? How much time did you spend preparing yourself physically? How careful were you with the words you spoke? How much energy did you exert serving and trying to please your date? You know as well as I do that we all "broke our necks" trying to impress each other on the first date.

This shows clearly that it was *not* simply chemistry that caused your relationship to be so satisfying at the start. It also involved a lot of hard work. One normally works very hard at a relationship until one is secure in the love of the other person. When the relationship seems secure, one gradually reduces the effort and begins to take it for granted. That point marks the beginning of the end of the deep feelings and strong attraction that characterized the initial stages of the relationship.

Just because you live in the same house or share the same checkbook does not mean you will feel anything for your spouse or have a strong relationship. For the rest of your life, you must work every day at your marriage for it to be rewarding and healthy. When you stop working at it, it will stop working for you.

In many ways, marriage is like the muscles in our bodies. When we exercise them regularly, our bodies become strong and attractive. However, when we lie around and do not exercise, our bodies become weak and unattractive. The more we lie around, the less we feel like exercising, and the weaker our muscles become.

Exercise Is the Key

It does not matter how out of love you are today, because if you will begin to work at your relationship, you will soon see the resurrection of feelings and experiences that you thought were gone for good. Regardless of how you feel, don't let your emotions lead you to wrong decisions. Even if you have bad feelings toward your spouse, your feelings will change as you obey God's commandment to cleave.

You may object, "No, I'm sorry. I just don't think it will ever work. I'm going to get a divorce and get on with my life."

I understand your feelings, but may I tell you something? If you divorce, more than likely, you will marry again. When you do, you will work hard to attract a wife or husband. Once you are remarried, the excitement of the relationship will carry you for a while. But the day will come, just as it did in your previous marriage, where work and faithful commitment, not just emotion, must fuel the relationship.

Wouldn't it be simpler to begin again with the one you now have? Why not just go ahead right where you are and commit to the hard work needed to renew your relationship? You can get on with your life a lot quicker and easier than in another relationship after a hurtful divorce and the accompanying sense of failure.

You are going to have to commit to work at it sooner or later, if you ever hope to have a happy marriage. Why delay the inevitable? Don't put off until tomorrow what you need to do today.

One man I (Jimmy) counseled had been married seven times and was in the process of marrying his eighth wife! The reason for his many failed relationships was his unwillingness to work at marriage. He would meet someone, get excited about her, marry her, and do well for a time; then he would begin having problems and, finally, divorce her.

When trouble began, rather than working things out, he ran away from it—or so he thought. Instead, he really was ensuring that he would have continuous problems. The only way to get rid of a problem for good is to solve it—not ignore it or divorce it.

We once ran into a woman in a shopping mall whom we had known previously but had not seen for a long time. Immediately, we thought how much better she looked than the last time we saw her. We estimated that she had lost about 50 pounds and had gotten a total makeover. We complimented her on how good she looked.

As she thanked us, she said, "I guess you know K—— and I got a divorce? Well, when we did, I knew right away that I had better get to work, lose some weight, and do something to myself, or I'd never catch another man!"

What instantly flashed through my (Jimmy's) mind was this thought: "I wonder why she wouldn't make the effort to lose that weight and look that good for her ex-husband? If she had, I'll bet they wouldn't be divorced today, and she wouldn't be looking for *another* man."

Why is it that we will work so hard to impress total strangers but will not work at all to please the ones we have vowed before God to love and cherish for the rest of our lives?

Someone may be thinking, "You don't understand. I know it's wrong, but I've been having an affair. I have never experienced such great love in all my life. We get along so well. I have never felt this way about anyone, so this must be God's will for my life. After having experienced *this* relationship, I don't know if I ever could be satisfied with my spouse again."

If so, we must tell you this: Affairs always are wrong in God's sight, *and* they are destructive. They don't solve anyone's problems, and they stir up a world of trouble for everyone involved. It does not matter what good feelings you experience through an affair or how valid you think your reasons may be—affairs are *never* of God! Also, any relationship initiated through an affair is on very shaky ground.

Consider this: If you met the person you are married to or are in love with now through an affair, what makes you think that person will be faithful to you? And when the great feelings stop and the work has to start (and this point will always come in every relationship sooner or later—mostly sooner), what makes you think your lover will work it out with you anymore than he or she did with the one before you?

Get smart! Sin never *solves* any problems; it simply breeds newer and bigger ones.

No matter what the state of your marriage is today, if you will work hard at loving your spouse and meeting his or her needs (even if that spouse is not doing the same for you), you will begin to see a real difference in your marriage. Even better, if both spouses commit to working hard at the marriage every day, the results will be incredible.

We know this is a fact, because we have lived out the process. We don't resent the work we do for each other; we consider it a joy. I (Jimmy) know Karen is going to meet my needs in an energetic and prioritized way, and Karen knows the same about me. What a wonderful way to live; what a permanent and satisfying way to love!

If you are planning to marry soon or were married recently, please don't allow your marriage to slide into apathetic slumber. Decide right now that your spouse is the right person for you and that, from now on, you are going to work to keep him or her happy and fulfilled.

As emotions come and go, you will enjoy a stable and satisfying permanent relationship, and you will experience intense and deeply satisfying feelings. In fact, working at your marriage ensures healthy feelings will be present more frequently and permanently than if you permit your marriage to drift on life's troubled seas.

However, perhaps you are in the stage where you are losing or have already lost your feelings and desires for each other. Perhaps you have wounded and damaged one another in the process. If this is where you are and you want your marriage healed and restored, God has a three-step plan to restore the first love of your relationship. This is a guaranteed method, because it is found in the Bible.

The good thing about God's plan is that, when He commands us to do something, He always teaches us how to do it; and, by His Holy Spirit, He gives us the strength to accomplish it.

Three Steps to Renewal

In Revelation 2:5, Jesus was speaking to the church at Ephesus concerning the deficient state of their relationship with Him. Once intense and rich, their love for Him now was cooling off. In response to this situation, Jesus instructed them to restore their love for Him.

Here is the three-step plan Jesus gave to Ephesian Christians for the renewal of their fervent love for Him.

Remember therefore from where you have fallen, and repent and do the deeds you did at first . . .

The same three steps will heal and revive the love of any couple. They are:

1. Remember Therefore from Where You Have Fallen

As new Christians, we are willing to do almost anything to serve Christ. We are the boldest evangelists and cannot wait to seek God at every opportunity. However, as time goes on, other things begin to compete for our attention. If we give in, and most of us do at some point, we find ourselves cooling off toward God.

Most people think this is simply a necessary maturing that every Christian must experience. However, Jesus called it the sin of "losing your first love for Him." He knows why we lost it, too! We stopped working at the relationship.

It is interesting that Jesus does not tell us to try to work up some emotion to restore our love for Him. He knows the essential strength of true love is not emotion. He knows it is a decision of the will. In fact, the word most often used in the New Testament for "love" is the Greek word *agape*, which means "a commitment to do what is right for someone else regardless of emotions."[2]

God's standard and foundation for love is a commitment to act in another's best interests regardless of how you feel. Although many times feelings are good and proper, they are unreliable as the foundation of a relationship. Feelings are a harsh taskmaster in your life. If you always do what you feel like doing, your life will become a vicious cycle of pain and confusion. When you make the decision to do what is right regardless of how you feel, your life will be blessed and secure.

Knowing this truth, Jesus first commanded the Ephesians to "remember" the place from which they had fallen. In other words, He wanted them to recall their actions at the beginning of the commitment to Him when their love was so intense. He did not try to get them to remember their *feelings*; He wanted them to remember their *actions*.

As it applies to marriage, this first step means remembering the joyous details of your happy and giving actions at the beginning when the relationship was so exciting and fulfilling. Remember how you honored the other person and were so sensitive in your speech? Remember how you did little things to impress the other person? Remember how both of you thought of each other all day and anticipated and prepared for your times together?

Once you have remembered the actions your first love was built on, then you are ready for Step Two.

2. Repent

The word translated "repent" in the Bible means "to turn around, or to do an aboutface."[3] This implies that we are going the wrong way and must change our direction. When we are losing the first love we once had for our spouses, it should be evident that we must be doing something wrong or going off in a direction other than before. Therefore, we must change directions, or *repent*, in order to be healed.

When Jesus tells us to repent, here is what He means. Remembering the fervent actions and right attitudes you displayed at the beginning of the relationship, you are to change any actions and attitudes currently being displayed that are different from those at the beginning. True repentance includes three ingredients: (1) acknowledging the truth (revelation), (2) admitting you were wrong (confession), and (3) adjusting your direction (action).

If this situation applies to you, when you have compared your present condition to your original state and have become willing to take responsibility for the failure by repenting, then you can conclude the process of restoration with Step Three.

3. Do the Deeds You Did at First

Note the fact that Jesus requires no emotion of us. He did not say, "Buster, you had better work up some deep feelings for Me right now, or you are in big trouble!"

He simply said to act the way they had when their relationship with Him was young. Once again invest your time and energy into the relationship, regardless of how you feel in the process. Joy will come when the work is done.

When we began the healing process in our marriage, the Holy Spirit led me (Jimmy) to this Scripture and told me to begin to pursue Karen with energy and sensitivity just as I had in the beginning. The only problem was that I had lost all feeling for her. Although we repented to one another and forgave one another, both of us had serious reservations about becoming emotionally vulnerable again.

At that point in our marriage, we were at a standoff. We needed to do something—we needed to *act*—yet our feelings were telling us *not* to act or to do the wrong thing. We simply had to stop listening to our unhealthy, wounded emotions and begin to obey the Word of God. So even though neither of us had any positive emotions or good feelings at the time, we began to do the things we knew were right for each other.

The result? After just a few days, we began to see significant changes in our relationship and in our feelings. After a few months, our marriage was totally different and deeply satisfying. After a few years, we were far beyond any height or depth of love we had ever experienced together before.

We don't want to give the impression that we have never since experienced any problems or frustrations in our marriage. If you get the erroneous impression that we are superhuman or different in some way from you, you may think we only succeeded because of some special ability or a special act of God. We are just like you. If God can do it with us, He can and will do it for anyone else, including you.

We are able to share our story with you right now, not because of who we are or what we did, but because God's Word is true, and He is faithful. If you will begin today to obey His commandment to cleave to your spouse and work at your relationship, you still will have some problems. However, as you remain steadfast and obedient, your problems will get less and be easier to overcome, and your blessings will grow larger and more enjoyable.

We still have few problems today. But we don't have many disagreements of any significance; and when we do, we are able to work through them without damaging our love and trust for one another. This is a big change from before. We have so much pleasure together and so many blessings in our lives, all because of the power and truth of God's Word working daily in our marriage.

Make a commitment today to work at your relationship as you reject any wrong information from the world about its false brand of love. You can live in a marriage where love and satisfaction are the rule and not the exception. It all depends on your willingness to obey God's commandment to cleave to your spouse.

If you make the decision to pursue your spouse with energy and diligence, you will quickly find it is a labor of love to which you will become addicted, not hard, grueling work. You will experience the wonderful truth that marriage gets stronger and more satisfying every day when you do it God's way.

In all labor there is a profit, but mere talk leads only to poverty (Prov. 14:23).

Notes
1. James Strong, *Hebrew-Chaldee Dictionary, Strong's Exhaustive Concordance of the Bible* (Iowa Falls, IA: Riverside Book and Bible House), Hebrew #1692.
2. Ibid., Greek #26.
3. Ibid., Greek #3340.

THE LAW OF POSSESSION

And they shall become one flesh.
GENESIS 2:24

The portion of Genesis 2:24 above is an obvious reference to sexual union. According to 1 Corinthians 6:16, when we experience sexual intercourse with a member of the opposite sex, we physically become one with that person. The context of that verse to the Corinthians is a warning from the apostle Paul to notoriously immoral Christians in Corinth not to join themselves with prostitutes in sexual promiscuity. He called this a "sin against a man's own body."

Beyond the obvious meaning of becoming "one flesh" through sexual intercourse, Genesis 2:24 states a law of marriage that permeates every area of life. This law, which I call the *law of possession*, is the key to establishing trust and intimacy in a relationship.

Once we understand and submit to this law, we will experience a significant depth of unity and bonding in marriage. However, if we break this law, even innocently, the damage to the trust and intimacy of the relationship can be severe, if not fatal.

To understand the full meaning and implications the law of possession has in marriage, consider this observation: Marriage is a complete union in which *all* things previously owned and managed individually (separately) are now owned and managed jointly. There are no exceptions. Anything in marriage that is not willfully submitted to the ownership of the other person is held outside the union, producing legitimate jealousy.

The act of becoming one flesh involves much more than sex. It involves merging everything owned by and associated with two persons into one mass, jointly owned and managed. If there is something a spouse is unwilling to merge into the marriage, that spouse is breaking the law of possession and violating the rights of the other spouse.

Because of the great importance of the law of possession and the concept of becoming one flesh, we will try to explain them more completely.

To avoid missing the full meaning of God's design for oneness in marriage, we need to look at what Paul wrote in 1 Corinthians 7 about sex and the marriage covenant. There, Paul not only continued his comments from the sixth chapter but also explained them more fully:

> The husband should fulfill his marital duty to his wife, and likewise the wife to her husband. The wife's body does not belong to her alone but also to her husband. In the same way, the husband's body does not belong to him alone but also to his wife (1 Cor. 7:3-4, *NIV*).

Did you notice what Paul said about the ownership of our bodies in marriage? We are to change ownership and control in the management of our bodies from sole, personal ownership and control to shared ownership and control with our spouses. This is not a license for abuse or getting weird; it is simply God's law of possession in operation.

Anything that is not mutually owned and controlled by both partners will lead to division and problems. Each area of our marriage that we willingly surrender to joint ownership and control will build a spirit of trust and intimacy in the relationship.

Here are three real-life examples to illustrate the results and consequences when the law of possession is violated. (These do not involve actual case histories, but are common problems that have surfaced in my counseling ministry.)

Example Number One

Fred desired to be intimate and enjoy sex, but Marilyn would not participate when he did something that angered her. Then, she would tell him, "I'm going to cut you off for a week if you do that again!" She meant it! Fred and Marilyn came to my office when the problems in their relationship grew to the point that they were on the verge of separation.

Fred resented Marilyn deeply because she was aware of his strong sex drive, and she used her body as a means to punish and manipulate him. In other words, Marilyn used sex to control her husband and their marriage. Not only did she cut Fred off when he misbehaved, but she also bargained for things with sex.

Fred angrily related to me an incident concerning a budget they had established to help work out their tight financial situation. Both had agreed to this budget and agreed to limit their spending.

One day, Marilyn saw a dress she wanted, but she knew buying it would throw off their budget. After agonizing over the issue for a while, Marilyn confronted Fred and asked to buy the dress anyway. Fred politely said no and explained why.

Immediately, Marilyn began to bargain seductively, "Fred, if you'll let me buy that dress, I will let you have sex twice a day for a week!"

You might think this scenario would be any man's dream, but you would be mistaken. Although Fred admitted to playing the "bargains-for-sex game" for a while, he described his real feelings this way: "Why can't Marilyn make love to me because she loves me and wants me, or at least because she loves me and wants me to be happy and satisfied? Why does sex have to be a weapon or a bargaining chip to get her own way? I have come to resent sex with Marilyn because I feel she withholds her body from me and does not understand or honor my sexual needs."

While there are times of the month when a woman's body may not be available for intercourse, a woman should never communicate to her husband that her body does not belong to him in an unqualified manner to meet his sexual needs. Of course, this does not mean or even imply that a man may sexually abuse his wife by physical force or mental anguish or force her to do something that violates the Word of God or her conscience.

It does mean exactly what the apostle Paul expressed: In marriage, our body no longer belongs exclusively to us. We must give it to our spouse for the purpose of mutual sexual satisfaction. Two brief statements should be made here before going on to the second example.

First, we want to point out emphatically that this principle works both ways. It is just as true for husbands as it is for wives. Although many cases involve a wife's withholding sexual relations with her husband for various reasons, marriage counselors today report that almost as many wives come to them for help because their husbands withhold themselves physically.

Obviously, it is easier for a woman to participate when she does not care about sex for her own sake than it is for a man. A husband with strong resentment toward his wife, or one whose manhood has been affected in some manner—either as a boy and young man or within the marriage—needs to seek in-depth counseling with a Christian pastor or leader. Impotence rarely can be cured by reading a book, no matter how good the information or advice is in that book.

Second, we hope you have recognized by now the essential role trust plays within marriage. *Trust* is the foundation that promotes and protects the ability to give oneself and one's body unconditionally to a spouse.

Every person should ask this question before marriage: Can I trust this person completely with every area of my life?

Unless the answer is yes, you will have difficulty giving yourself to that person. If you cannot give yourself to your partner completely, at some point, you will feel violated. Therefore, the issue of trust is of major importance to the success of every marriage.

Example Number Two

At my (Jimmy's) first meeting with L.C. and LaDonna, they seemed to be a young couple with everything going for them. They were both sweet, God-fearing people, but they had a serious problem, a wedge that was deeply dividing their marriage. LaDonna had received an inheritance from her father who had died recently, but L.C. controlled the finances.

At first, she did all of the talking, describing her deep resentment toward her husband. "My father died last year and left me $65,000," she told me, as L.C. looked uncomfortably toward the floor. "When we received it, I knew I needed to submit to L.C. as the financial leader of our home, and I did," she said.

As she continued, her voice began to break and tears streamed down her face. "When we got the inheritance check from my father's estate, L.C. spent half the money on a new truck for himself without even asking me what I thought. Then he put the other half in investments. I felt betrayed," she said in a trembling voice, as she reached toward the box of tissues on my desk.

After a short and awkward silence, LaDonna concluded her remarks with this statement: "I didn't mind him getting a truck, and I know we needed to put some in investments. But two things really bothered me. First, L.C. never even asked me what I wanted to do with the money. He simply took possession of it as if it were all his. Second, I had told him several times I wanted to take a few thousand and fix up our house. After buying the truck and investing the rest, he told me we didn't need to fix up the house because the kids were still young, and we couldn't afford it right now. That was more than I could take!"

With the gauntlet obviously thrown toward L.C., he offered this defense, "Well, I know she's upset because I wouldn't let her buy the furniture and stuff she wanted, but I just didn't think it was practical right then. And every time I tried to talk to her about the situation, she got emotional like she is now, and I couldn't reason with her."

For the next 30 minutes, I explained two things to L.C. First, the way he had spent the inheritance money showed LaDonna very clearly that he had taken sole possession of it and did not care about her opinions or desires, although it came from *her* father. He did not ask her advice, and what little she offered was ignored.

Although he was to lead the family, that did not mean he was a dictator who dominated the decisions or handled their circumstances as he pleased. Everything in their lives belonged to them *both*, so they must be partners in the decision-making process.

L.C. was typical of many men in that he had misused his position of authority to selfishly control rather than lead for the benefit of all. While the husband has final authority in the home, that position exists for him to build up and serve those under him, not to rule for his personal comfort or gain.

Second, I explained to L.C. how important a woman's home is to her. When he denied his wife's request to fix up the house, he was saying, "I really don't care about your world. I have my truck, and my world is doing great."

He obviously wrestled with the advice I gave him that day, but finally, he agreed to pray about the situation and to discuss it again with LaDonna. Later, she told me everything had been worked out, and they were getting along fine.

Example Number Three

Greg and Tamara both had been married previously, and Tamara had two children from her earlier marriage. They were seeking counseling, however, not for the sake of their own relationship but because Greg and her children were not getting along. This is a common scenario that causes significant problems in marriages where one or both spouses have had previous marriages.

Both of them were warm, intelligent people who had been attracted to one another because they complemented each other well. They were so articulate and polished, it was difficult at first to determine the seriousness of their situation.

Unfortunately, Greg and Tamara ended up getting a divorce rather than resolving the problem, because Tamara *would not share the ownership and control of her children with Greg.*

You might say, "But the children were not Greg's. Their father was Tamara's previous spouse."

That is true; however, once Greg and Tamara married, the children became part of the new household where Greg was their resident "father." As Greg confided during a counseling session, he felt that his rights had been violated in two ways:

1. He felt Tamara did not trust him enough with her children to allow him to correct them or to give input to their lives. She responded by saying they had been hurt enough emotionally by the divorce from their father, and she was only trying to protect them. Still, Greg could not understand

how she could trust her own life to him, but not the lives of her children. I agreed with him.

2. Greg felt violated by the way Tamara's children treated him. Knowing he had no authority over them, they were disrespectful and disobeyed him constantly.

When confronted by their mother about their treatment of Greg, the children would instinctively accuse him of wrongdoing and try to pit their mother and Greg against one another.

It worked! Caught between her children's confused feelings and Greg's legitimate frustrations, Tamara chose her children and divorced Greg.

This Law Has No Exception

The law of possession must cover every area, aspect and detail of a successful marriage. Anything not submitted to joint ownership and control will produce violation of the marriage bond. It does not matter what it is. From my counseling experiences, I could relate dozens of examples of couples who had serious problems and divorced, simply because they did not observe this law of possession.

For some, the thing they refused to surrender was money; for others, it was family. Still others fought about careers, sports, education, time, future plans, children, and many other issues.

In order that you will not think your spouse is being petty and unreasonably resentful when you withhold an area of your life from joint ownership and control, consider what Jesus said to those desiring to become His disciples, to those wanting a relationship with Him:

In the same way, any of you who does not give up everything he has cannot be my disciple (Luke 14:33, *NIV*).

Applying this statement to our lives, Jesus is not requiring us to get rid of everything we have before we can have a relationship with Him. However, He is saying that we must submit everything we have to His authority, or we cannot follow Him. If there is anything in your life that you cannot or will not submit to Jesus, you are saying that thing is more important to you than He is, whether you realize it or not.

The things we will not give to Jesus become idols in His sight, and He refuses to compete with them. He is insulted when we value other things or people more than Him, when we will not trust Him with everything in our lives.

The same thing is true on a different level with our spouses. When there is something we have that we will not share with them, it is like telling them that they are not as important to us as that thing. Also, we are implying that we do not trust them enough to let them share it.

One of the most flagrant violations of the law of possession today is the use of prenuptial agreements. That is a legal document signed before marriage to prohibit one spouse's access to the other spouse's wealth.

To put it bluntly, a prenuptial agreement is a death certificate for a marriage, because it is a clear statement that the one initiating the agreement does not trust the other enough to give up his or her entire life.

Not only does there occur the problem of a spouse not wanting to surrender something he or she owns and controls to a spouse, but there also occurs the problem of a spouse who will not *accept* something the other person has.

For example, one man would not accept his wife's parents. He was wrong. Unless it is a sin or something illegal and very wrong, you must accept ownership of everything in your spouse's life. The law of possession only works when it is applied to both parties. Selective possession leads to hurt, mistrust and a loss of intimacy.

Another example is subtle but obvious: Have you ever noticed how a parent is willing to say proudly, "That's my child," when a child behaves or does something great? But when some children do wrong things or misbehave, have you ever seen a parent look at a spouse and say, "Did you see what *your* child just did?"

Sorry! Good, bad or indifferent, both spouses must take responsibility for everything in the marriage.

So far, I have addressed this issue mostly from the negative side. Now consider what happens in a marriage when two people give themselves completely to the relationship. Plainly, God knew what He was doing when He set forth the law of possession, because He provided for deep intimacy when He designed marriage to be a place of oneness.

The greatest benefit of putting everything we have into marriage is that we now share everything. We belong to each other totally. There is not a door we are not allowed to enter, so we share life completely.

Intimacy is not built solely or primarily on great sex or deep conversations. True intimacy is created when two people so intertwine their lives with one another that one cannot determine where one life ends and the other begins.

If you insist on independence and personal rights, that is your choice. However, you will not find real intimacy in that choice. Intimacy flows from a selfless, giving, sacrificial heart that is completely open and devoted to the object of its affection. Most members of today's society are desperately searching for intimacy in relationship, but they are too selfish to pay the price.

As you consider the issue of oneness in marriage and seek to become one flesh, let us ask you the following questions:

- Are you completely surrendered to your mate?
- Is there something you are holding back?

If you detect an area of your marriage that is presently violating the law of possession, quickly repent to God and to your spouse and make it right. On the other hand, if there is sin in your life, do not ask your spouse to accept it. Get rid of it! Although we need to be understanding and gracious with one another, we must realize how deadly sin is to any relationship.

Remember, the words "mine" and "thine" are fine when you are single. However, when you marry, you must get a new vocabulary. In marriage, those two little words start problems, but the word "our" can solve them.

Regardless of how precious something in your life is to you, ask yourself, "Is this important enough to sacrifice my marriage for?"

If you are honest, you will admit that no matter what else you must surrender, when paying the price "buys" an intimate relationship with God or with your spouse, it is worth the sacrifice.

Marriage is designed by God to be a total sharing of life between two people. It is a lifelong bond that can be surpassed only by a person's eternal bond with the Creator. The price is laying down one's entire life to the one we are covenanted with in marriage.

That may seem a high price until you compare it with the cost of loneliness and disillusionment that accompany selfishness and personal protection. Do not be robbed of a rich, rewarding marriage by the enemy telling you to "Look out for Number One." Give it all to God and to your spouse. Once again, you will find that you cannot improve on God's wonderful plan for marriage.

> For whoever wants to save his life will lose it, but whoever loses his life for me will find it (Matt. 16:25, *NIV*).

THE LAW OF PURITY

And the man and his wife were both naked and were not ashamed.
GENESIS 2:25

After God created Adam and Eve in the Garden of Eden, He did not clothe them. He did not intend to prepare artificial coverings for them. God's perfect will was for them to remain naked. Before you get nervous, we want to tell you that we're not nudists, and we do not support or condone the practice. However, this important biblical truth will help couples greatly if they understand its real meaning and significance for marriage today.

In the beginning of time, God intended marriage to be a place of total "nakedness"—physically, mentally, emotionally and spiritually. This is the condition Adam and Eve enjoyed in Genesis 2:25. They were completely exposed before God and before one another. In that condition, they shared themselves totally in an atmosphere of intimacy and openness. That is God's picture of a perfect marriage relationship.

Although we were not created to completely expose ourselves to most of the people we meet through life, a marriage partner is the exception. In fact, in addition to the relationship with God, there is no other relationship in life that affords the potential for as much "nakedness" as marriage.

In marriage, we start out instinctively desiring to share ourselves with one another. However, for this to take place, there must be a prepared and protected atmosphere providing an environment where we can regularly "get naked."

God designed the nakedness of marriage to include every area of our lives: body, soul and spirit. When we are able to undress ourselves in every area before our spouses without shame or fear, we are in a healthy place for strong, intimate relationship to develop. If we cannot expose ourselves completely before our spouses, it means we are hiding something. This hidden thing needs to be exposed. The reason is simple: God created us with a need for nakedness.

Perhaps you have never realized that you have a need for nakedness before your spouse, but you do. This is not simply physical exposure, but rather, the exposure of everything about you. You need to open up and reveal yourself, but you cannot do that in just any place or with just any person.

Healthy nakedness must happen in a special place with the right person. Although special friends and family can accommodate the need for exposure to some degree, marriage is the singular place God has created for us to fulfill the need for total nakedness.

At this point, you may say, "Well, I'm married, and I certainly can't expose every area of my being to my spouse!"

You may *not* be able at this time to fulfill your inner desire to become completely open and vulnerable in marriage, yet the truth remains that God created a need in mankind for complete exposure. The fact that your situation does not make that feasible does not wipe out the need or change the fact that God created marriage as the place for it to be met.

On the other hand, we need to look at some of the problems with making God's plan work. To begin with, we need to recognize what caused Adam and Eve to become "unnaked" in the beginning, to coin a word. Before the first couple sinned, they were able to totally expose themselves to God and to each other without shame or fear.

However, when Eve ate the fruit and gave it to Adam, and he ate, something in their relationship changed immediately. According to the Bible, they lost their innocence instantly. Their unimpaired nakedness was lost to shame and fear.

As the taste of fresh fruit was still on their lips, Adam and Eve searched for leaves to cover their genitals. Before they ate the fruit from the tree of knowledge of good and evil, their genitals were shamelessly uncovered.

This signifies three things:

1. Their differences could be openly expressed. (The genitals were the most obvious physical difference.)
2. They could have unhindered intimacy. (There was no clothing to remove for sex.)
3. Their most sensitive areas could be exposed without fear. (Genitals are the most sensitive area of the body.)

Conversely, the fig leaves with which Adam and Eve clothed themselves after sin entered their relationship with God represent three truths:

1. Our differences cannot be safely expressed where sin is present.
2. Sin damages and often destroys the atmosphere necessary to breed intimacy.
3. The sensitive areas of our lives and delicate issues in our relationships cannot be safely exposed when sin is present.

Sin Is the Greatest Obstacle to Openness

In any relationship, sin is the single greatest hindrance to the ability to openly relate to one another. This is where the *law of purity* applies.

The description of Adam and Eve's being naked and unashamed was not written simply to reveal their nudity. It was written to show us the original purity of mankind and of marriage. We need to understand how God designed marriage and apply ourselves to conform to His original design.

To understand how to bring our marriages into compliance with God's requirement for purity, there are several issues that need to be discussed.

1. *Sin is always deadly.* Romans 6:23 states, "For the wages of sin is death." The penalty for sin remains constant. When we allow sin into our lives or our relationships, we swallow a deadly spiritual poison. No matter how small the dose, it hurts. Also, without a healthy respect for the deadly effects of sin, we are open targets for Satan's lies and destructive schemes against us.

2. Purity must be upheld by both partners in order for the relationship to provide a climate for total exposure. Genesis 2:25 says both the man and woman were naked. Purity isn't just for women and children; it is for men as well. Both partners in a marriage must be careful about what is allowed into their lives. Marriage is such a close bond between a man and woman that everything each person thinks, says or does affects the other person and the spirit of the relationship. There is no such thing as "private sin."

I (Jimmy) have counseled many couples in which one of them insisted that his or her sin was not affecting the other. It would be absurd to say that you could roll in the mud, then hug your spouse, and not transfer any of that mud to her (or him), would it not? It is just as absurd to think you could harbor the "mud" of sin in your life and not have it affect your spouse.

Because of this very practical spiritual truth, a spouse has a right to be concerned about every area of a partner's life. Anything that person does will directly affect the other.

3. Purity is for every area of marriage. When a robber wants to get into your home, he doesn't need you to leave *every* door and window open. He only needs one way inside. If he can gain only one entry point, he can burglarize your entire house. The same is true of sin.

The devil doesn't need a person to sin in many areas in order to destroy that life or marriage. He only needs one good entry point to give him a stronghold from which to bring destruction. I have seen people devastated and marriages destroyed because someone allowed sin into just one area.

Whether it is your sex life, your finances, the words of your mouth, addictions, or something else, you need to understand that sin from that one entry point will ultimately cause destruction. It may not happen overnight, but it is inevitable.

Consider this illustration of the destructive nature of sin. When you buy a new car, the owner's manual from the manufacturer will be in the glove box to inform you how this new machine should be operated. We trust the manufacturer to provide this information, because he understands every detail of the vehicle.

If a warning is in the manual from the manufacturer not to do a certain thing, or to take care of the car in a certain way, otherwise damage will result, then we know it must be true. We realize those instructions are not personal. The manufacturer isn't telling us *dos* and *don'ts* because he doesn't want us to have fun. The manufacturer tells us these things in order for us to (1) get the most out of the car, and (2) keep from damaging our vehicle.

This is an excellent illustration of God and marriage. God is the Designer and Manufacturer of marriage. His instruction manual is the Bible, in which He has told us to do and not to do certain things.

Some people apparently think God doesn't know what He's talking about; others think He is an ogre trying to keep us from having fun. The truth is that God is a loving Creator communicating to us through His Word so that we can enjoy life to the fullest without damaging ourselves and others.

Sin is against God's design. While it may produce temporary pleasure without immediate destruction, participating in sin begins a destructive process. For example:

- A little social drinking today often becomes alcoholism tomorrow.

- A little dabbling with light pornography today easily can progress to perversion, adultery, social diseases, and possibly AIDS later on.

- A little overspending today becomes financial bondage or even bankruptcy after a period of time.

- Cute, sarcastic remarks aimed at a spouse early in marriage become cutting and even vicious words as the relationship progresses.

The best way to keep the end result of sin from occurring is to stop it in the beginning. The initiation of sin is the same as it was for Adam and Eve. It begins with the devil presenting himself as something he isn't—innocent and harmless.

As Satan disguised himself in the Garden to seduce Eve, so he does today. Just as he lied to Eve, telling her that sin would enhance her life, he tells us the same today.

Remember, however, that before Adam and Eve sinned, they had a perfect marriage. They were one flesh, naked and unashamed together in an intimate wonderland of love. Remember, also, that after they sinned, they were *two* lonely people hiding from God and from each other. What a picture of the world today!

In Peter's first epistle, he warned his readers to be cautious of Satan's presence in their lives. He wrote:

> Be self-controlled and alert. Your enemy the devil prowls around
> like a roaring lion looking for someone to devour (1 Pet. 5:8, *NIV*).

This doesn't mean Christians should be paranoid or extremely devil-conscious. It does mean they should be alert and wary of the real enemy who hates to see healthy marriages.

Even more important than being aware of Satan's schemes is the need to know and understand that Satan's power isn't as great as the power of God. When a marriage is built upon God's Word in an atmosphere of purity, the devil cannot harm it. But when a spouse is seduced by Satan's lies to allow sin or disobedience to God into his or her life, that person is then on Satan's turf—and the devil lives in a bad neighborhood!

I (Jimmy) remember many of my attitudes about sin when Karen and I first married. Although I considered myself a good person, I really believed some sins were not so bad and could even enhance our marriage. I had an image of Karen and myself having a marriage where we went to church and were socially respectable, but one in which we also could "have a little fun."

It wasn't long before I found out that the "fun" of sin has a severe backlash. In fact, many problems we had early in our marriage could be traced to the roots of sin allowed in my life. Rather than giving pleasure, sin seriously damaged, and soon would have destroyed, our relationship.

The only answer was to banish it from our lives. When we did, we found the most fun and the most enjoyable lifestyle in the world is one of purity and obedience to God. I lived more than 20 years of my life seriously in sin or dabbling in it. Since then, I have lived more than 20 years of my life for the Lord. Although I am still far from perfect, I have found a truth that I simply did not believe in those first 20 years: Purity is a blast!

In case you have the same belief and attitude that I had in the beginning, here are some general guidelines concerning sin in marriage and some steps to take to either establish or restore the atmosphere of purity in your relationship.

Seven Steps to Purity in Marriage

1. Take Responsibility for Your Own Behavior

Don't focus primarily on your spouse; focus on yourself. You cannot change his or her behavior, but you can change your own behavior with God's help. Just as Jesus expressed it, when we judge others, we are trying to "remove a speck" from someone else's eye, while we have "a plank" in our own (Luke 6:41-42, *NIV*). Take responsibility for your own words and actions and build an atmosphere of purity and trust from your side first.

2. Do Not Return Sin for Sin

God's Word tells us to return evil with good and even to love our enemies (Luke 6:27-36, *NIV*). Revenge and retaliation will never solve a problem in marriage. Those attitudes and behaviors will only perpetuate a problem and even make it worse.

Make up your mind that you are not going to sin in response to anything your spouse says or does. In that way, your behavior can be used by God to help your spouse respect and trust you. The power of love and righteousness are greater than the power of evil.

The person who believes this truth and puts it into practice will be blessed; the person who doesn't believe or act on this truth will be bruised and battered in a lifelong exchange of evil for evil. Consider and apply to your life the words of 1 Peter 3:1-2:

> Wives, in the same way be submissive to your husbands so that, if any of them do not believe the word, they may be won over without words by the behavior of their wives, when they see the purity and reverence of your lives (*NIV*).

Wives and husbands alike must commit to using purity, not sin, in dealing with their problems.

3. Admit Your Faults

The heartfelt and sincere expression, "I'm sorry. I was wrong. Will you forgive me?" can heal a marriage quicker than almost anything else. However, the person who refuses to say he is sorry will suffer in marriage. (Sometimes, *both* parties in a marriage will not admit their faults. Then you really have trouble!) John wrote:

> If we confess our sins, he is faithful and just and will forgive us our sins and purify us from all unrighteousness (1 John 1:9, *NIV*).

In other words, if we will admit our faults to God, He will forgive us. Jesus died on the cross to pay for our sins. Therefore, when we have sinned against God, we do not have to pay for them or do penance. However, we *must* honestly confess sin for Him to forgive us.

The same cycle of purity begins in marriage when one spouse admits that he or she has been wrong. Even if your spouse doesn't reciprocate or respond positively, you must admit your mistakes in order to be right before God. Humility and honesty are two virtues in marriage, investments that pay high dividends.

On the other hand, pride and self-deception lead to an atmosphere where exposure to one another is too risky. The epistle of James offers two Scriptures related to this issue that are important for us to remember:

> God opposes the proud but gives grace to the humble. Therefore confess your sins to each other and pray for each other so that you may be healed (Jas. 4:6; 5:16, *NIV*).

4. Forgive

In Matthew 6:14-15, Jesus said:

> For if you forgive men when they sin against you, your heavenly Father will also forgive you. But if you do not forgive men their sins, your Father will not forgive your sins (*NIV*).

Forgiving other people is a serious issue with God. Repeatedly throughout the New Testament, we are instructed and warned concerning forgiveness. Not only did God tell us we would not be forgiven if we do not forgive others, but He told us that unforgiveness poisons our hearts as well (see Heb. 12:15).

If you have ever been around unforgiving people, you surely have heard them speak venomous words concerning the people they resent. Unforgiveness shows on our faces, in our words, and in our actions.

The poison of unforgiveness damages the vessel it is stored in worse than it hurts the one it is spit upon. In other words, the one hurt most when you do not forgive others is *yourself*. Even if you are forgiving toward your spouse, feelings of resentment and bitterness toward others in your life will still affect your marriage negatively.

In fact, many times a spouse becomes the whipping post, the outlet for anger and frustration harbored against others. If you are unforgiving concerning things in your past—parents, jobs, friendships, previous close relationships, or anything else—it will negatively affect everything in your life, especially marriage, unless you deal with the past righteously.

Unforgiveness is like a dead rat in the attic: *It makes the entire house stink.* The opposite is true of forgiveness. We are blessed and refreshed when we forgive others and get rid of unhealthy thoughts and feelings.

Here are five steps to forgiveness:

1. *Release the guilty person from personal judgment.* Do not keep rehearsing the offense in your mind. Let God be the judge.

2. *Love the person who has offended you.* Let your behavior reflect your decision to forgive.

3. *Bless and pray for that person.* Jesus told us to bless those who curse us and to pray for those who mistreat us (see Luke 6:28). This is one of the most powerful ways to change negative feelings. Deep resentment and hurt are turned to love and compassion as words of blessing and prayer are spoken for those who have wronged us, even if they have not apologized to us.

4. *Do not bring up the hurt in the future.* When God forgives us, He removes our sins as far as the east is from the west (see Ps. 103:12). In other words, God doesn't simply forgive; He forgets. Although we cannot erase things from our memories, we can make a decision not to bring up past offenses. This decision alone can enhance a marriage greatly.

5. *Repeat this process as many times as necessary.* Keep going through these steps until you sense a genuine release of unforgiveness.

5. Speak the Truth in Love

There are many times in marriage when couples need to sit down and tell one another about something that bothers them or has offended them. This is not "retrieving" old hurts. It is taking care of problems as they arise in order for the couple to live in purity. Ignoring a significant sin in a spouse is dangerous both for oneself and for the sinning spouse.

Allowing hurts and frustrations to build up is just as dangerous, because one day those things surely will explode out into the open. In order for purity to exist, a couple must commit to speak truth lovingly to one another about those things that affect the marriage and are of concern to the other person. That doesn't mean that both of you always will agree on everything, but you should allow free expression of your spouse's feelings without being turned off and without feeling attacked.

Early in our marriage, we would wait to confront one another until we were angry. Then our words were hurtful. Since then, we have learned to take care of problems daily. We do not attack each other's problems, and we do not ignore each other's problems. We share lovingly what we think is important to us and to our relationship. Then we talk and pray about that issue until it is resolved.

This attitude toward communication and sharing is one of the main reasons we have so many positive feelings and experiences today with one another. The ability to talk about sensitive areas of our lives with one another has greatly enhanced our lives. We are able to relate to one another as best friends, to confess sin, or to reveal deep feelings without being accused or mistrusted. Some might say this is dangerous, but we say it is God's design.

However, some Scriptures from Ephesians ought to be remembered when spouses confront one another. They are:

> Instead, speaking the truth in love, we will in all things grow up into him who is the Head, that is, Christ. Therefore each of you must put off falsehood and speak truthfully to his neighbor, for we are all members of one body. In your anger do not sin: Do not let the sun go down while you are still angry, and do not give the devil a foothold (4:15,25-27, *NIV*).

6. Pray for Each Other

There may be some things in your spouse's life that you simply cannot change. Only God can. Once you have spoken the truth in love, sometimes your spouse will understand and change immediately; but sometimes he or she will not. Rather than trying to enforce your feelings through manipulation, intimidation or domination, *pray for your spouse.*

The best you could possibly do alone would be to conform your spouse's outward behavior to your desires; but, in so doing, you will harm your relationship. If you will pray for your spouse, God can change the hearts of both of you. Then, not only have you won that other person completely, but also you have not damaged the relationship in the process.

After counseling hundreds of couples, I (Jimmy) can tell you for sure that there is no perfect mate. However, as we speak the truth to each other and pray for each other, God can build a pure marriage on the foundation of our faith in Him. Consider again the advice in James 5:16:

> Therefore confess your sins to each other and pray for each other
> so that you may be healed. The prayer of a righteous man is pow-
> erful and effective (*NIV*).

7. Seek Righteous Fellowship

First Corinthians 15:33 says, "Do not be misled: Bad company corrupts good character" (*NIV*).

It is most difficult to keep a marriage pure when our main fellow-ship and association are with people who are impure. On the one hand, we are not advocating a legalistic separation from any friend, relative or associate who has problems; but on the other hand, we are saying we must be very careful about our environment.

The Bible tells us clearly that we will become like those whom we are around. If we don't believe this, we are misled.

I (Jimmy) remember one couple who thought it innocent fun to go out dancing and drinking on Saturday nights. They joined a few other "good" couples simply to have a little fun. Their fun turned into drunk-enness and adultery.

You need friends who will encourage you to seek God and love your spouse, not encourage you to "divorce the jerk" when you have prob-lems. You don't need friends who will seduce you into sin.

Marriage was designed by God as a place where two people can be completely naked before one another without fear or shame. This nakedness is to include the thought-life of the mind. God wants part-ners in a marriage to be able to share any thoughts with one another without fear.

Nakedness also is to be emotional. God wants us to be able to share and express our feelings like little children without being rejected or embarrassed. Also, He designed mankind to be spiritually naked in marriage. He wants us to be able to pray and worship together in the most beautiful and intimate way. Finally, God wants us to be able to be physically naked together without shame. He wants us to enjoy our bodies together sexually with optimum pleasure and oneness.

Before we can experience all of the beauty and holiness of purity, we must be in an *atmosphere* of purity. Is there something in your life that could be introducing impurity into your marriage? Is there something in your spouse's life that you have not confronted and have not forgiven, but you know it is affecting your ability to love one another as you should? Then don't ignore these issues.

In a loving manner, seek to make your home and marriage a safe place where you and your mate can come to "get naked." As you commit to seek God's will for your life and marriage, seek His forgiveness daily for your sins. Although none of us is perfect, we can be forgiven by the blood of Jesus.

As you walk with a daily respect for God's law of purity in marriage, you will see a marked difference in the atmosphere and pleasure of your relationship. Purity is the atmosphere where love and intimacy find their deepest and most beautiful expression.

Don't allow yourself to be robbed of God's best for your marriage by Satan's lies. Be diligent to remain pure, and God will bless you beyond your wildest dreams.

Blessed are the pure in heart, for they will see God (Matt. 5:8, *NIV*).

HOW TO BUILD YOUR DREAM MARRIAGE

GOD'S BLUEPRINT FOR MARITAL BLISS

What is your idea of a perfect mate? Whether you are a man or a woman, I can pretty much guess what your answer will be. After having counseled married couples for many years, I have learned all of us essentially are the same. With the exception of some minor personal preferences, both sexes have universal standards for what they desire from the opposite sex.

For a man, the ideal woman is someone who makes him feel like a king. He wants a cheerleader to tell him how great he is and to encourage him throughout his life. This ideal woman aggressively meets his sexual needs, looks her best at all times, and provides a home environment to which he can look forward all day.

She shares his hobbies and interests as often as she can. To put it simply, she is a good-looking, sexy, husband-honoring, domestically centered "fishin' buddy"!

For a woman, the ideal man is sensitive and affectionate. She wants a strong leader, someone who makes decisions after prayer and while honoring her opinions. She wants a man who opens up his mind and spirit and communicates with her in an intimate and open manner.

The ideal man is a hard worker, who faithfully provides for her financially. He is generous but also manages money wisely. He is a good father, and he helps around the house. In other words, her dream man is a strong leader with a soft heart.

Although you may not totally agree with every point we made about the ideal mate, we'll bet the above descriptions are very close to your own ideal. Our certainty is not based only on our observations through counseling; it is based on God's Word.

The Holy Spirit inspired the apostle Paul to write a description of the ideal mate in Ephesians 5:22-33. In addition to being an important doctrinal source concerning marriage, this passage is a blueprint for marital bliss. Read these verses very carefully:

> Wives, submit to your husbands as to the Lord. For the husband is the head of the wife as Christ is the head of the church, his body, of which he is the Savior. Now as the church submits to Christ, so also wives should submit to their husbands in everything. Husbands, love your wives, just as Christ loved the church and gave himself up for her to make her holy, cleansing her by the washing with water through the word, and to present her to himself as a radiant church, without stain or wrinkle or any other blemish, but holy and blameless. In this same way, husbands ought to love their wives as their own bodies. He who loves his wife loves himself. After all, no one ever hated his own body, but he feeds and cares for it, just as Christ does the church. For we are members of his body. "For this reason a man will leave his father and mother and be united to his wife, and the two will become one flesh." This is a profound mystery—but I am talking about Christ and the church. However, each one of you also must love his wife as he loves himself, and the wife must respect her husband (*NIV*).

For years, I (Jimmy) have read these verses while counseling husbands and wives to show them how beautiful their marriages can become, if they will fulfill their biblical roles. In many years of using this passage, I have never had anyone tell me he or she disagreed with what the Bible said their spouses should do. However, many have resisted or refused to accept their own biblical roles.

I have never had a man tell me that he did not want his wife to honor or submit to him "as to the Lord." I have never had a woman tell me she did not want her husband to "give up his life" for her as Jesus did for the Church.

What I have heard, however, were complaints about what the other person in the marriage did or did not do and why those actions made it impossible for the speaker to do what he or she should do!

By the time most couples seek counseling, they already are in a vicious pattern of accusations and frustrations. He will tell me what he doesn't like about her, and she will tell me what is wrong with him. After I listen carefully to both parties and deal with surface issues, I always bring them to Ephesians 5:22-33 to show them the kind of marriage God wants for them.

Three Reasons for Resisting Change

There are three general reasons why people resist making changes in their own lives:

1. Fear of Going First

They are afraid to commit to their own biblical roles until their spouses change. They do not want to go first, because they are afraid of being taken advantage of if they become vulnerable. The more pride and hurt are present in relationship, the more stubborn the standoff.

2. Society's Influence

The second reason people tend to reject their own roles in marriage is social influence. When I tell men that the apostle Paul wrote for them to sacrifice for their wives and selflessly meet their needs, many of them look at me like, "Rambo wouldn't do that!" Society has modeled a perverted view of manhood to this entire generation of men. Because of that perverted image, many men have abandoned their God-appointed roles as sacrificial overseers to become selfish, pseudo-macho egomaniacs.

In the same manner, many women respond bitterly to being told that they are to submit to their husbands as unto the Lord. Although most Christian women realize they are to believe what the Bible says, submission to their husbands is the ultimate test of faith.

Much of this dilemma is caused by the ungodly, man-hating spirit of radical feminism that has misled and intimidated today's women. While it is true that many men in this generation have violated their roles of leadership in serious ways, that fact does not justify the ungodly and unbiblical response of many women.

3. Lack of Belief

The third reason why spouses reject their own biblical roles is unbelief. In some instances, it is not because of fear or deception that a person refuses to carry out his or her appointed role in marriage. It is simply because of a lack of belief that it will work.

> And without faith it is impossible to please God, because anyone who comes to him must believe that he exists and that he rewards those who earnestly seek him (Heb. 11:6, *NIV*).

To those who balk at making a commitment to fulfill their biblical roles in marriage, I pose two questions: Do you believe in the Bible? When most of them answer yes, I ask, Is what you are doing right now in your marriage working? Then they almost always answer no.

At that point, I try to explain lovingly why faith in God's Word is the only logical choice for any Christian.

Examine your own heart:

- Do you have fears that hinder you from giving yourself totally to your spouse as you know you should?

- How about society? Do you have a biblical concept of what a true man and woman should be like, or have you been tainted by a deceived and self-destructive world?

- Do you sometimes question if the Bible still works? Is there something lacking in your faith?

All of these questions should be reflected upon and discussed with your spouse in order to properly fulfill your role in marriage.

If we can get past the hindrances that keep us from seeing the picture clearly, we will begin to understand God's genius. The way He designed marriage is perfect. In fact, the description of marriage in Ephesians 5 is the description of a dream marriage, where both partners are doing exactly what the other person wants and needs him or her to do.

If we would only commit by faith to fulfill our own roles in marriage for the rest of our lives, we would experience something incredible.

Results of Fulfilling Proper Roles

Here are three things the proper roles of husbands and wives accomplish as found in Ephesians 5:22-33.

1. Biblical Roles Provide

We cannot provide for our own needs completely. If we could, we would not need to get married. But our spouses can provide for many of the needs we cannot meet ourselves. When our spouses fulfill their biblical roles, our needs are met.

A man's foremost marital need is the need for honor. Isn't it interesting that God commands a woman to submit to a man "as to the Lord"? When a woman honors a man and submits to him with a joyful attitude, she meets his deepest marital need.

Likewise, when a man sacrificially gives himself to nourish and cherish his wife, he meets her deepest marital need—the need for security. A woman needs a leader who will protect and provide for her. When a man does this with a joyful attitude, a woman's inner longings are satisfied.

2. Biblical Roles Protect

Many women fear submitting to their husbands in a biblical way, because they do not want to be abused by a dominating, selfish man who will take advantage of them. But, ladies, what if the husband to whom you submitted was a sacrificial servant who loved you and met your needs with sensitivity and humility? That would be a different story, would it not?

Likewise, many men fear humbling themselves before their wives and giving themselves sacrificially, because they don't want to be washing dishes and ironing clothes for the rest of their lives. But, gentlemen, what if the woman you sacrificially served treated you like a king? What if your wife served you and met your needs eagerly and with great honor? Would you feel vulnerable around a woman like that? Of course not!

When a man and a woman fulfill their respective roles, each spouse is both provided for and protected. The longer you refuse to do it God's way, the more you are encouraging your spouse to do the same. Be the one in your marriage who puts a stop to the vicious cycle of unmet needs and begins a victory cycle of blessing.

When you do your part, it makes it safe for your spouse to do his or her part. Even if your spouse does not follow your example overnight, have faith in God and persevere. God will reward you. Anyway, any alternative has no chance at all of working.

3. Biblical Roles Promote

When two people love one another as Paul described in Ephesians 5, the result is deepened love, intimacy and trust. Biblical roles keep a relationship growing year after year. When you don't think it can get any better—it does. Sometimes you have to pinch yourself to see if your marriage is real. Your feelings are so healthy; your respect is so deep; your desire is so strong.

The entire relationship keeps getting better the longer you fulfill your role. When you do not fulfill your biblical role, the opposite happens: Everything begins to deteriorate, and hope for a dream marriage turns into a nightmare.

If you look around you today, you will see that an atmosphere of mistrust surrounds the institution of marriage. Although marriage is still fairly well respected, people generally are pessimistic about their chances of enjoying a long-term, successful relationship. So when they hear of another divorce or another miserable couple, their fears are reinforced.

Ask yourself, how many bad marriages that you are aware of are made up of two people who love one another as the Bible says they should? None, right? However, also think of how many bad marriages consist of a selfish, "out-to-lunch" man and/or an angry, dishonoring wife. Although no one description will fit every problem marriage, it doesn't take long to realize bad marriages begin with people who are unbiblical in their role functions.

Be encouraged with this truth: Marriage still works! Even better, marriage is wonderful.

God's design for marriage is a sacrificial male leading an honoring female. Their love directed selflessly toward one another was meant to perpetuate their relationship throughout life. God's design for marriage creates a perfect friendship between a man and a woman. Although this is far from what many people experience, it is not out of reach for anyone.

A blissful, biblical marriage begins by putting faith in God's Word and believing He has the answers you seek. You must obey God's design for marriage that leads to experiencing the blessings of love as God has designed for all to enjoy.

As you give, your love will be returned manyfold. As you serve, God will honor and exalt you. As you lay your life down for your mate, you will find the life you have been seeking. Do not delay any longer. Build your marriage according to God's blueprint. Your dream marriage is waiting!

Give, and it will be given to you; good measure, pressed down, shaken together, running over, they will pour into your lap. For whatever measure you deal out to others, it will be dealt to you in return (Luke 6:38).

The Destructive Husband

Husbands, love your wives, just as Christ loved the church and gave himself for her.
EPHESIANS 5:25, *NIV*

One evening I saw coverage of a women's march in Washington, D.C., on a national news program. The march was sponsored by the National Organization of Women (NOW), a radical feminist group with an aggressive agenda to "liberate" women in America.

The most notable thing about the march was not the cause or the number of women present, but the obvious anger reflected in the body language and expressions of those women. At one point, the camera zoomed in for a close-up of one of the veteran leaders, who had an intimidating demeanor.

She was shaking her fist and shouting at the crowd of women present. Her words were anti-men, anti-establishment, and pro-women's rights rhetoric; and the women gathered before her were responding enthusiastically. They reflected her spirit and her aggression.

What happened in this country to create such a vast number of angry, anti-men women?

Of course, a good deal of the problem began in the Garden of Eden, when sin entered the human race, but why have America's male-female relationships taken such an incredibly bad turn in recent years? Why has the divorce rate soared from 5 percent to more than 50 percent in the past century?

Although there are many spiritual and social factors that have had an adverse effect on the relationships between the sexes in America, the greatest single factor is *unrighteous men*.

When you see a young person walking down the street with pink, spiked hair and tattoos all over his body, you almost always are beholding the reflection of his feelings about his father. The same is true of women. When you see an angry, man-hating woman, who is burning her bra and demanding her rights, you almost always are witnessing the product of the men who have most influenced her life.

Whether men like it or not, they must realize they have been entrusted by God with the leadership of families, churches and society as a whole. Whenever men are righteous stewards of this authority and use their influence to provide for and protect those in their care, their spouses and children will reflect appreciation and contentment through their behavior.

American society was relatively stable for about the first 200 years of our history, *because men were basically God-fearing, sacrificing individuals who had a strong work and family ethic.* However, over the past four or five decades, things changed. Rather than men following the model of selfless overseers of their families and communities, they followed a more selfish and corrupt pattern.

Throughout the history of the world, there have been evil men and women, but something about the general spirit of manhood in America definitely changed over the past 40 years. The women of America, like women worldwide, are reflections of the men in their society.

When the men are godly, sacrificing agents who protect and provide for women, then the women are generally content. However, when the men are lazy and ungodly, the women will begin to reflect the men's sins. The ungodly model of many men today has provoked women and children in our society to respond in kind.

When we see a rebellious and destructive culture growing worse every day, we are looking at a mirror image of the men in that society. The same is true of churches, homes and other institutions. They are the reflections of the men who lead them. In fact, in many cases, they are the reflections of the men who do not lead, because the men either are absent or apostate in their functions.

The purpose of this chapter is not to male-bash or to belittle men. God knows we hear enough of that already! Rather, the purpose of this chapter is to honestly review and assess the reasons why marriage is being destroyed and to find some answers.

The root problem in unstable and broken homes today is a lack of righteous male leadership. The only source of hope to solve the problem is God's Word. Ephesians 5:25 tells men how to love women.

The primary reason we love Jesus is not because He commanded us to, nor is it because He threatens us if we do not. It is because He died on the cross for us. We are attracted to Jesus because He was willing to sacrifice His life for us. The same thing is true of women where men are concerned.

Society Reflects a Generation of Selfish Men

A woman falls in love with, and stays in love with, a man who will sacrifice to meet her needs—not because she is commanded to love him. Nothing in this world can endear a man to a woman more than the quality of sacrificial love. By the same token, nothing can embitter a woman's spirit more than a selfish or abusive man.

Our society presently is reeling from the effects of the abusive and selfish men of today and from the recent past. When men change, so will our society.

On a more personal note, I (Jimmy) have experienced the reality of an angry and embittered woman in my life. As sweet as Karen was on the day we met, it was hard for me to believe that she had turned into such a different person after only five years of marriage. Rather than greeting me at the door with a kiss, she met me in the kitchen with a stare. Rather than whispering sweet nothings in my ear at bedtime, she spoke bitter complaints from her side of the bed. Was this woman the reflection of me? Unfortunately, yes.

I must admit I tried my best to win Karen's heart at the beginning of our relationship, but once I knew she was mine, I stopped trying so hard to please her. Where I once gave 100 percent of my efforts to pursue her and meet her needs, that percentage dropped considerably.

By the fourth year of our marriage, I had almost stopped pursuing Karen at all. The little energy I did direct toward her was primarily for the purpose of gaining sex. But once I had what I wanted, I lost interest in serving her. Before long, she began to complain of being used for sex. I then accused her of being unreasonable.

For the first five years of our marriage, as I wrote earlier, I worked, played golf, and went home to rest. Most of my memories surround those three events. I had the basic attitude that when I finished working and was home, I had finished my job and the rest was up to Karen. I expected her to cook, take care of the kids, clean the house, pay the bills, and also do as much of the yard work as she could to take the load off me.

When I came home in the evenings, I would sit in the same chair and watch television until I went to bed. If Karen asked me to help her around the house or do something with her or the children, it annoyed me. I would tell her, "I'm really tired, and I need to rest."

Later that evening, when I wanted sex, she would tell me the same thing—and I would get furious. Remember what we wrote about a woman being the reflection of her husband? In addition to being lazy and taking my wife for granted, I was a chauvinist. Without even realizing it, I carried an attitude that women were not as important or as special as men.

Their feelings were not as important as men's feelings. They were not really as intelligent as men, and so on. I am ashamed today to think I ever believed those lies. What was worse was that my chauvinistic attitudes fueled much of my neglectful and hypocritical behavior toward Karen. Rather than using my position of authority to serve her and exalt her as I should have, I used it to order her around and use her for my own selfish purposes. Therefore, the angry woman in my house was definitely the reflection of her unrighteous husband.

Someone might say at this point, "But you make it seem as if women do not have minds of their own. Are you saying all a woman does is react to her husband?"

The last thing in the world I am trying to say is that women do not have minds of their own! Women were created by God as equal to men in every spiritual, moral and intellectual sense. Emotionally and physically, women are not inferior or superior—they are just different from men.

Women are unique, intelligent creatures, who have been designed by God to fulfill a special role in life. Please understand that my desire is to honor women, not to cast any shadow on their uniqueness or equality. To illustrate this point in a way that will disassociate from the male-female issue, consider this biblical analogy.

Think back to the stories in the Old Testament about the kings of Israel. Throughout their history, Israel had many different kings ruling them. Beginning with Saul, then David, Solomon, and so forth, the well-being of Israel for centuries was dependent upon the quality of the person who sat on the throne.

When the king was unrighteous and rebellious, the people not only suffered as a result but also reflected the sinful attitudes of their king. When the king was righteous and submitted to God, the people prospered as they mirrored the wholesome lifestyle and attitudes of their ruler. History, as well as reality, proves the point that a society, institution, church or home always is responding to the presence or absence of righteous male authority.

To deduce that women are inferior because they naturally respond to their husband's behavior is to say the same about the nation of Israel. Obviously, Israel comprised many intelligent, strong and unique individuals who did not always follow exactly the leanings or leadings of their kings. However, even if they did not, they still were powerfully influenced by the dictates and spirit of the man in power.

For each strong person who resisted the influence of the king, there were many others who were susceptible to being overwhelmed by the tide of spiritual and social forces released by the person in authority. Using as a backdrop the nation of Israel and their kings, we are going to describe four different types of destructive husbands: the dominant husband, the passive husband, the immoral husband, and the distracted husband. These are four types I (Jimmy) see most in counseling.

Actually, many times I never see the husbands; I only hear about them from their wives. Regardless of whether I see them or not, I witness the destructiveness of their behavior. The emotional agony, insecurity, the general suffering that I see in the wives and children of destructive men are sometimes overwhelming.

Sometimes I am tempted to physically shake such a man and say, "Don't you see what you are doing to her?"

But whenever I begin to feel that way, I recall that it wasn't that long ago when I was a destructive husband myself. But for the grace of God, I would either still be destroying our marriage or, even more probably, be divorced. Each time I remember my former behavior, I immediately become more humble and appreciative.

Also, I am reminded that God did not save me from my problems so that I could condemn others. He saved me so that I could turn back to help them. This book is offered for that very purpose: to change lives and save marriages.

Four Kinds of Destructive Husbands

1. The Dominant Husband

The book of 1 Kings records the death of King Solomon, who reigned in Israel for 40 years. Upon his death, his son Rehoboam was to take the throne, but there was a problem. When Solomon died, the people gathered together before Rehoboam at Shechem. They were weary from the heavy labors Solomon had forced them to endure. They were hoping to find a more sensitive ear with his son.

So they said to him:

> Your father put a heavy yoke on us, but now lighten the harsh labor and the heavy yoke he put on us, and we will serve you (1 Kings 12:4, *NIV*).

Upon hearing this request, Rehoboam told the people to return in three days for his answer. After they left, he called in the elders who had served his father to ask their advice, which was direct and good.

> If today you will be a servant to these people and serve them and give them a favorable answer, they always will be your servants (v. 7, *NIV*).

Unfortunately, the new king rejected the wise counsel of the elders and chose instead to act on foolish advice from his young friends.

> The young men who had grown up with him replied, "Tell these people who have said to you, 'Your father put a heavy yoke on

us, but make our yoke lighter'—tell them, 'My little finger is thicker than my father's waist. My father laid on you a heavy yoke; I will make it even heavier. My father scourged you with whips; I will scourge you with scorpions'" (vv. 10-11, *NIV*).

When Rehoboam announced his decision to the Israelites, they rebelled, and the nation of Israel was split on that very day. The majority of the people split away from Rehoboam and made a man named Jeroboam their king. It is interesting that, previously, Jeroboam had been honored by Solomon because of his distinguished service.

In other words, the people rejected the "boss" and exalted the servant over them. This happened because Rehoboam did something that is natural for many men. Instead of humbling himself before his people and being sensitive to their needs, he chose to dominate them into subjection. The result was a disaster.

Because of Rehoboam's refusal to humble himself and serve the people as the elders had advised him, God gave the nation over to a man who *would* serve the people. Out of the original 12 tribes of Israel, 10 tribes went with Jeroboam, and only Judah and Benjamin stayed with Rehoboam as king.

The moral of this historical event is this: *A servant's heart is the most important quality in leadership.*

At the Last Supper, Jesus Himself washed the disciples' feet as one of the last things He did with them (see John 13:4-15). He also commanded them to "wash one another's feet." In other words, they were to remain humble and be one another's servants.

Jesus gave His disciples another powerful teaching on the subject of leadership after the mother of James and John asked that they might have the high seats next to Jesus in His kingdom. Of course, the other disciples were indignant over this.

Jesus called them together and said, "You know that the rulers of the Gentiles lord it over them and their high officials exercise authority over them. Not so with you. Instead, whoever wants to become great among you must be your servant, and whoever wants to be first must be your slave—just as the Son of Man did not come to be served, but to serve, and to give his life as a ransom for many" (Matt. 20:25-28, *NIV*).

Husbands have choices to make related to their leadership styles: to choose the way of pride or the way of humility, to get in front and lead or to stand behind and push, to listen to the wisdom of God's Word or to take someone else's advice as Rehoboam did. The choices husbands make will determine not only their leadership styles but also *whom* they lead.

I (Jimmy) will never forget one night when I received a phone call from a church member informing me that a couple in our church was in the process of breaking up that very evening. He asked if I would go with him over to their home immediately and try to keep them together. Of course, I agreed.

In a few minutes, I was sitting across from this couple in their living room. Individually, they were two of the nicest people I had ever met, but as a couple, they were miserable. I saw a side of both of them that I had never seen before. Both were angry and defensive and seemed to be immovable in the stand they had taken to separate.

After I tried everything I knew to work out the situation, the wife still declined to open up very much about what she thought or felt. The only thing she said during a long period of time was that she would not put up with him any longer.

Finally, I asked her a question that apparently opened a floodgate to a chasm of heartache and anger within her. I asked a very simple question: "What does he do that makes you feel the way you do about him now?" She immediately responded as she turned toward me from the sofa and began to recite her grievances against him, one by one. I knew instantly that I was dealing with a dominant husband.

She had no idea how much money they had or where it was, because he would not tell her. She had absolutely no access to their finances, and when she asked for money, he would grill her as to what it was for and whether she really needed it. Although they were an upper middle-class family with a great deal of financial security, she felt like a pauper under the control of a harsh master.

In addition to his dominance over finances, she also told me he controlled every other area of their lives. Everything they ate, everything they did or she did, everywhere they went, and every person with whom they had contact was decided by him.

Once she had finished exposing her grievance, she concluded with this statement, "I'm ready to get out of this prison and start living!" Once she said that, I looked at the husband and asked him to respond to her grievances. He made no real defense. In fact, he admitted everything she said was true—but he thought he was doing the right thing! He thought the problem was all hers. She did not appreciate his "looking after" her.

From his point of view, she did not *need* to know about their money. He was doing a good job of managing it. His attitude was, "I don't think she's got it so bad."

I counseled this couple over a period of weeks, but he would not acknowledge that he was in any error at all. As a result, his wife refused to live with him any longer and moved out. Thankfully, today they are back together, but that only happened after he became willing to repent and change.

Like Rehoboam, the dominant husband uses carnal thinking to rule those around him. As a result, he is resented by those under his authority. Even worse, many times, he is rebelled against and deserted, like Rehoboam and the Israelites or like the husband in the above incident. Regardless of the outcome, *domination* in authority does not work, whether it is as a government ruler, a boss, a husband or a father.

Dominating through carnal authority instead of using spiritual authority makes one a petty tyrant, when God wants men to be benevolent authorities. You may wonder, "What causes a man to become controlling and dominating?" Typically, the dominating husband has been strongly influenced by one or more of the following factors involving his own father or his parents.

1. Undernurturing or Detached Parents
When a boy is growing up, he needs physical affection, words of love and affirmation softly spoken to him, and a lot of attention from both parents. When this nurturing influence is weak or absent in a boy's life,

he will overdevelop his sense of independence and identity. In order to be healthy, all of us need to maintain a balance between individual identity and group acceptance.

The boy who is undernurtured and underled by his parents will begin to respond by developing his own personality and identity as an emotional defense that results in an independent individual with a strong personality.

When he marries, almost always he will be attracted to his opposite—the overnurtured, overdominated female. He is attracted to her for two reasons. First, he needs the nurturing and belonging strengths she has, and she becomes the nurturing, accepting parents he never had. Second, because she typically has low self-esteem and a lack of confidence, she needs his sense of identity, and therefore accommodates the strength of his personality.

Although at first it seems to fit, this really is a very unhealthy codependent relationship. Neither spouse in this type of relationship will find long-term satisfaction. The man eventually will lose respect for his wife because she is weak, and she will grow to resent him because he dominates her.

The only healthy type of relationship is one in which both spouses have a balanced sense of identity and belonging, and neither has to seek that balance in an unhealthy way through overdependence upon the other.

If you have identified yourself, or if you are a woman reader who has recognized your husband as having a dominant personality, that means there are problems on both sides of the relationship that need to be healed.

2. Mismodeling

The strongest models a boy has in his formative years are his parents. There are other role models a boy or young man sees on television and in the movies, in addition to a significant amount of peer pressure among boys and men to be macho.

Primarily though, whenever a man has been strongly influenced by dominant parents in his past, he will seldom be healthy. The dominated boy typically will grow up having a weak personality with an underdeveloped sense of identity, or he will become like his dominant role models. The biblical description of this is the term "iniquity."

In Deuteronomy 5:9, God told the people of Israel that He would visit the iniquities of the fathers on their children to the third and fourth generation. The Hebrew word *avon* (pronounced "aw-vone" and translated "iniquity") means "to bend" or "to twist."[1] If you have ever seen a tree that has been blown by a prevailing wind from the same direction for many years, you have seen how the tree becomes bent permanently. This is a perfect analogy of what happens to children when they grow up in a sinful environment.

As a child is constantly influenced by harsh words, immoral behavior, abusive treatment, neglect, and so on, he becomes influenced by it. Unless the behavior of the parent is, at some point, properly dealt with by the affected child, it will have a permanent influence on his life.

The example that parents set is powerful in developing the identity and behavior patterns of their children. Society also plays an important role in this process. When parents and society have been a positive role influence to children, they become upright in their behavior. There is nothing to bend them or twist their understanding of life.

However, when a child grows up in an unhealthy home and/or society where he knowingly or unknowingly accepts the values shown him, he will carry those belief systems and behaviors into his marriage, thus creating many unhealthy homes.

Every person whom I (Jimmy) have ever known or counseled has iniquities from his or her past. Perhaps it is prejudice, negativity, spiritual pride, religious tradition, gossip, abuse, substance abuse, chauvinism, anger, or one of many other things. The main thing that must be realized is that, whatever it is, it is not right, and it is something that was picked up from the home environment as a child or young person.

3. Ignorance or Insecurity

Ignorance or insecurity causes a man to overcompensate for his lack. When a boy has grown up without a father present in the home, he lacks the appropriate knowledge of how to love a woman from daily observations. Not only is this lack of knowledge dangerous, but he often will feel insecure around women. If a boy has been dominated by a mother or has had negative experiences with women in general, his sense of confidence especially can be lacking.

One of the most dominant husbands I (Jimmy) ever encountered illustrates this point. This man acted around his wife as if he were totally in control. He behaved arrogantly and dominatingly. When I confronted him in counseling and finally succeeded in getting him to lower his super-macho-man guard, he confessed that actually he was very insecure around women.

He told me three things about himself that explained the dominance: his father was a traveling salesman who was never at home when he was growing up; his mother tried to dominate him but he rebelled; and he had been rejected as a young boy by several girls. Consequently, he had developed a rejection complex.

Combining those three influences had produced a young man without a male role model who did not want to be dominated by women. He had built walls between himself and the women around him to keep from being hurt again.

It was impossible for this man to have a healthy relationship with a woman without being healed. His healing came out of a process of counseling that addressed three basic needs in his life:

1. He needed to recognize the problems of his early family life. I carefully outlined the dysfunction of his absent father/dominant mother home until he understood it in his own terms.
2. He needed to forgive his parents, which I carefully led him to do.
3. He needed to understand his own dominant behavior.

From Ephesians 5, I explained to him the type of sensitive, servant-leadership a woman needs and how to walk in that. Because he basically had a good heart, it didn't take long at all for his marriage to be healed and transformed.

4. Sin and Deception

Another influence that creates dominant men is sin and deception. There are some men who have no good explanation from their pasts as to why they are dominant. For these men, it is simply a matter of sin, usually beginning with pride. Chauvinism, false manliness, and selfishness are the roots of their personalities. To make things worse, these men are open targets for the deception of Satan as he tries to destroy marriages by lies, accusations and darkness.

The only solution for the deceived or sinful man is the same as for the others: repentance and acceptance of God's Word as the standard of truth for manhood and marriage. The prayer of a righteous wife is greatly beneficial in this type of case; however, ultimately, the sinful man himself must make the final decision.

5. Dominant Temperament

The final explanation, factor or influence for a dominating husband is simply being born with a *dominant temperament*. In many secular and Christian studies, four basic temperaments (personality types) have been found. The strongest and most aggressive is the "choleric" or "lion" temperament (sometimes called a "Type A" personality). A person with this basic temperament is typically aggressive, strongly opinionated, and desires to be in control.

The positive aspect of this type is naturally strong leadership qualities. However, when this personality is not submitted to God and is unchecked by biblical standards of love and order, it almost always leads to abusive treatment of others.

A man with a choleric temperament needs to use his natural leadership qualities in his home, but he must be careful not to dominate his wife and children with his personality. The choleric man normally will have to make a serious effort to allow his wife and children the opportunity to express themselves around him. He will need to learn to balance his strong leadership qualities with a soft and sensitive love for his family.

2. The Passive Husband

One of the worst kings in Israel's history was Ahab. Not only is he known for being ungodly in his own right, but he is even better known for his evil, conniving wife, Jezebel. She was the daughter of Ethbaal, king of the Sidonians, and as such, high priestess of the cult of Baal.

After marrying her, Ahab began to worship her god and follow her spirit of evil. Jezebel really controlled Israel throughout Ahab's reign as the power behind the throne. He was king; she was boss.

Ahab was a passive leader, and while it looked as if he was in control, he really was not. Throughout his reign, he allowed Jezebel to terrorize and destroy God's people and to act in such a way as to provoke a curse on herself, Ahab and the entire nation.

He had the power to stand up and be a righteous leader and husband. If he had done that, there would have been times of peace and prosperity for Israel. However, because of Ahab's sin and weakness, his reign was a season of famine and destruction.

One prime example of how his personality enabled his wife to be in complete control is found in the story of a vineyard owned by a man named Naboth, which Ahab wanted. This vineyard was close to the palace, and Ahab wanted to turn it into a vegetable garden.

When the king confronted Naboth about trading the property or selling it to him, the vineyard owner refused. It was his family inheritance from generations past. Upon hearing this, Ahab went home despondent. Now, read the biblical record of what happened next:

So Ahab went home, sullen and angry because Naboth the Jezreelite had said, "I will not give you the inheritance of my fathers." He lay on his bed sulking and refused to eat. His wife Jezebel came in and asked him, "Why are you so sullen? Why won't you eat?" He answered her, "Because I said to Naboth the Jezreelite, 'Sell me your vineyard; or if you prefer, I will give you another vineyard in its place.' But he said, 'I will not give you my vineyard.'" Jezebel his wife said, "Is this how you act as king over Israel? Get up and eat! Cheer up. I'll get you the

vineyard of Naboth the Jezreelite." So she wrote letters in
Ahab's name, placed his seal on them, and sent them to the
elders and nobles who lived in Naboth's city with him. In
those letters she wrote: "Proclaim a day of fasting and seat
Naboth in a prominent place among the people. But seat two
scoundrels opposite him and have them testify that he has
cursed both God and the king. Then take him out and stone
him to death" (1 Kings 21:4-10, *NIV*).

Did you notice how Ahab reacted to Naboth? He went home and
sulked until someone else took care of the problem for him. As a little
boy, his parents probably ran his life for him. As an adult, his wife did.
This passive leader loved to wear the uniform and swing the sword, but
he didn't want to do any of the dirty work. This is a common scenario
for the passive man.

For every dominant man I have dealt with in counseling, I have
encountered two passive ones. Passive husbands seem sweet and sensitive to their wives at first, but later drive them crazy because they will
not lead. Whether it is finances, their spiritual lives, children, romance,
or whatever, the passive man ultimately destroys any sense of security
as well as the respect his wife once had for him. As long as the problem
remains, destruction continues.

The first thing the passive husband needs to understand is his wife's
need for leadership. For healing to begin, the passive man needs to realize
that he cannot remain passive and truly meet any woman's basic needs.

In stating this, let us describe some of the contributing factors that
most often produce a passive man.

1. An Overled or Overnurtured Past

Many passive men are simply acting out the programs of their pasts. If
their parents made their decisions and constantly controlled their behavior as boys, they never learned to act for themselves and never built real
personal identities.

In some instances, this "overled" aspect actually can be domination in
itself. If a young boy has parents who dominate and control his life, he is

never allowed to express himself or to learn to take responsibility for his own life. Regardless of whether a boy has been overnurtured or dominated, the result is that he is not ready to meet the demands of adulthood.

The overled, overnurtured boy almost always is attracted to his opposite in a woman—the dominant, aggressive female—for two reasons. The first one is that she gives him the leadership and sense of identity he needs. She is the replacement for his parents. The second reason is that he is attracted to her because his passive personality blends in well with her outgoing aggressiveness.

If he doesn't want to talk, she will talk. If he doesn't want to make a decision, she will make the decision. A match made in heaven, right? *Wrong!* These are the ingredients of a bad relationship.

Although the aggressive, dominant female is attracted to the passive male, she ultimately will resent him for his weakness in leadership and his passive temperament. Also, the dominant, aggressive personality that once attracted him will eventually cause bitterness because of her lack of honor and respect for him. This type of relationship cannot work because it is unbiblical and violates the greatest needs of both partners.

For a man in this position, the answer is for him to begin to exert his leadership. He should not *overswing* to a dominant position, but he should stop letting others run his life and make his decisions.

As King David said to his son Solomon before his death, "Be a man!" (see 1 Kings 2:2).

It may be difficult at first to change, but pray for God's strength and do it. It may even surprise the dog when the husband starts making decisions around the house, but he and everyone else will get used to it very quickly and be much happier and secure.

The husband must be sensitive and humble but act in a godly, aggressive manner to lead his home. He should forgive his parents, break family iniquities, and begin a new family system that works.

2. Mismodeling

Many times the passive man has been raised in a family system of passive men. Early in life the men of the family were taught to memorize the phrase, "Yes, dear," in a whining, submissive tone. Men who come from this type of system will either rebel against it and find a woman to dominate, or they will follow it and seek a woman to dominate them. Either way, it is an unhealthy pattern.

The answer is to recognize the unbiblical male role model in your past life, confess passiveness as sin, forgive your parents or whoever were your caregivers, and break the iniquity from your life.

3. Intimidation

Many men in America have been intimidated by the women's rights movement and all of the ensuing media coverage. As men have been constantly chastised for opening doors, not allowing women to pay their own way and to reveal their equality in every sense of the word, or even for not allowing women to fight in wars, many men have become frozen with fear of doing the wrong thing.

What do we do? Well, men, the first thing *not* to do is become passive. We realize many women are frustrated by the way they have been treated by men. However, the answer is not for men to change places with women so that they can dominate us for a while! The answer is to correct the problem, not to switch male/female roles.

The only lasting solution to the male-female problems in America is for men to assume once again their places as righteous and sacrificial leaders. Any other action is only an accommodation to the problem, not a solution. Men, if you have harmed women by abusing them or mistreating them in any way, you need to repent to them and ask their forgiveness.

After you have repented, *be a righteous man*. Just as Paul wrote in Ephesians 5, Jesus is the ultimate role model for husbands. Fix your eyes on Jesus as you ask the Holy Spirit to teach you how to be a righteous leader.

If you have not sinned against a woman, yet she gets in your face and angrily blames you for everything every man on the face of this earth has done to her—don't accept the blame. You can sympathize with her feelings, but don't try to solve the problem by becoming the opposite of what she hates. Don't become an overly submissive, female-dominated slave simply to prove you are not a chauvinist. It will not work!

4. Sin or Laziness

Some men become passive to punish their wives for something they feel the wives have done wrong. Rather than yelling or stomping around, these men sit and torment their wives with silence and inaction.

Other men are passive because they are lazy. Their wives' aggressiveness makes it possible for them to rest, and so they do. Men who are apathetic and passive because of a root of sin or laziness simply must repent and get to work.

5. Passive/Phlegmatic Temperament

Of the four basic temperament types, the most laid-back of all is the phlegmatic personality. People with this temperament are easy to get along with generally and make great friends. They are slow to anger and less inclined to change or to become unstable. This provides for a lot of good qualities in a relationship.

However, the husband who has a naturally passive, phlegmatic personality will typically be a poor leader in his home. It is not that he cannot lead; it is that normally he is much more inclined to let his wife lead, or just go with the flow. This tendency creates major problems for a marriage.

A man with a phlegmatic personality needs to first of all realize that he must lead his home in an assertive manner. Not only is this a commandment of God, but it also is a major need in a woman. It may not be as natural for a phlegmatic man to assert his opinions and his direction; nevertheless, he must change to have a biblical marriage and to do God's will for his life.

As you pray and ask the Holy Spirit to give you wisdom and power, begin now to lead your home. Your naturally gentle personality gives you a solid foundation to become a good leader, but you must learn to act and lead with courage and skill.

3. The Immoral Husband

Although David had many great character traits and did great exploits in the service of God, he made a terrible mistake that brought destruction to his family and to the nation of Israel.

According to 2 Samuel 11:1-3, King David was walking around on the palace roof one evening in the spring of the year gazing upon the city of Jerusalem. As he scanned the surrounding rooftops, he noticed a woman bathing.

Rather than turning and walking away, David continued to study her nude body. Finally, he couldn't stand it any longer. Not only was his curiosity piqued, but his lusts were ablaze with desire for the woman. He sent hurriedly for someone to tell him who she was. Before long, a man came forward and told David the woman living in that house was Bathsheba, the wife of Uriah the Hittite.

David was now in a dilemma. As she was married, he knew it would be adultery to have sex with her. Pacing around on his roof, he suddenly turned and commanded his servants to go get Bathsheba and bring her to him immediately.

When she arrived at the palace, David had her brought to his sleeping quarters. As she arrived in his room, and the servants were sent away, David gazed upon this beautiful woman who had aroused his lust minutes before on the rooftop.

Without delay—and apparently without any resistance from her—David took Bathsheba and fulfilled his desire for her. Afterward, Bathsheba gathered up her garments, cleansed herself, and returned home. Believing no harm was done, David went on about the business of being king and tried to forget his indiscretion.

However, there was a problem. Bathsheba was pregnant with David's child. After a few months of relative calm, David was shaken early one morning with the news of her pregnancy. Rather than facing the problem honestly, David compounded his sin. He sent for her husband to come home from battle and spend time with her, in order to make it look as if it were his child.

When Uriah came home, instead of solving the problem, he created an even greater crisis. As a man of great integrity, he refused to sleep with his wife while his fellow soldiers were sleeping in the fields. David faced a tough decision. Should he confess his sin to Uriah and perhaps lose a good general, as well as cause Bathsheba to be stoned (the penalty in Israel for a woman found in adultery)? If he didn't, the only other alternative was to have Uriah killed in battle and marry Bathsheba.

As everyone who has read or heard this biblical event knows, David opted for the choice of murder. Once Bathsheba heard her husband was dead, she mourned for him. When the mourning period was over, David took her as his wife.

However, all of that was not done without God being aware of it, of course. He was displeased by all the wrong choices David had made. One comparatively small sin of lustfully eyeing a nude woman glimpsed accidentally had mushroomed into great sin. God sent the prophet Nathan to confront David. Nathan told David a story that exposed David's own sin; then he delivered this word:

> Why did you despise the word of the Lord by doing what is evil in his eyes? You struck down Uriah the Hittite with the sword and took his wife to be your own. You killed him with the sword of the Ammonites. Now, therefore, the sword will never depart from your house, because you despised me and took the wife of Uriah the Hittite to be your own (2 Sam. 12:9-10, *NIV*).

Immorality is a growing problem in America and is greatest among men. The $13 billion-a-year pornography industry is almost completely supported by men. In addition to hardcore pornography, there are prostitution, dial-a-porn, R-rated video rentals, and plain old adultery.

Also, more men are becoming involved in homosexuality than ever before. Bisexuals are transmitting the AIDS virus quickly across America. Like King David, we have refused to deal honestly with the problem, and now we are faced with destruction right at our front doors.

One of the most serious cases of immorality that I (Jimmy) personally have encountered involved a man addicted to pornography. He
began with popular men's magazines, which today are called "light
porn," or are not considered pornography at all, but "art." He explained
to his wife that the pictures turned him on, thereby making him a better lover. Although she didn't like it, she allowed it.

Five years later, he was watching quadruple X-rated movies and hiring
prostitutes to have sex with him and his wife. Finally, his wife could no
longer go along with his perverse immorality, and she came for counseling.

Sin can never be satisfied! The more you get, the more you want. The
more you indulge in sin, the more it takes to even temporarily satisfy. The
farther you go, the less satisfaction you receive, until finally, you have to
quit or be dominated completely by whatever sin you are into.

Over the years, I (Jimmy) have counseled many men and women
who were battling immorality in their marriages. In most instances, the
man was the source of the immorality. Whether he was having an affair,
watching in-room adult movies on the road and trying to get his wife to
match what professional actresses were doing for money, or into some
other sexual sin, the immoral man brought destruction to his home.

Here are some of the influences that contribute to the making of an
immoral man:

1. Rejection

Rejection by parents is one of the strongest influences that drive some
men toward pornography and immorality.

When a growing boy has been deprived of wholesome physical affection and attention, it will create a greater appetite for physical contact
than in other boys. As we are sexual creatures, the innate need for affection and touching by other human beings often becomes a need for sex.

A great deal of homosexual tendencies can be traced to rejection or
a lack of male bonding. The lack of emotional and physical contact
with a man at a young age leaves a boy hungering for male love. If there
is a strong female influence present where the male influence is absent,
a boy can grow up sexually confused. This is why some men identify so
much with women that they view other men as the opposite sex.

The answer to rejection is a process of forgiveness and healing and, most important, identification of the root of sexual immorality. After having identified it, one must deal with it directly in a biblical manner.

2. Visual Enticement

Men are much more visually stimulated than women. This is why pornography appeals to men more than to women. The entire entertainment and advertising media have relentlessly targeted this male attribute. The result is naked or near-naked bodies everywhere you look. Even wholesome television programs can be littered with unrighteous commercials. But, beyond television, today's world is full of sexual temptations for men.

The answer to this problem begins with blatant honesty. Men must honestly admit to being tempted by visual stimuli. Many men who today are in deep bondage tried yesterday to make it look as if they did not have a problem. After honesty comes restraint. Men must remove temptation by not watching impure television programs and movies, by dropping certain magazine subscriptions, and by staying in motels and hotels that do not have "adult videos" in the rooms.

Next, men must become accountable. This is one of the most important steps in the entire process. The man who is not accountable to someone for where he is and what he is doing is in a dangerous position. Find someone to whom you can talk and become accountable. It could save your life and your marriage.

3. Mental Bondage

When a man sees an erotic image, there is a chemical called epinephrine released in his brain that locks in the image permanently. That is why many men can remember vividly certain sexually erotic pictures or movies that they saw years ago. God designed epinephrine to help men become excited by their wives and remember them. Satan tries to use this natural creation of God to fill men's minds like a museum of perversion with every image possible that will inspire lust and filthy thoughts.

A man can never overcome lust until he has won the battle for his mind. Not only must men overcome the sinful images already there, but men must also battle unclean thoughts as they try to enter their minds.

There is only one answer: meditation on God's Word. Men, we can save you a lot of time and heartache right here, if you will just believe us. Cold showers and self-abuse will never work. You must change the way you think, or you will never change the way you act.

That is why Paul wrote in 2 Corinthians 10:4-5:

> The weapons we fight with are not the weapons of the world. On the contrary, they have divine power to demolish strongholds. We demolish arguments and every pretension that sets itself up against the knowledge of God, and we take captive every thought to make it obedient to Christ (*NIV*).

This passage explains a vital truth: The beginning of every major battle is fought in our minds with the Word of God.

Begin in the mornings by reading the Bible 5 to 25 minutes a day. As you go about your daily work, reflect upon what you read that morning. Let it sink into your heart and mind. As you do this, you will see a huge difference in your life. Not only is meditation upon God's Word able to destroy the sexual strongholds in your mind, but God also promises in Psalm 1 that He will cause everything you do to prosper, if you meditate on His Word day and night.

4. Sin and Deception

Satan works overtime to convince us that sin will enhance our lives. If we believe his lies, we become sitting ducks for destruction. The only answer to our sinful flesh is to crucify it by submitting it to Christ, as the Bible says we should. The only answer to Satan's lies is to refute them with the truth of the Word of God.

The greatest sexual fulfillment for any man is a pure, monogamous relationship with his wife. Don't accept the same lie that fooled King David, or you will be forced to swallow the same bitter pill of reality that he swallowed. We live in a dangerously deceptive world. God's wisdom and the exercise of caution will prevent you from becoming its prey.

4. The Distracted Husband

In addition to Jesus, probably the wisest man who ever lived was King Solomon. The second son of David and Bathsheba, Solomon was appointed to reign on the throne of David. In the very beginning of his reign, he was humbled and blessed by God with extreme wisdom in every area of life. During his reign, the nation of Israel continued to grow and prosper at an astounding rate.

Kings and queens from around the world traveled to Israel to hear the wisdom of this great man and to see his kingdom. Unfortunately, it did not last. Solomon had 700 wives, plus 300 concubines.

This brings up a very interesting question: Why would he have so many wives?

Even with the knowledge that kings of the time gave their daughters in marriage to neighboring rulers as one way of keeping peace or as a way of making an alliance with a powerful king, a thousand such alliances seems extraordinary. So we don't know that anyone can answer that question completely, but one thing seems clear, and that is that somehow Solomon became a driven man.

Apparently, this began innocently enough. Solomon was a greatly gifted man with opportunities to do many great things for God and for his people. His first major project was to build the first temple in Jerusalem, which was completed to perfection and was instrumental in reviving the faith of the people.

When Solomon finished that project, he began another and another—and on and on for the rest of his life. When he got a little time off, he married another wife, then another, and so on.

Finally, toward the end of his life, he had a nation full of completed projects—for which he had taxed the people greatly and worked them very hard—and a palace adorned with wives. But there were two things missing: an intimate relationship with God and with one woman.

Solomon's distracted and driven existence left him spiritually and emotionally bankrupt and without God's blessing at the end of his life. Because of Solomon's failure to follow God faithfully, God took most of the kingdom from Solomon's line.

First Kings 11:4-11 records his final days:

As Solomon grew old, his wives turned his heart after other gods, and his heart was not fully devoted to the Lord his God, as the heart of David his father had been. He followed Ashtoreth the goddess of the Sidonians, and Molech the detestable god of the Ammonites. So Solomon did evil in the eyes of the Lord; he did not follow the Lord completely, as David his father had done. On a hill east of Jerusalem, Solomon built a high place for Chemosh the detestable god of Moab, and for Molech the detestable god of the Ammonites. He did the same for all his foreign wives, who burned incense and offered sacrifices to their gods. The Lord became angry with Solomon because his heart had turned away from the Lord, the God of Israel, who had appeared to him twice. Although he had forbidden Solomon to follow other gods, Solomon did not keep the Lord's command. So the Lord said to Solomon, "Since this is your attitude and you have not kept my covenant and my decrees, which I commanded you, I will most certainly tear the kingdom away from you and give it to one of your subordinates" (*NIV*).

A truth to be learned from the life of King Solomon is this: If he could fall, anyone can. God appeared to Solomon twice and spoke to him audibly. He was the wisest, most intelligent man (except Jesus) who ever lived. He possessed every material asset imaginable. Yet, he fell. That should put the fear of God into us all!

The most important thing we need to understand about the fall of Solomon is *why* it happened. The answer is simple: He was distracted by the busyness and pursuits of life and had no time left to pursue God. His once-rich and intimate relationship with God faded to nothing because he stopped pursuing Him.

The same mistake affected Solomon's relationship with women. He had time to drop by for a chat and some quick sex with one of his many wives, but not for prolonged conversation or true intimacy. Solomon would fit right in with the American culture today. Our driven, over-achieving society would make him king within two weeks, because we are just like him in many ways.

I (Jimmy) often counsel couples who are suffering terribly because the man is distracted by his job, a hobby, recreation or entertainment. The wife is frustrated because he will not tune in to her. As a result, the woman begins to nag him to get his attention. This response often drives her husband even farther away.

As I try to get the distracted husband to turn his heart toward home, I normally deal with the following root issues that cause the problem.

1. Performance Motivation

Many men are taught by their parents that they are not accepted unless they perform. This happens when a parent communicates love and approval only when a child excels at something or in some way. It also happens when a parent drives a child to excel. Many children are taught to bring home straight *As* on their report cards, or it is not good enough. Although the parent intends only good things for the child, often the child's self-esteem is damaged in the process.

Parents should communicate their love to a child at all times, not just when he does something great. Parental love, properly communicated, builds a child's self-esteem and security. The child knows he does not have to perform to get his parent's approval. When a parent communicates conditional acceptance to a child, the child feels he must perform to be loved.

Because all children want to be accepted by their parents, they perform to win approval; in doing so, children learn to perform for acceptance in society later on. This is a dangerous motivation because society is so conditional in its acceptance anyway.

Society wants us to drive the right car, look a certain way, and so forth, in order to be accepted. Although all of us should perform to some degree to obey God and maintain social responsibilities, no one should have to jump through a hoop to get people to like him or her.

When I (Jimmy) counsel men who are driven and distracted, I am often dealing with men who have never felt accepted by their fathers.

One man was a driven athlete who had played major college football. He confessed that the thing that motivated him to excel in sports was to win his father's approval and attention.

You may have had a father who didn't accept you as you were, but God does accept you! Of course, He wants you to do your best and keep His commandments, but before you do, He loves you and accepts you if you are His child. Stop performing to gain man's approval and start doing what God tells you to do. Remember, according to Jesus in Matthew 11:30, His yoke is easy and His burden is light.

2. Greed

Some men work a lot or play a lot because of greed. In most cases where men work too much, they feel they are doing their families a service. Although men should be good providers, the first thing every man should give his wife and children is himself. If work keeps you from doing that, money or the things it buys will not solve your problems.

Although many men feel they are overworking for their families, the truth is—it is mostly for themselves. They derive either emotional gratification, material reward, or both from what they are doing, and that keeps them going. When confronted by their wives to slow down and come home, many husbands cop out with the "I'm doing it for you" routine, when it really is greed motivating them.

Instead of work, other men golf, fish, hunt, and so forth to excess at the family's expense. These men are greedy for pleasure. One couple was on the verge of divorce because the husband played slow-pitch softball six nights a week. He congratulated himself in front of me and his wife because he had the discipline to take one night off!

The only answer to greed for money and possessions or for fun and self-satisfaction is repentance that will lead to contentment. Repent for turning your heart away from God and your family because of misguided or unrestrained desires. Turn your heart toward God and your family, being content with them and giving them their rightful places in your life.

3. Perverted Values

Many men simply believe their families are an outgrowth of their work. I (Jimmy) counseled one man whose wife was furious because he worked seven days and six nights a week. She had to go to his place of employment to see him. Most of their time together was spent around his job.

She finally became fed up and told him she was going to leave if he did not change. His response was to take an hour out of his "busy" schedule to come to my office and ask me to "talk some sense" into his unreasonable wife.

When I agreed with his wife's belief that he worked too much, he became obviously disgusted with me. It got even worse when I told him he should change jobs, if necessary, to meet his wife's needs. But the absolute high point of our discussion came when I told him his work was supposed to support the home, not the other way around.

He turned beet-red with anger. It was as if I had slapped his grandmother! I could have said almost anything about his wife without making him mad, but his job was another issue. No wonder his wife wished he was only having an affair with another woman so at least she could compete.

But, as she exclaimed, "I simply can't compete with his work!" She shouldn't have had to.

The man with perverted priorities needs to read the Bible. Jesus said in Matthew 22 that the greatest commandment is to love God, and the second greatest is to love others. Loving work did not even make the top 10. Repentance and making the required lifestyle adjustments are the most important steps in turning a man's heart toward home. If his heart isn't there, it doesn't matter what else is.

4. Unresolved Conflict

When there is unresolved conflict between a husband and wife, the husband often responds by turning his attention toward his work. The longer this takes place, the more unhealthy their relationship becomes.

Some men are not honored or respected at home, but they are at work. So they gravitate to the workplace as a surrogate home atmosphere to meet their most basic needs, or at least to protect them.

Regardless of the reason, a man does not find the correct answer to his problem by turning away from home.

If you are hiding from family problems by working excessively, you need to repent and go home. Ask God to help you overcome your problems at home. As you persevere in prayer to face the challenge of working through problems, God will honor you, and you will be much happier for having faced the issues head-on.

Iniquities Can Be Broken and Cleansed

Here is how to break iniquities in your life and keep from passing them on to your children:

1. You Must Take Responsibility for Your Own Behavior
Although your parents have influenced you, your sins are not their fault. They are yours. Therefore, you must take responsibility for yourself and not shift the blame to your parents, society, or anywhere else.

2. Specifically Identify the Problem
For example, a man reading this chapter might say, "My father was dominant and abusive. I realize now that I am the same way. My iniquity is dominant and abusive behavior."

3. Having Acknowledged the Sin Causing Problems in Your Life and Marriage, You Must Specifically Repent
God has promised that, if we confess our sins, He will forgive us (see 1 John 1:9). Therefore, you must confess your sin to God and sincerely attempt to turn away from it.

4. You Must Forgive Your Parents
This step is critical if you are to change and truly turn away from that pattern of dominance.

In some instances, this may be very difficult, because the sin of your parents may have been severe abuse or neglect, even sexual abuse. However, regardless of how severe the problem was, you will not be healed and released from that destructive pattern until you forgive your parents.

Forgiveness is as much or more for your sake as it is for theirs. Unforgiveness is like an invisible umbilical cord that forever ties you to them, as it also perpetually feeds your problem. However, when you forgive, the umbilical cord is cut, and you can be free.

Also, God cannot forgive your sins against Him unless you forgive other people's sins against you (see Matt. 6:15). When you have not forgiven your parents, you cannot become healthy or balanced in life.

Unforgiveness is like an intoxicant in the bloodstream that causes a staggering drunk to move from side to side and not be able to walk a straight line. When you have not forgiven your parents, you either will become just like them or you will become the opposite of them, which normally is damaging and unhealthy. In other words, unforgiveness causes you to be bent to one extreme or the other in life and not to be able to grow straight and tall.

Many people pride themselves on the fact that they are not like their parents because earlier in life they made vows to themselves not to ever be like them. What those people often fail to realize is that, although they may be quite different from their parents, their personalities are just as unhealthy. So, like drunks trying to mount a horse, we—and generations after us—will keep falling from side to side until someone repents and forgives.

Stop holding your parents in judgment. Do not rehearse your past and their failures. *Release them from guilt in your mind.* Once you have done this, bless your parents. Regardless of how you feel, pray for them and bless them. Even if they are dead, this step is important for you. If they are alive, not only bless them in prayer often, but also honor them. According to Ephesians 6:3, God will greatly bless us when we honor our parents.

5. Finally, Break the Iniquity over Your Own Family

This is done in two ways. First, in prayer, proclaim your freedom from this family iniquity by the atoning blood of Jesus. Receive His forgiveness by faith and remain steadfast in that position of purity.

Second, be a righteous model to your children in order not to produce a "bend" in their lives. You do this as you repent quickly for your sins and are careful about your behavior around them and example in front of them. Also, love them and lead them with great care and sensitivity.

Perhaps you have recognized one or more of these examples in your own life or marriage. Early in our marriage, I (Jimmy) was dominant, immoral and distracted. Today, I am different because of God's grace and a willingness to deal with my problems.

We hope you have read something in this chapter that will benefit you. Whether you are a wife who needs to understand and pray for your husband or a man trying to understand your relationship with your wife, we pray that you have been encouraged and strengthened.

Note
1. James Strong, "Hebrew-Chaldee Dictionary," *Strong's Exhaustive Concordance of the Bible* (Iowa Falls, IA: Riverside Book and Bible House), Hebrew #5771.

How to Understand and Meet Your Wife's Needs

So husbands ought also to love their own wives as their own bodies.
He who loves his own wife loves himself; For no one ever hated his own flesh,
but nourishes and cherishes it, just as Christ also does the church.

EPHESIANS 5:28-29

When a young person gets his first car, he is mesmerized by the thought of more independence and mobility. He has dreamed about it, fantasized about it, talked about it, and even pretended he was driving it. Now the big moment has come.

Our daughter went through this phase shortly before her sixteenth birthday. As we made nightly rounds to every car lot in the city, it didn't take long to see that our daughter was looking for only one thing—style.

She would see one that struck her fancy and say, "Oh, I really like that one!"

We would respond, "Okay, honey, let's look at it and see how much it costs. If we like it, we will read about it in the consumer magazines, pray about it, and then make a decision."

Although she kept a sweet and submissive spirit through the entire process, we could tell she was a little put out with all of the technical aspects of looking for a car. She was ready to buy the first flashy car she could find and get on the road.

Although we knew we needed to take our time and get the best car for our money, we really could empathize with our daughter. I (Jimmy) remembered feeling as she did when I got my first car. I wasn't thinking about maintenance expense, gas mileage, resale value, or upkeep. I was thinking about speed, independence, and girls!

Most people prepare for marriage like a teenager shopping for his or her first car. Teenagers look first for exterior and other immediate qualities, showing little concern about long-term maintenance. Rather than asking about important things such as mileage and resale value, they are preoccupied with speed and flashy accessories. Marriage often is approached the same way.

So when people get married, they usually haven't prepared themselves for the expense and maintenance aspect of the relationship.

After our daughter had her first car for about a month, something went wrong with it.

She immediately asked us, with a perplexed look on her face, "What are you going to do about this?"

We smiled and said, "Honey, it's your car. What are you going to do about it?"

Although we knew we would help her get the car fixed, we were trying to bring a little reality into her thinking. She had experienced the fun of the car; now it was time to take responsibility for keeping it operable and in good shape.

Immaturity causes us to enjoy the pleasure of something without assuming responsibility for it. It is even more immature to get rid of something, or to reject it, simply because it needs maintenance or has broken down. Anyone who drives a car or owns a home realizes you cannot sell your car or move every time you have a problem. We learn to be responsible for the maintenance if we are going to use and enjoy material possessions.

Likewise, the answer for marriage problems is not to reject your spouse or to get a new one. The answer is to assume responsibility for fixing any problems. If we took our God-given responsibilities to provide for our partners' needs and to maintain our relationships properly, there would be few—if any—serious problems to face in our marriages.

A tremendous number of marital problems are due to shallow thinking and irresponsible attitudes. Most of us want marriages without maintenance, thrills without responsibilities, and fun without faithful devotion. Sorry! That is simply immature and unrealistic thinking.

When a man marries a woman, he has acquired a precious gift from God. He has a lifelong friend, lover and helpmate. He is drawn to such a relationship because he needs a woman with whom to share life. But if he thinks for a minute that his precious bride will not require regular maintenance, he is sadly mistaken. No matter what woman a man marries, his wife will require essentially the same care.

Women's Basic Needs Are the Same

After 18 years of marriage and having counseled thousands of women, I (Jimmy) can tell you emphatically, women are all basically the same. Like automobiles, there may be a few different options available on some models, but under the hood, the equipment is the same.

Some men don't believe this, so they keep trading wives, hoping each time to get a newer or better model that performs 100 percent of the time and never needs care and maintenance. Such a man is headed for multiple disappointments simply because that particular model does not exist—automobile or woman.

Before a man marries, he should understand that he automatically assumes the responsibility for his wife's needs.

There are two significant issues about women that men must learn and accept in order to have a harmonious marriage. The first issue is the essential difference that exists between men and women. The second is learning the four major needs of a woman and how best to meet them.

We realize men understand the basic sexual and physical differences in men and women and recognize certain other differences as well. However, our goal is for men to understand and accept the fact that women are essentially different from men in almost every area.

Beyond the issue of physical sexual difference, many men are totally frustrated by the overall mystique of a woman. I (Jimmy) am a good example. After several years of marriage, I was almost convinced that God didn't make women!

I thought, "God is smarter than that!"

I was totally frustrated with everything about Karen. She was so different from me. How could she be normal? I wanted a woman who had all of the right physical and sexual attributes, but who thought and acted like a man.

While I didn't realize it then, I spent the first five years of marriage trying to make my wife be like me. I would lecture her, browbeat her, tell her, and show her—but she just would not catch on. Finally, I gave up. I thought I had made a mistake in marrying Karen. Out of three billion women on this planet, I thought I had picked the only weird one.

In my ignorance and arrogance, I was fighting against God's perfect design. Like a child trying to assemble a nuclear bomb without instructions, I egotistically knew how to make our marriage work if only Karen would listen to me. But I was deceived. I was unwilling to accept and honor the essential differences God had designed in my wife to make her a woman.

Many women feel and act the same toward men. Observing the inherent differences, they respond with the "men are weird" attitude. Both sexes need to realize neither one is weird. We are the way God made us. We can either accept this truth and learn to function in it, or we can continue generations of frustration and fighting.

Even when we have realized and accepted the differences in the opposite sex, we must be careful not to translate their differences into our own language.

For example, suppose your wife says to you, "Honey, I want you to hold me."

Almost immediately, a normal man will think, "Oh, boy, she wants sex!" And he will begin not only to hold her but to make sexual advances.

As your wife slaps your hand out from under her blouse, she says, "Can't you keep from touching me there all of the time? I just want you to hold me!"

Although you hear the words correctly, your mind keeps trying to translate woman-talk into man-talk. The feminine words, "I just want you to hold me," translate to the male mind as, "Doesn't compute. She must mean she wants sex. That computes!"

Men have a natural need for sex. A man's brain thinks this way, because sex is one of his primary needs. But sex is *not* a primary need for a woman. Women need affection. While totally different from men, it is true. So when a woman says she only needs to be held, that is exactly what she means.

Any translation into man-talk is inappropriate. If a man does translate what she is saying into man-talk, he will only frustrate her and himself as well.

How does it make you feel when you express a need to your wife, and she belittles it or translates it into her language?

For example, suppose you said to your wife, "Let's go have sex right now," and she responded with, "You pervert!" or, "No, honey, you don't need sex. What you really need is some non-sexual affection. Here, let me hold you." How would that make you feel?

Many of you know the feeling of rejection, because you have experienced it. When recently married couples seek counseling, those who had no formal preparation before marriage often state their problems like this: "He's a pervert!" says the wife, and the husband counters, "She's a prude."

What each really is saying is, "I do not understand nor accept our differences."

She can't understand why he wants sex all of the time, and he can't understand why she doesn't want sex all of the time. Each is convinced something is gravely wrong with the other.

If husbands and wives would simply *listen* to each other, take each other at face value, and apply themselves to meeting one another's needs, happiness would prevail. Husbands would get the sex they need in an energetic and satisfying way. Wives would get the tender affection they need. No one could wipe the smiles off their faces with a soap pad.

Not only does a woman need affection, but she also has a deep need for intimate conversation. Whenever I (Jimmy) learned to be affectionate with Karen and communicate with her as she desired, I came to enjoy it as much as she did. Today, I love and need such affection and communication. I can't believe I ever lived without them. Also, when Karen began to aggressively meet my sexual needs, she began to enjoy sex as much as I did. God's plan is wonderful. Not only do we get to fulfill each other, but we discover things about ourselves and life that we never knew existed.

When spouses reject each other and call each other names, lives are damaged. The only way to successfully live with and love a spouse is to honor and accept the inherent differences and meet the other's needs aggressively. When this is done, spouses can become best friends and intimate lovers. When this is not done, spouses become bitter rivals and mutual victims.

The remainder of this chapter will discuss the four major needs of a woman and the ways they are met. A woman's four basic needs are security, affection, open communication, and leadership. Because security is the most basic need, we will discuss that first.

Security Is More Than Finances

Although security is a very broad term and general in meaning, nevertheless, it is a woman's greatest need. Whether a woman is growing up with her parents or living with her husband, she has the genuine need to be secure. A woman needs to know she is safe and well provided for in every aspect.

A wife's basic need for security is satisfied by adequate protection and provision given by God through her husband. The husband must communicate four things to his wife to satisfy her need for security.

1. He Must Communicate That He Cares for His Wife Above Anyone or Anything Except God

When a woman senses her husband is preoccupied or detached from her in some way, she will immediately feel insecure. She wants to know her husband is tuned in to her needs and concerns. A woman can discern instinctively if her husband truly is caring for her properly.

The best way a husband can determine if he is caring for his wife properly is simply to ask her, "Honey, do you feel like I'm caring for you properly? Do you feel provided for and protected?"

If she says yes, he can know he is meeting her needs, but if she says no, then he should listen carefully as she explains why not. Most men are too preoccupied with trying to "get my wife off my back" and keep her from demanding too much, rather than being totally committed to meeting her needs, regardless of the cost.

A woman learns to recognize when a man is not really committed to caring for her. Her situation is similar to the man who has a selfish and greedy boss. All men want to get the most they can out of employment, and their employer holds the keys. If they work for a selfless and generous employer, they feel secure and optimistic. If they have a boss who is distracted, overly demanding, or selfish, they lose a sense of security and joy.

Your wife's well-being and prosperity are greatly dependent upon you. She is very sensitive to your actions and attitudes for good reason. You need to understand and accept this. Consider what it would be like for a sensitive, caring employer to come up to you tomorrow and say, "You know, I've really been thinking about you lately. I wonder if there is anything I can provide for you to make your job more enjoyable. Also, am I paying you enough?"

That would be any employed person's dream. Well, every woman's dream is to have a husband who will manifest this same attitude. Regularly communicate to your wife that you are available and desire to meet her needs. Then, care for her. You will be pleasantly surprised by how well your wife responds to her new atmosphere of security.

A man often fears what his wife will do when he makes himself totally available to meet her needs. That is the last thing to fear. You simply cannot imagine what a woman will do for her man if he will envelope her in an atmosphere of total security by laying down his selfish ways to meet her needs.

Again, think about your employer. Wouldn't you do more and sacrifice more for a boss who served you and cared for you sacrificially? Or do you think you would lounge around the workplace while ordering your boss around and abusing him?

Simply because you have become humble and have committed yourself to meeting your wife's needs doesn't mean you lose your authority or manhood. True and lasting authority is built, not broken, upon the foundation of sacrificial servanthood. It is leadership by example, not ego.

2. A Husband Must Communicate His Admiration and Love for His Wife

A woman can never hear too often how pretty she is or how much her husband loves her. A woman blossoms fully in an atmosphere of praise and adoration, but she wilts and dies in the presence of perpetual silence or criticism.

Although a man must speak at times some words of correction or displeasure to his wife, these words must come from a source the woman knows is supportive and friendly. When you praise your wife and convince her of your love in real ways, you have then earned the right to also correct her. However, if all you do is point out her flaws and bad points, your wife will become insecure and bitter.

Every woman is the reflection of her husband. Women reflect in their faces, attitudes and appearances how they feel about their husbands and their environments. When a man creates an atmosphere of praise and respect for his wife, it makes a noticeable difference in everything she does. She radiates and reflects love and respect from every area of her life.

When a man constantly criticizes his wife or makes her dig for shallow compliments, she will reflect her insecurity. Women naturally gravitate to people and places where they will receive compliments about themselves. Men do, also. For a woman to have to go outside her home to receive praise is an indictment on her husband. What often comes next is even more serious.

I (Jimmy) have counseled many married couples who have had affairs. Sometimes it is the man, and sometimes it is the woman. Although affairs are always sinful and devastating to a marriage, you need to understand what tempts a woman to have an affair. It isn't sex. Women have affairs because they meet a man who will talk to them and make them feel special.

Women are turned on by men who compliment them and make them feel good about themselves. The best insurance a husband can possibly have that his wife will never have an affair is an atmosphere of praise and encouragement that he creates in which she can live. If he will do this, his wife will be drawn to him, and she will not be hungry for love when someone else comes along offering compliments and affection.

If he does not, although she may not participate in an affair, her hunger for love will cause her to wrestle with unnecessary temptations and fantasies.

Here are some simple rules for praising your wife:

- *Be sincere.* Say good things you really mean, and say them a lot.

- *Say something about every area of her life.* Do not just concentrate on physical things, although she needs you to physically affirm her often. Compliment her mind, her heart, her character, her motherhood, her cooking and so forth. Let her know that you are totally proud of her.

- *Never use sarcasm.* Never compliment your wife in a backhanded manner. It isn't cute; it will damage her spirit. For example, don't say, "Hey, you have a great body—under all that fat!"

- *Earn your words of correction.* For every one thing you correct or confront, give numerous compliments.

- *Praise your wife every day and never stop.* Send cards, flowers, love letters, anything that will communicate your love and respect.

3. A Husband Must Communicate His Faithfulness

Whistling at pretty girls walking down the street is understandable for teenage boys, but it is inexcusable for a married man. Jesus said that if a man even looks upon a woman with desire for her in his heart, it is the same as adultery. Adultery is not simply a physical act; it is an attitude.

Many men have never slept with a woman outside of marriage; nevertheless, they may carry a spirit of unfaithfulness. Women can pick up on this immediately, and it makes them insecure. A man's heart must remain faithful, not just when his wife is present, but also when she is absent. You need to communicate regularly to your wife that she is the only one you desire. You must convince her that she is the most beautiful woman in the world to you.

Unfaithfulness also is communicated by comparing your wife with other women. This is the kiss of death. Whenever you compare your wife's anatomy, behavior, intelligence or cooking to those of another woman—especially your mother—you have made a big mistake. The only time to compare your wife with another woman is when you are complimenting her.

Another no-no is to habitually watch other women through magazines, television shows, movies or real life. Although you may think it is harmless, it isn't. It's the same as your wife looking at or talking about other men all of the time. It is dishonoring and sinful. In any relationship where one person is out of control in an area, the other person normally will compensate.

Men want their wives to be sexually responsive. Did you know that a dirty movie or other pornographic material is the very worst thing to use in an attempt to make a woman sexually responsive? When a woman feels you are looking at other women or have other problems with unfaithfulness, she will instinctively withdraw from sex to compensate for your problem.

When you demonstrate sexual purity and restraint outside the bedroom, your wife can be free and responsive in the bedroom. Your purity will provide the security she needs to actually blossom.

Also, a husband should never threaten to divorce his wife. Don't even talk about divorce. Lose the word. Many married people discuss divorce as a threat to get the other spouse's attention. The only one to profit from such threats is the devil.

He loves divorce because it damages God's creation so terribly. So, when divorce is even a remote possibility in your mind, the devil works overtime to make it a reality. Also, your wife will become insecure if you talk about it, especially if you use it to manipulate or scare her.

4. A Husband Must Communicate His Dedication to Provide Financially
Finances are one of the most important areas of security for a woman.
A wife needs the assurance that her husband is committed to providing
for her financially. A man communicates his commitment to provide
financially in four ways:

1. *Praying for God's blessing and direction.* A woman is tremendously comforted to know her husband is praying and seeking God for financial direction and provision. It also is very helpful when a man leads his wife in prayer when financial pressure comes. If he will, he can avert many problems from occurring in their relationship as well as invoking God's blessing and provision. The old saying, "The family who prays together stays together," is true.

2. *Aggressively seeking the best employment possible.* Although we know that God is our provider, it still is important to knock on doors and seek opportunities.

3. *Being a hard and faithful worker.* A wife needs to know her husband is honest, faithful and hard-working. When a man is dishonest, lazy or changes jobs too often, he violates his wife and makes her insecure. Even if it means foregoing some income or benefits, a husband needs to be careful not to sacrifice his wife's security. This is very important.

4. *Being a wise money manager.* When a husband is a diligent steward of God's money, his wife feels secure. This is not a license to be stingy or unreasonably tight with money but an opportunity for wise money management. The husband should take responsibility for managing the money and paying the bills. (More specific information is in chapter 18.) It is extremely important to your wife for you to manage the family's money and resources wisely.

Non-Sexual Affection Is Important

An essential need of all women is non-sexual affection. Understanding and dealing with this truth was particularly tough for me (Jimmy), because I grew up in a family that was not very outwardly affectionate. My older brothers and I fought all of the time. So one of my weakest skills in marriage was in the area of affection.

For the first eight years of my relationship with Karen, I seldom held her or touched her for any length of time without becoming rough or sexual. She constantly complained about my being too rough or only touching her in sexual ways, but I honestly didn't know how to stop. In fact, I really didn't want to.

One time, when Karen was standing at the sink washing dishes, I came up behind her and grabbed her breasts.

In total frustration, she turned around and said, "Can't you touch me anywhere but there?"

I smugly replied, "Sure, but I don't want to." Not only was I constantly grabbing her and being rough about it, but I was complacent about changing or about meeting her needs.

Beginning with our dating days, I wasn't able to hold her hand without squeezing it or pinching her between her thumb and index finger. I really didn't think I was squeezing that hard, but she kept telling me I hurt her. I was just uncomfortable being physically affectionate, especially in public.

Over and over throughout our marriage, Karen kept telling me how she wanted me to hold her and touch her in non-sexual ways. I did not understand that non-sexual touching is a major need in a woman. I just thought she was strange or going through some phase. In fact, for a long time, I though she needed to toughen up and learn to enjoy wrestling around and rough play, because I enjoyed it.

But Karen never changed, because that was her basic nature. My attitudes toward affection were learned behavior. For a long time, I thought I couldn't change, because I "just was not that way." But then the Holy Spirit began to convict me that He was able to change anything if I would have a willing heart. Finally, I gave in and decided to give it a try.

The first time I seriously attempted to be affectionate with Karen in a soft, non-sexual way was one afternoon as we were sitting alone in our living room. I had been praying about how to begin to be affectionate. All of a sudden, the Holy Spirit nudged me and told me this was the time. I know this sounds stupid, but I had knots in my stomach.

Before acting, I thought about what I was going to do for at least 20 minutes. Finally, I got up and started across the room to where Karen sat on the couch, folding clothes. When she saw me coming, I knew exactly what she was thinking, "He must want sex or something."

However, for the first time in our relationship, I sat on the couch beside her, then put my arm around her and cuddled her affectionately without being sexual. Karen kept glancing at me with a smirk on her face.

I knew she was wondering, "Okay, what is it going to be this time? Sex or wrestling?" But I kept my arm around her and held her lovingly.

After five or ten minutes, I moved my arm, and she looked at me, and said, "What are you up to?"

I replied, "Nothing. I'm just trying to be affectionate with you in a non-sexual way."

She smiled and whispered, "Well, keep it up. I like it."

You can be sure that I did keep it up. The first few weeks were the hardest, but before long, I was completely comfortable with showing my affection in a soft, non-sexual way, and I began to really like it, too. To my surprise and delight, the more affectionate I was, the more sexually responsive Karen became.

My obedience to God and honoring Karen's wishes in this area was a real breakthrough for both our relationship and me personally.

Another benefit to being affectionate with your wife is that it makes your children secure and provides them with a good role model. Children need a lot of affection, and they need to see affection between their parents.

If you don't normally touch and caress your wife in soft, non-sexual ways, you need to begin to do that. Regardless of your past or present likes or dislikes, it fulfills and satisfies an extremely important need in your wife's life.

Beginning in the morning and throughout the day, look for opportunities to hug her, hold her hand, put your arm around her, and to be physically close. Such expressions of love will be great for both of you. Specifically ask what she desires in the area of affection and then do what she requests.

The Need for Open Communication

Wives have an inner need for detailed and honest communication with their husbands. They aren't looking for a once-every-two-or-three-days overview on how their husbands are doing. A wife wants a detailed conversation on what is going on in your life and mind every day. Although chapter 17 deals with communication in marriage, this is an appropriate place for a few specific pointers on husbands communicating with wives.

Every man first needs to accept the fact that communication is a bona fide need of his wife, not merely a want. She isn't being nosy or unreasonable when she grills you for information. She is simply trying to be a part of your life. Sharing information is one of the most powerful ways a wife is made to feel one with her husband.

Anything a wife does not know that she should know is a barrier to fulfilling her need for security and communication. So when a husband doesn't open up and tell his wife what he is doing, feeling or thinking, she becomes insecure and frustrated. For a man to understand this, he needs to try harder to see the world from a woman's perspective.

A wife is dependent upon her husband in many ways. She isn't in the position of headship. Therefore, a wife feels very vulnerable when she is not aware of what is going on in her husband's life. Not only does she need to hear the honest truth about what is happening with him, but she also needs to share with him what is going on in her life.

When a husband will not talk sensitively with his wife or listen attentively to her, their relationship deteriorates significantly and often very quickly. Remember that women seldom have affairs because of sex. They have affairs because they find a man who will communicate with them in a sensitive, open manner, thus making them feel special.

As a woman talks to such a man, she begins to feel intimate with him. Although the man usually is communicating with her in this way to eventually have sex, most of the time, she will end up giving him what he wants simply because he is communicating.

Affairs are extremely sinful and damaging, so understanding what leads to many of them can be a preventative measure. Once you understand the importance open communication plays in a wife's life, you need to tell your wife you recognize this need in her and accept your responsibility to meet it.

Doing so will make your wife feel special and secure while knowing her husband is committed to meeting her needs in a sensitive, sacrificial way.

After I (Jimmy) recognized and accepted this responsibility to Karen, the next thing I did was set aside a time every day to meet this need. We agreed to spend one hour every day before bedtime just talking. We put the children to bed about 8:30 or 9 P.M. when they were small. This gave us an hour to talk before our own bedtime. As the children grew older, we simply required them to be in their rooms by 9 P.M., reading or studying, so that we could have our time alone.

We normally would have popcorn or some other snack and sit together in the living room or bedroom to talk. The television always was off so that there would be no distraction. We talked as long as we needed to about anything.

At first I believed I was sacrificing for my wife, but soon that time became the highlight of my day. I now thoroughly enjoy our time together and need it as much as Karen does.

Early in our marriage, I would walk in the door after work and Karen would start grilling me with questions such as, "How was your day? Who did you see? What did they say?" and so forth. Not only did I not want to be interrogated when I entered my home, but also Karen would not accept "headline" answers such as, "Nothing," "Fine," and "No one special." She wanted everything explained in detail.

When we decided to be alone and talk for at least one hour a day, we made a compromise. I agreed to completely open up and talk in a sensitive, detailed manner, and Karen agreed not to grill me when I first came in from work. That not only worked perfectly then, but it is still working.

One small thing changed with time. In addition to our regular evening sessions, we walk for an hour together three or four mornings a week. It is not only good exercise, but also an excellent time to talk and pray together. It makes another special time for being together.

Open, frank and honest communications are essential for marital success. I have counseled many couples where the husband would not open up and talk. Sometimes it was because of unhealed wounds from his past. Other times it was because his wife had a sharp tongue, and he was afraid of being vulnerable. Probably the worst situation is the naturally quiet man with a wife who really needs his conversation.

One of the worst forms of abuse for a woman is silence by her husband. I have had wives in my office beg and plead their husbands to talk as the husbands sat quietly, refusing to open up.

Husbands, you must open up and talk honestly with your wife. If she has harmed you in some way, forgive her. Tell her she is going to have to be more careful with her words, if that is the issue. Afterwards, confront her when she does not choose her words carefully, but don't withdraw.

If you have unhealed hurts from your past or some hidden thing in your life hindering your opening up, either get it out and talk about it with your wife or find a pastor or some other professional counselor who can help you. You must work past any hindrances for the sake of your marriage and your own personal health.

Men who internalize their problems and don't talk about them have a greater incidence of heart problems, alcoholism and stress. The cornerstone of addiction and many other problems is a lack of honesty and openness about feelings and problems. Break the bondage of silence and begin to talk with your wife.

There is no such thing as the strong, silent type, because true strength is displayed in the courage to open up, not in hiding thoughts and feelings in fear. If you are the type of person who is naturally silent, *make* yourself open up and start communicating. Get in touch with your own thoughts and feelings and begin to express them openly.

Ask the Holy Spirit to help you learn to communicate and to give you the courage to change. He will answer your requests, because He is interested in you and your marriage.

Leadership Is Important

Regardless of how passive or dominant a woman is, she has a deep desire to be led by a caring, righteous man. She naturally wants to find a man who will care for her and lead her through life. This doesn't mean she wants to be dominated or controlled. In fact, a woman feels violated and insecure when a man begins to dominate her.

The same is true when a man doesn't properly lead in every area of the marriage. A woman desires her husband to lead in the spiritual life of the family, the finances, discipline and training of the children, and in every other area. When a man does not exercise such leadership, a wife becomes insecure and frustrated.

Lack of leadership is one of the more common complaints I (Jimmy) have heard from women in marriage counseling. Many women have complained that their husbands will not help with the children, take care of the money, lead them in prayer and in the things of God, and so forth. The husband often resents the wife's expectations of leadership.

Interestingly, men who will not lead usually are the very ones who deeply resent their wives challenging their authority by acting in their places.

God hasn't given the man the ultimate authority in the home to make sure he gets the best chair in the living room. God has given him authority in order for him to have the ability to lead. Authority without leadership is like an engine without a car body to contain it and make it useful.

So, use the authority God has given you to lead. As you become responsible for the leadership of every area of your family, your wife will love it, and she will love you more. However, you must be careful not to dominate your wife or family.

Listen carefully to what your wife says and how she feels about issues in your marriage. Ask her advice and pray with her about major decisions. Then make the decisions you believe God is telling you to make. I can assure you, your wife is going to be very supportive as you take this attitude and action. Not only that, God is going to reward you more than you can imagine for taking your rightful position in the home.

Women, for the most part, have gotten a bad rap for being rebellious and nagging their husbands. Although they may do a lot of regrettable things when they feel insecure or are left to themselves, almost all women readily accept and honor righteous authority in their lives. So, men, if you will lead, they will follow. But, if you will not lead, you definitely will have problems, and your wives will be just one of them.

We hope this chapter has helped male readers to understand their wives' needs better and how to meet them. In addition, we hope it has helped female readers to understand themselves better. Husband, when you understand how to apply yourself in an energetic way to fulfill your wife and then do it, both of you will be blessed beyond your wildest dreams. Without question, the best thing God did for all mankind was to send Jesus to die for us on the cross and then raise Him up again. But besides that, creating women has to rank way up there.

What a blessing women are when they are properly understood and cared for by righteous men!

The Destructive Wife

In the same way, you wives, be submissive to your own husbands so that
even if any of them are disobedient to the word, they may be won
without a word by the behavior of their wives, as they observe your chaste
and respectful behavior. And let not your adornment be merely external—
braiding the hair, and wearing gold jewelry, or putting on dresses;
But let it be the hidden person of the heart, with the imperishable quality
of a gentle and quiet spirit, which is precious in the sight of God.
For in this way in former times the holy women also, who hoped in God,
used to adorn themselves, being submissive to their own husbands.
Thus Sarah obeyed Abraham, calling him lord, and you have become her
children if you do what is right without being frightened by any fear.

1 Peter 3:1-6

As I (Jimmy) have spoken to women's groups over the years on the subject of women's roles in marriage, I often have sensed a feeling of caution in the audience. I understand this concern, so usually I begin by saying some things to help eliminate any barriers or defenses that might prevent women from receiving the message. The following are some of these introductory comments.

First, we all are equal in Christ. Although wives are to submit to their husbands in marriage, husbands are to submit to the authorities in their lives. It is hypocritical for a woman to be treated with contempt for not submitting to her husband when he is rebelling against and resisting the authorities in his life.

In fact, the context of Ephesians 5:22, which has been quoted several times already in this book, is found in the preceding verse, verse 21: "Submit to one another out of reverence for Christ" (*NIV*).

Second, although some information in this chapter may be painful for some women, it is God's truth that can bring healing. No one wants to be confronted by a self-righteous, mean-spirited person, even one bearing truth. Therefore, we will try our best to deliver God's healing truths with the utmost care and respect for the women receiving it.

Most women are intensely interested in the subject of relationships. That is why women are the foremost purchasers of books and self-help materials on marriage and relationships in general. In most cases, women are the first ones in troubled marriages to seek help.

The loving, nurturing instinct of women not only provides a relational focus designed to build healthy marriages and families, but it also protects our society from becoming relationally detached and uncaring. Therefore women play an extremely important role within society at every level.

In fact, a great dilemma facing women today is how they can most influence society without detaching from their domestic roles. Women desire to be involved and important in every level of our culture. Whether it is business, education, church or government, women need to be honored for their intelligence, equality and ability to give wise input.

However, as women more and more begin to seek positions of authority outside the home, two problems develop.

First, the more women detach from a domestically-centered environment, the more unhealthy society becomes. Although we may understand why a woman would want more from life than domestic responsibilities, we must realize that caring for a home, husband and children are extremely important functions society cannot do without.

In fact, the degrading fashion in which motherhood and being a housewife are generally depicted today is shameful. A woman who is a good homemaker and mother is doing a great service to God, her husband, her children, her community and society at large. As long as society looks down on domestically-centered women, society is perpetuating a curse upon itself.

Also, as more women are changing from domestically-centered to career-centered lives, they are becoming less satisfied personally. Some of this stems from a sense of guilt. When a woman must often leave her children with a babysitter or day-care center, that mother instinctively knows she needs to be with the children herself, no matter how excellent the temporary caregiver of the children is as a substitute.

If you are a working mother, please don't feel condemned by this statement. You may be working because you don't have a choice. We are not saying a working woman cannot be a good mother. The truth is that many women who work are wonderful mothers and wives. However, the truth also is that the more a woman detaches herself from a nurturing, caring home environment, the less satisfaction she will derive from life.

The answer is not for a woman to stay at home all day except for running errands connected with the home. Instead, a woman should strive to keep her focus of attention at home and to carefully monitor her activities outside the home so that all of the family unit will benefit from her care and attention.

Second, the reason women are less satisfied when they become detached from a home-centered environment is that women have a natural desire to be provided for by their husbands. While a woman may volunteer for church or charity activities or may even get a job to make some extra money, most women like to do such things on a voluntary, extracurricular basis. Most do not appreciate being forced to make money or to lead the household.

As men were instructed in the previous chapter, one of the primary needs of a woman is to be righteously led. When a husband is not leading his wife properly, an emotional void results. Although the severity of this void varies, one thing is common: Women feel insecure when they are not being taken care of properly.

This insecurity can be caused by an unrighteous husband, boss, school principal, mayor, police chief, governor or president. The point is that women have a need to be cared for in a righteous manner through responsible male leadership.

In the next chapter, four types of destructive wives will be described: the dominant, the enabler, the distracted, and the emotion-motivated wife. A wife may possess more than one of the four destructive traits, but even one of these traits in a wife can cause severe damage to a marital relationship. Possessing more than one trait means the chances of damaging the marriage are even greater.

Society's Problem: Lack of Male Leadership

The root cause of women feeling the need to leave their homes, and in many cases being forced to leave the home, to seek financial and/or political security is the lack of male leadership. If men were leading today in the manner in which they should, women would be much more secure. Therefore, women would not feel such intense pressure to learn vocational skills and to become as personally and socially protective.

However, today's void of righteous leadership places many women in vulnerable positions.

We have three goals for this chapter and the next:

- The first is to reveal the important responsibility society has to protect a woman's need to be domestically-centered.

- The second is to expose the fact that because women have a God-given need to be highly domestic while being under righteous authority, they will become less satisfied the more they are removed from such an environment.

- The final goal is to educate women on the way to deal with their own destructive tendencies in marriage, most of which are in response to their husband or to men in general.

As discussed in chapter 8, "The Destructive Husband," because a wife is dependent upon her husband for leadership and provision, she naturally will respond to what her husband does or does not do. The reason is that, in the beginning, God created Adam to be the initiator and Eve to reflect Adam's glory as his helpmate and companion.

This reflective quality of women is beautiful to behold when a woman has a righteous husband. However, when a husband sins or does not fulfill his responsibility to lead his wife and love her sacrificially, she is put at a tremendous disadvantage. In fact, one of the greatest challenges a woman will face in her lifetime is how to respond correctly to an unrighteous husband or authority figure.

This is why America is seeing such an enormously frightening social trend of women becoming more masculine and independent. Because the men of our society have been so disobedient to the call of God to righteously lead and provide for their wives, women have become insecure and have responded through a major change in their behavior and social position.

While it is apparent why women exhibit many negative feelings and fears arising from insecurity in their marriages and a general inability to trust men, the answer for women is not to respond to the problems of men with *more* problems.

The answer is to respond in obedience to God's Word. More specifically, in marriage a wife must respond to the atmosphere her husband provides for her in a righteous manner. Review the Scripture verses printed at the beginning of the chapter. They instruct that a woman is to respond righteously to her husband, even if he is not being obedient to the Word of God. Never has this passage been as important as it is today.

After counseling married people for years, I (Jimmy) can tell you without a doubt that the most common conversation has been with a hurting wife concerning her disobedient or sinful husband. I have learned there are two essential things a woman must do to change her marriage: 1) She must be willing to obey God's Word for wives, regardless of her husband's behavior; and 2) she must deal properly with the problems in her own life.

While many women are in marriages they want to see changed—and we have a great deal of sympathy for their plights—some of those wives are as destructive as their husbands without knowing it. They must learn to take responsibility for their part of the problem.

As Peter wrote in the verses at the beginning of this chapter, the solution to the problem of a sinful man is not an angry, obstinate woman, but a righteous woman who is beautiful from the inside out. This woman can not only build a godly home, but she can also powerfully influence the society in which she lives.

FOUR KINDS OF DESTRUCTIVE WIVES

A wife of noble character who can find? She is worth far more than rubies.
Her husband has full confidence in her and lacks nothing of value.
She brings him good, not harm, all the days of her life.
PROVERBS 31:10-12, *NIV*

1. The Dominant Wife

Better to live on a corner of the roof than share a house
with a quarrelsome wife.
PROVERBS 21:9, *NIV*

Better to live in a desert than with a quarrelsome and ill-tempered wife.
PROVERBS 21:19, *NIV*

Brad and Sue were a couple no one would have dreamed had the problems they were experiencing in marriage. On the outside, they seemed to have a perfect relationship. Brad was an outgoing, handsome man with a gentle and personable manner. Sue was a fun-loving family woman who was faithful to God and to Brad.

Everyone loved to be around them because they both were so easy to get along with. However, few people seemed to notice their deteriorating relationship.

Brad's sweet and gentle nature was what attracted Sue to him in the first place, but now she found him to be greatly lacking as a leader. Although he was kind and personable, he was a people-pleaser.

As a result of his being such a good listener and so kind, many people went to him with their problems. However, Brad lacked the depth of character and convictions that would enable him to give any solid answers. If you wanted a loving smile and a listening ear, Brad was your man; but if you needed leadership he was not very strong.

Lack of leadership was the root of the problem that grew between Brad and Sue. She appreciated his good qualities but found herself losing more and more respect for him because he would not lead. As she became more frustrated, she complained increasingly about the things he was not doing. Brad resented her remarks, thought she was nagging, and resisted the changes she sought. But Sue persisted.

Without realizing it, Sue was as much of the problem as Brad. From the beginning of their relationship, it was her dominant personality that enabled Brad to be passive. Rather than keeping her naturally aggressive and opinionated personality in check, Sue exploited Brad's personality as a facilitator to enhance the exercise of her dominance.

However, she found two problems arose from her being in control: First, the sweet man she married was not able to fill the role God expected him to fill, thereby frustrating Sue's need for male leadership; and, second, she found that her personality grated on Brad more of the time.

Where, at one time, he had seemed to enjoy her strong personality and opinions, now it seemed he resented them. Sue was confused. How could she have gotten into such a mess? With the best of intentions, she had married a good, Christian man whom she felt any other woman would be proud to have, yet she was miserable.

To begin to understand the serious problems a dominant woman faces in marriage, consider this excerpt from an excellent article by Dr. Marlin Howe, entitled "Will a Wife Respect a Husband She Can Control?"

What is the most common complaint that married couples have about each other?

In my counseling practice, the most repeated complaint is this: For the man, he feels he gets little respect from his wife; for the woman, she feels she gets little love from her husband. How could this be since their feelings for one another were so strong when they first met? They really were in love, weren't they?

Strong feelings for each other, yes! Love, no! Couples who share the above complaint are usually trapped in what counselors call a "dependent/co-dependent relationship." One spouse is dependent upon the other, who appears more independent. The independent spouse, however, is dependent upon the other spouse's dependency.

God designed marriage to have a healthy, dependent/co-dependent relationship (Gen. 1,2). The wife is to be dependent on her husband. He is to be dependent on her dependency. In doing so, she feels feminine, protected, and cared for. He feels masculine, needed, and important. She feels loved. He feels respected (Eph. 5).

The unhealthy dependent/co-dependent relationship occurs in sex-role reversed marriages. The husband is dependent upon his wife. The wife, who appears independent, is actually dependent upon his dependency. As such, she feels an awesome responsibility to cover for him, to protect him, to decide for him, even to rescue him. She is in control. He is out of control.

I have never yet met a woman who respected a man she could control. So, from her innermost soul swells a basic need to disrespect her husband, to find fault with him. I have never yet met a man who truly loved a woman who controlled him. So, from his innermost soul swells a basic need to separate from his wife, to ignore her, to find significance elsewhere. Thus, both spouses are pushing each other away—the wife through fault-finding and the husband through neglect.

You ask, "Why did these two people marry in the first place?" The answer: They had to! The man usually comes from a home where his father was either weak, passive, or remote, and the mother had to wear the pants in the family. Since the boy experienced more of his mother than his father, his emotional system was over-mothered—too well-cared for. Science discovered that by late teens, the internalization of a person's identity is complete (Prov. 22:6). So, a boy who internalized a too-high level of care will try to find a wife who could continue that level of mothering.

Will he ever find her? Dr. Voth, chief psychiatrist of the Menninger Clinic in Topeka, Kansas, says that she probably will find him first. A dependent boy is highly attractive to an independent girl. They marry. Why? Because his dependency allows her to be in control, responsible, significant, and not vulnerable. In contrast, her independence allows him to remain dependent, irresponsible, vulnerable, and secure.

You ask, "If this arrangement works, who cares?"

The problem is that it does not work! In time, the wife will become weary of being so responsible, and the husband will become weary of being so controlled. Lacking a sense of masculinity, he will seek to distance himself from his wife. As her husband separates from her, she will feel a strong, inner resentment that she is not being loved by him.

Feeling the need to be feminine, she will then pursue him. To the degree in which she pursues, he separates—hunting, fishing, working, drinking, fighting, carousing, watching television, and so forth.

Once her spirit is sufficiently crushed, she will begin to separate herself. Feeling too much distance, her husband will then pursue her. He may promise reform, even the moon, and guarantee the impossible. She is repulsed at his manlessness but does not recognize her womanlessness.

If they come together, it is but for a brief time. The marital push-pull recycles. Once broken down, there is divorce—be it emotional or physical.[1]

As you can see, the problems created by a sex-role reversal of a dominant female/passive male relationship are vast. To understand the answer to this problem, consider the most common reasons that a woman becomes dominant, and the solutions for them.

1. Sin Nature/Rebellion
In the Garden of Eden, sin entered the human race when Adam and Eve ate the fruit from the tree of knowledge of good and evil. When God

confronted them about their sin, He said to Eve, "Your desire will be for your husband, and he will rule over you" (Gen. 3:16, *NIV*).

The word "desire" in this passage means "a desire for authority."[2] So, since the Garden of Eden, women have had a natural, sinful tendency to usurp the authority of the men in their lives. Notice how God told Eve, "and he will rule over you." Eve was given notice that, although her desire was for authority, neither God nor man would allow her to have it. Therefore, every woman must understand her own instinctive nature to rebel against her husband and try to gain authority over him.

The primary solution is for all women to crucify that desire by not allowing it to work in them. The less opportunity one gives it, the weaker this desire will become. The next step, if you are a dominant woman who is not submitting to all authority in your life, is to repent. You must honestly confess your sin and begin to submit yourself to your husband, as well as to other authorities in your life.

2. Fear

First Peter 3 exhorts women to be submissive to their husbands as they adorn themselves inwardly with a gentle and quiet spirit. Peter reminds women that the great women of ancient times did this. Specifically, Sarah honored Abraham, even calling him "lord." Peter concludes his statement about Sarah with this interesting comment:

> You are her daughters if you do what is right and do not give way
> to fear (1 Pet. 3:6, *NIV*).

Since women already have a sin nature prompting them to resist their husband's authority, Satan does everything he can to tempt a woman to rebel. His number one weapon to incite women to rebellion is *fear*. Although all of us have sin natures, as well as natural fears, there also is a demonically inspired fear that the devil breathes into our lives to incite us to sin.

Paul wrote this truth in 2 Timothy 1:7:

> God hath not given us the spirit of fear; but of power, and of
> love, and of a sound mind (*KJV*).

In this Scripture, fear is referred to as a spirit force. We are also told it does not come from God. On the contrary, God gives us power, love and a sound mind. Satan inspires us to react unrighteously, but God gives us the power to act righteously.

When I (Jimmy) counsel with a woman who dominates her home and/or who is embittered about her husband's lack of leadership, I almost always am dealing with a woman strongly influenced by fear. Whether it is fear of financial failure, fear of loneliness, or fear of personal harm, fear is one of the main motivations of a dominant woman.

She wants her husband to be in control, but she fears what will happen if he takes control; therefore, she either stays in control and dominates her husband or constantly interrupts his authority.

For women in this situation, the answer is for them to stop giving a place to fear in their lives by keeping their eyes on Jesus and allowing their husbands to fail. In a later chapter is an example of a woman who began her marriage by allowing her husband to fail. She committed to love him no matter what he did and to allow God to correct him.

This couple has now been married more than 30 years, and they are still madly in love. After failing in almost every way, her husband is now a success in almost every way. The reasons are these:

- He did not have to constantly battle with his wife for the authority of the home. She gave it to him.

- He did not have to worry about failing. She loved and supported him anyway.

- He grew to love and respect her for her faithfulness in supporting him through good times and bad. Therefore, he desired to please her.

- Because she trusted God to be big enough to correct her husband, He did.

- She constantly crucified her desire to sin and resisted a demonic spirit of fear with the Word of God. Therefore, God's power worked through her so that she could love her husband and respect him, as she knew she should.

Do not allow fear to control your life. *Fear* is anti-faith, anti-love, and anti-peace. Submit yourself to God. Resist the devil, and he will flee from you (see Jas. 4:7). Not only that, your marriage will prosper greatly as you put faith in God and His Word.

3. Detached/Undernurturing Father

When a young girl is being reared, she needs her father to affirm her in every way. She also needs her father to lead her and help her make decisions in life. When this influence is present in a young girl's life, she grows up with healthy self-esteem, as well as with a capacity to depend upon a man in general.

But when a father is not present and affirming in his daughter's life, she will be forced to compensate somehow. In most situations, this means she will become much more independent and opinionated because she will have to work things out for herself. That can create an intensified craving for male affection and affirmation. When you combine these two ingredients, a woman with a strong personality and a strong desire for affirmation emerges.

So how will she be able to function in life with her strong personality and intense need for love? Without correcting the root problems of her life, this woman will only be able to function by finding a man who is very nurturing and whose personality is weak enough to accommodate hers. This will result in the classic dominant female/passive male relationship.

The woman in such a relationship must first realize the problems of the family system in which she was raised. In fact, she needs to realize that she was sinned against by her father and forgive him. Perhaps you already realize you were wronged by your father. Well, then, you must forgive him.

If you do not forgive him, you will damage yourself and those around you much more than you will ever damage him. You see, when we have not forgiven someone, we automatically respond to life based on a distorted perspective. So forgive your father.

Next, recognize the problems arising from your *response* to his absence. Perhaps you became masculine and abrasive to hide your hurts or to punish him. Or, perhaps you made a vow to yourself that you would never let a man hurt you again. However you responded, if you realize the way you reacted was wrong, repent and ask God to give you the strength to change.

Finally, although you will still need love and affirmation, you also need leadership. You must submit to your husband and allow him to be the man God wants him to be. Let him fail, as you support him in prayer. Pray daily for God to heal you and your husband as you submit to his authority. Use the strengths of your life to support your husband's leadership, but never usurp his authority.

4. Wrong Training

When a young girl has been brought up watching her mother dominate her father, it creates many unhealthy images in her young mind. Not only does she begin to think a woman should control a man, but she will begin to despise and disrespect the weakness she sees in her father, thus perpetuating the generational cycle of female dominance.

This is particularly true in some cultures where women have dominated families for centuries. For a woman to understand the Scriptural problem called "iniquities" and how to deal with them, refer back to chapter 9 on "Four Kinds of Destructive Husbands," and read the section on the dominant husband. That section details how we are influenced by the behavior and sins of our parents and how to deal with them.

The woman who had a dominant mother must forgive her, realize what she did was sinful, and refuse to participate in the same sin herself. Remember, if you allow dominance in your life, you are passing a failed family system down one more generation. Do not let this happen. Realize the mistakes of your family, and deal with them in a righteous manner.

5. Dominant/Choleric Temperament

Some women are born with a naturally strong personality. The woman with a choleric temperament is typically strongly opinionated and aggressive by nature. Though there are some positive aspects to this type of personality, there also are some distinct dangers, especially in marriage.

The naturally aggressive woman must learn to submit her personality to the leadership of the Holy Spirit as she subdues her inherent desire to be in control. She also must submit herself by an act of her will to her husband's authority as she daily allows him to lead. A wife's strong temperament can be a wonderful complement to her husband's authority when it is submitted to and led by God's Spirit. When it is not, her temperament can cause her to usurp her husband's authority, which deeply damages the essence of the marriage bond.

2. The Enabler Wife

I (Jimmy) first met Natalie when she came into my office for counseling. It wasn't really marriage counseling, because her divorce was final on the Tuesday before our session. However, she came seeking counsel concerning some hurts and fears in her life, wondering how she should deal with them.

While Natalie was kind, she obviously was a very hurt person, for part of Natalie's problem was a history of abuse. Her alcoholic father had sexually and emotionally abused her all of her life, and it was still going on. The last time she visited her parents' home, her father had tried to fondle her.

Because of that early-life situation, Natalie had a history of problem marriages. This was her third divorce. She was not only wrestling with the hurts her father had dealt her, but she was also dealing with a string of failed relationships and the heavy toll they had taken on her life.

As she related the details of her past, Natalie first described the kind of man her father was—he had a good side to him that many people never saw, and she really loved him. However, the things he had done to her had wounded her deeply. Although she had tried to forgive him, it was difficult to forget.

I inquired about her husbands, beginning with the first one. Her story sounded like a broken record. Her description of each husband sounded like her description of her father. While one would think a woman like Natalie would find a man totally unlike her father, the opposite was true. Natalie was an enabler. She had been physically, sexually and emotionally abused by men all her life. Even more tragic, she had allowed it to happen—at least the abuse in her marriages.

Surely you have noticed women like Natalie. They are the salt of the earth themselves, but they are attracted to losers—men with problems. But why? Why would any woman naturally gravitate to a bad man or want to place herself in a dependent position to an undependable man? Why do some women seem to be magnets for bad men?

Before listing the contributing causes for the enabling woman, let's define the term "enabler."

When a person allows a loved one to behave in a destructive manner, they are "enabling" the other person to be what he or she is. Worse still, enabling occurs when a person provides the resources or atmosphere necessary to *promote* destructive behavior in another person. Therefore, any time one allows or provides for the destructive behavior of a person in one's family or of someone close, one is an enabler.

The opposite of an enabler is a person who refuses to watch another person self-destruct or abuse others, or refuses to become a target for her own destruction. The next chapter will deal with the issue of wife abuse and one's righteous response to it.

The following influences create the enabling personality, but there are appropriate responses to defeat them.

1. Low Self-esteem

Did you know that the majority of prostitutes in America come from abusive home environments? Have you ever wondered why a person would allow herself to be belittled and abused by a pimp, as well as being used by clients as a sexual trinket? The reason is that many of these women do not see themselves as deserving any better treatment.

Natalie was an example of this point. All of her life she felt dirty because of her father's sexual abuse.

Not only that, but each time her father got drunk, he told her, "You'll never get a man, as ugly as you are."

By the time she was 18 years old, Natalie believed what her father had told her. Truly believing she was not worthy of a good man who would love her properly, she pursued men whom she felt were as unworthy or even more unworthy than she was.

Natalie viewed herself from a low perspective. The only way she could feel secure in a relationship with a man was to find a companion equally as low or—even better—lower than herself. As long as she was with a "bad" man, she felt worthy and needed in the relationship.

Years with her father had taught her the survival skills she needed to deal with men like this. So, however hurtful her situation was, it was normal to her. However, her approach to relationships didn't work. She either had to flee her marriages because of physical abuse or she was abandoned by her unfaithful husbands. What a tragedy!

For a woman with low self-esteem, the solution is for her to stop believing what people tell her about herself, what she tells herself about herself, or what the mirror tells her about herself and start believing what God's Word tells her.

When Karen and I married, she had lower self-esteem than almost any woman I have ever seen. Nothing helped her until she began to read the Bible and allow God to transform her mind. Day by day, as Karen read God's Word, His love and affirmation sank deeper and deeper into her heart. Words of criticism and discouragement were replaced with words of comfort and praise. Hurtful words and thoughts were replaced with healing words and thoughts.

According to God's Word, He thinks so much of you that He sent His only Son to die for you on the cross. If you are a child of God, you will one day be "married" to Jesus as part of the corporate Bride, the Church. And, if you are good enough for Jesus, don't you think you deserve a righteous, godly husband?

Now, these concepts don't give you the right to divorce your present husband. Stop enabling your husband's destructive behavior. You deserve better, and so does he.

The enabling wife will also normally enable her children's destructive behavior. Allowing destructive tendencies in your children to make you feel needed in the home is an expensive way to soothe your own wounds. Believe God's Word for yourself and your family. As you do, you may not always be popular with your children, but you will be with God. Later in life, your children will thank you for loving them enough to discipline them with love and to tell them no, when it is necessary.

2. A Distorted View of Love

One woman I (Jimmy) counseled had lived in a home with a dominant, abusive mother. She told me, with tears in her eyes, that her mother was a harsh and legalistic disciplinarian. So, early in life, she swore to herself that she would never rear her children the way she was reared.

Being true to her inner vow, she refused to criticize or correct any problem she saw in her husband or children. Although she felt a growing anger and sense of violation coming from her abusive husband and rebellious children, she had decided it must be her problem. She came for counseling to see how she could learn to overcome her anger and depression.

As I counseled this woman, I first led her to break the inner vow she had made to herself as a child. I shared Matthew 5:34-37 to show her that we are not to swear to, or by, ourselves or anyone else. I explained that, when she had vowed not to be like her mother, not only had she judged her mother, but she also had acted independently of God.

After she understood the danger of inner vows and had renounced her vow, I explained the nature of true love. I shared Hebrews 12 where God's Word tells us He disciplines everyone He loves, and if we are not disciplined by Him, we are not His children. In other words, love is not revealed only through care and affection but also by correction and confrontation.

The problem with this woman's mother was that she had *only* corrected and confronted her family. Seeing the extreme behavior of her mother and judging it to be wrong, she had swung to the opposite extreme. Her healing came from forgiving her mother, renouncing her inner vow, and learning from Scripture that real love is demonstrated by a balance of acceptance and accountability, not exclusively one or the other.

If you truly believe you are loving your husband by allowing him to self-destruct, abuse your children or yourself, you are deceived. Although you should not *sin* against your husband, you should stand up to him in love and refuse to be a partner to his problem. As you do so, you are not rebelling or refusing to love him; you simply are loving him enough to not allow him to destroy himself and those around him.

3. Fear of Rejection
Rejection is one of the deepest hurts a person endures throughout his or her life. So fear of rejection is typically one of our deepest fears. Some women do not become enablers out of a low self-esteem or out of not understanding love properly. They become enablers out of fear of rejection and fear of being alone. Therefore, they put up with abuse and tolerate and encourage serious problems in their husbands and loved ones. For them, remaining silent is a ticket for love and acceptance.

Once again, *fear is of the devil.* Unless it is the healthy fear (awe and reverence) of God, fear drives you to do the wrong thing. Rather than fearing what people are going to do if you speak the truth to them and refuse to enable their sins, stand up and have faith in God. Even if you are rejected, do you not think God is big enough to protect you and reward you if you do what is right? He really is.

While all of us need to love those around us and be gracious to everyone, there comes a time when we simply cannot go along. Whether it is sin, abuse or ungodliness, our highest authority is God. He will never reject us for doing what is right. On the contrary, regardless of what men do or threaten to do, God will powerfully work on our behalf if we only will put our faith in Him.

4. Passive/Phlegmatic Temperament
Many women are born with a very sweet, laid-back personality. Women with this phlegmatic type of temperament are typically very accepting and forbearing. In fact, the greatest strength of this type of personality is its strong relational loyalty and sensitivity.

Although the woman with this type of temperament has the potential for deep, stable relationships, she also has the potential to be an enabler. The same kind and gentle tendencies in the phlegmatic person that create the natural acceptance of others also create a tendency to not confront others when necessary.

The woman with the passive/phlegmatic temperament needs to use her natural strengths to love as she also learns to stand up for herself, speaking the truth in love as she expresses her real feelings. In this manner, the phlegmatic woman can be both a loyal companion and a strong, active partner at the same time.

3. The Distracted Wife

Likewise, teach the older women to be reverent in the way they live, not to be slanderers or addicted to much wine, but to teach what is good. Then they can train the younger women to love their husbands and children, to be self-controlled and pure, to be busy at home, to be kind, and to be subject to their husbands, so that no one will malign the word of God.
TITUS 2:3-5, *NIV*

Joan was a well-groomed woman who had lived all her life in a high-income bracket. From the minute she stepped into my office, I could tell she was confident and articulate. After greeting one another and sharing some general words to break the ice, I asked Joan about her relationship with her husband, Al. Joan was an extremely honest woman, so it was an easy job finding the problem and the solution to their difficulties.

From Joan's point of view, she and Al had never had a close relationship. Al was in college when they married, and that kept him away from her a lot. After he graduated from law school, he became an associate with a law firm and immediately became absorbed in upward mobility. While Joan lived in financial security and had all the social trappings of any woman's dreams, there was one thing she did not have: her husband's attention.

As soon as I detected Al's "distracted-husband syndrome," I asked Joan how she had dealt with this attitude during their marriage. She replied that, early in the marriage, they had fought regularly about all of the time he spent away from home. She had expressed her feelings to him, but although he made promises about the future, the present never seemed to change. So she had learned to stay busy in order not to hurt so badly over this situation.

Joan absorbed herself in her children, friends, family, social activities, charity work, and church work. In fact, she was well-known throughout the community for her incredible contributions in many areas. The problem persisted, however. Her activities were undertaken as a replacement for her husband's love, which, of course, didn't work.

Al sinned against Joan by putting his education and employment before her in his life. Joan had perpetuated the sin by filling her own life with distractions. Remember, sin never solves problems; it only perpetuates them.

Although there was a good explanation for the reason Joan busied herself with other things, to do so was the wrong decision. Rather than responding to Al's distraction, Joan should have kept her heart turned toward Al and acted and prayed in a godly way for the Lord to correct him.

Instead, she turned her heart *away* from Al and busied her life with other things, leaving no one to fight for the marriage. So it was no surprise to learn that Al had been having an affair for several years. It wasn't her fault, but a climate for adultery had been created by their mutually distracted relationship.

Just as a man needs to turn his heart toward his wife and home, a woman must learn to do the same thing. Since the husband has a higher priority than anything in a woman's life except God, she must faithfully protect the time and energy he deserves for the rest of their marriage.

To find God's solution for distraction in wives, one must know the root causes. The following are some of the root causes and solutions.

1. A Distracted Husband

A distracted husband leaves a wife emotionally vulnerable. Rather than filling the void left by a distracted husband with excessive activities and projects of her own, a woman must use her time and energies to pursue her husband and to create an environment in their home that attracts him. Also, the prayers of a righteous wife for a distracted husband are powerful.

The wife of a distracted man must fight and keep on fighting for the heart of her husband. The moment she turns her heart away from him in response to his distraction, she surrenders her marriage to defeat.

2. Motherhood

The primary reason many women do not have the energy and time they need for their husbands is because they expend them on their children. Knowing how demanding children are and how distracted men may be, a woman must seek every means available to protect her best time, energy and affection for her husband. Sometimes this means the husband must help more with the children. Also, it can mean training the children to respect your need to direct attention and affection toward your husband at certain times of the day or evening.

Remember, mothers, although children are very special and need much love and attention, your relationship with your husband is even more important. So don't allow yourself to be a mother at the expense of being a wife. Your husband needs you, and your children need to see a healthy relationship between you and your husband. When your children are grown and gone, you and your husband will still be together, if you work at your marriage.

3. Overload

When a woman has to work, raise children, keep a house and love her husband, she can feel overwhelmed at times. We especially don't want to seem insensitive about "overload," because some women don't have a choice, or they are sacrificing for the sake of their families. But, if you need help to give you more time to spend with your children and husband, seek it in an aggressive and creative manner. Specifically, if there is a way to lighten your load by dropping non-essential demands, do it.

Don't allow your busyness and the demands of your time and energy to rob you of the relationship God created with your husband. When people get busy, their tendency is to neglect the most important things in their lives. *You must not do this.* With all of your might, and for the rest of your life, fight for your marriage. Strive to protect and create the time, attention and energy needed to keep your marriage strong, even if it means sacrificing in other areas. It will be worth the effort.

4. Unrestrained/Misprioritized Relationships

For many women, relationships with friends, parents and other family members can pose a real threat to their marriages. While we all need these other relationships in our lives, they must be monitored carefully to make sure they are not violating our relationship with our spouse.

Specific examples of things that can cause real problems in a marriage are too much time on the telephone, too close a relationship with a friend or family member that replaces your spouse in many ways and takes time and energy away from him, and too much time spent at the homes of parents or friends or with them in your own home.

For a married couple to bond and to relate properly, they need time and energy for one another on a daily basis. Even if it hurts someone else's feelings, don't sacrifice your marriage for anyone else. If you are having problems in your marriage that have prompted you to seek other relationships, don't let those relationships interfere with your ability to pursue and provide aggressively for your husband.

4. The Emotion-Motivated Wife

A wife of noble character is her husband's crown, but a disgraceful wife is like decay in his bones.
PROVERBS 12:4, *NIV*

The wise woman builds her house, but with her own hands the foolish one tears hers down.
PROVERBS 14:1, *NIV*

As Paul cautioned Timothy about the difficult times coming to the world in the last days, he also told him how despicable men would become. One characteristic Paul gave of the last days was that evil men would take advantage of "weak-willed women, who are loaded down with sins and are swayed by all kinds of evil desires" (2 Tim. 3:6, *NIV*).

When a woman is "weak-willed," it means she is not led by her own convictions. Rather, she is led by her emotions or the forces around her that persuade her to do what she does. This woman is open prey for the devil's lies and deception presented by anyone working for him. She is vulnerable simply because she relies more on her feelings than on the truth to make her decisions.

Do you remember that God commanded Eve in the Garden of Eden to not eat the fruit from the tree of knowledge of good and evil? Because she did not cling to the truth God had spoken to her, Satan was able to convince her that God's words were not true and that it would be all right for her to eat the fruit.

As Eve heard the soothing, self-exalting words of the devil and saw the appealing beauty of the fruit, her feelings told her eating the fruit must be okay. Rejecting God's eternal words and placing ultimate faith in her feelings, she made a terrible mistake.

Because Eve acted on her temporary human emotion and not on what God had said, she ushered in destruction to her own life, her marriage, her children's lives, and ultimately, to all of her descendants. What a tremendously high price to pay for doing what one feels like doing!

Most of the people dying of AIDS today in North America contracted the disease doing what they felt like doing. Nearly everyone locked behind bars in prisons across America is there for doing what they felt like doing. Just as tragically, many women in destructive marriages today are living in misery, not because there is no way out, but because they refuse to do something contrary to their feelings.

Although feelings sometimes are good and helpful, they are completely unreliable as a source of permanent direction. When we allow our feelings to dictate the way we behave, we live on a roller coaster of ups and downs, as we learn to live in perpetual insecurity and confusion.

The answer to this dilemma is to do what is right regardless of what our feelings say. *Feelings make a great caboose, but a terrible engine.* Make God's Word the engine to motivate your actions now, and you will find that proper feelings will follow later.

As a result of counseling hurting, confused wives for years, I (Jimmy) have found emotional motivation to be a major issue in marriages. For many women, their fears and feelings dictate everything they do in their lives and marriages. Although they read and hear what the Bible says they should do, they do not obey God's Word because their emotions are guiding them differently.

For women to learn to break out of the bondage of being weak-willed and emotion-motivated, they need to become aware of the major causes of this problem. Then, they must use the ways to be free from them. Listed below are the major causes and ways to be free from them.

1. Unbelief

"And without faith it is impossible to please God, because anyone who comes to him must believe that he exists and that he rewards those who earnestly seek him" (Heb. 11:6, *NIV*).

The woman without faith is unwilling to take God at His word. Rather than believing God will be faithful to do what He says, she puts greater faith in her feelings. Rather than standing on His eternal words, she acts on her temporary feelings. Unbelief is not a *problem*; it is a *sin*.

The solution is to repent and act in obedience to God's Word. It does not matter nearly as much what one feels about God or His Word. The thing that matters is what one does. Regardless of your feelings, seek God and obey Him. Deny your feelings the right to control you and begin to exercise your will. As you do, you will see great improvements in every area of your life.

2. Lack of Discipline

Some people had permissive parents who never made them do any-thing or who never corrected them properly. The undisciplined, and often brattish, child learned to do whatever he or she felt like doing regardless of what was right or prudent. The woman who was reared without personal discipline needs to understand that, although her parents may not have punished her for disobeying or did not make her responsible for her actions, God will.

As we heard one man say, "My parents never spanked me, but when I grew up, life gave me a big spanking!"

Learn now to discipline yourself and to put some parameters on your life. The greatest parameter is the Word of God. As you seek to do what God says, He will forgive you for your failures as you learn to overcome. Do not give up! God loves you! He will give you the power to succeed as you seek Him and pray for His grace.

3. Deception/Wrong Information

Jesus referred to Satan as "a liar and the father of lies" (John 8:44). Satan specializes in filling our minds with as much disinformation as possible in order to produce resentment, fear, disgust, rebellion, and other negative emotions. God's Word is the opposite. When we read God's Word, it fills our minds with truth that works. His truths are words of wisdom that solve our problems and make our lives pleasant and productive.

No matter who is advising you contrary to the Word of God, do not believe them. As 2 Corinthians 10 instructs, bring every thought captive to Christ and make sure it is in agreement with His Word. Remember, any thought you do not take captive and bring into agreement with God's Word will end up taking you captive. Your marriage is too precious to allow it to be destroyed by the devil's sugar-coated lies. Use the Bible to find out what really is true, and you will find stability and success as your reward.

We hope this chapter on "Four Kinds of Destructive Wives" has helped you in some way. As we said at the beginning of the chapter, our intention is to bring words of healing and instruction. We hope you have received this through what you have read.

Also, remember that God is with you right now. He is available to work powerfully in your life if you will let Him in. It does not matter how bad your problems are or how long you have had them; the only thing that matters is God's great power and love for us. Only God can and will take a destructive man or woman and change him or her into a vessel of love and honor.

Let God have access to every area of your life today. As you do, He will begin to heal and restore your life in new and powerful ways. The result will be a healthier and happier you and a stronger, growing marriage.

Notes

1. *Pulpit Helps* (Chattanooga, TN: AMG International), March 1990, p. 18. Used by permission.
2. James Strong, *Hebrew-Chaldee Dictionary, Strong's Exhaustive Concordance of the Bible* (Iowa Falls, IA: Riverside Book and Bible House), Hebrew #8669.

HOW TO UNDERSTAND AND MEET YOUR HUSBAND'S NEEDS

*When he saw Queen Esther standing in the court, he was pleased with her
and held out to her the gold scepter that was in his hand. So Esther approached
and touched the tip of the scepter. Then the king asked, "What is it, Queen
Esther? What is your request? Even up to half the kingdom, it will be given you."*
ESTHER 5:2-3, *NIV*

Esther was a woman of remarkable beauty and strength. An orphan
reared by her cousin Mordecai (see Esther 2:7), Esther was a young
woman without a rival among her peers. Although she was a Jew living
in a heathen land, God blessed her and prospered her abundantly.

In fact, God's hand was upon Esther in a special way. He knew an
opportunity was approaching in the kingdom of Persia through which
a woman of character and godliness could be used to change history.
Because of Esther's submissive and godly spirit, she was chosen for
this purpose.

If you have read the story in the book of Esther, you know that the
previous queen refused to display herself at an official banquet and
consequently was killed or banished (so old Jewish stories go). The
king's advisers were concerned that all of the women of the kingdom
would not obey their husbands if the king let Queen Vashti get away
with her rebellion (see Esther 1:16-20). (Some ancient stories of the
time, based on the customs of Persia, say that the king was requiring
Vashti to parade naked before his guests. If so, she was very courageous,
risking her life for her convictions. Whatever her motivation, the king
and his counselors viewed it as rebellion, and she lost her queenship.)

Soon a search began among all of the beautiful young virgins in the kingdom for a successor to Vashti. Esther was one of the group chosen to be groomed for a year by the eunuch in charge of the king's harem. Then the king would choose a queen from among that group.

Esther won the heart of the eunuch; however, that did not improve her chances at all with the king. He was being especially particular about choosing a wife after being embarrassed by Vashti. So, after the time of preparation was over, a different virgin from the group would be brought to him every night, and the next morning, that girl would join the king's concubines.

In plain language, part of the tryout for queen was the king's seeing how good each girl was in bed. By the time it was Esther's turn, none of the girls had been summoned twice to the king's bed. All year long, I am sure Esther had prayed that she would get at least one chance and that God would give her favor with the king and wisdom as to how to please him.

Of course, God did not condone nor arrange for Esther to have pre-marital sex. In fact, it was not His will for kings to have all those wives and concubines, as we have seen in the story of Solomon. God's clear will for all mankind is one husband and one wife (see Gen. 2:24).

However, in a fallen world, bad things do happen to good people sometimes. We should have faith that, whenever possible, God will turn things for our good, if we are faithful and obedient. That is what He did in the case of Esther. He turned the sacrifice of her body into a victory for Him, and she became the savior of her people. Her attitude toward those set in authority over her in the king's harem showed that she had a sweet and submissive spirit.

The virgins were allowed to take anything with them that would make them more beautiful or that might please the king. I am sure that some had taken musical instruments, some had worn exotic costumes, and perhaps, some had even taken pets with them. But Esther would only take what the eunuch told her to take. The Bible does not tell us what that was, but perhaps it was precious jewelry. Because of his position, the eunuch knew the king's likes and dislikes concerning women better than anyone. Because Esther had found favor with him, I am sure he advised her accordingly. Whatever it was, that incident shows that Esther had a quiet and submissive spirit, which had endeared her already to the eunuch, causing him to stack the deck in her behalf.

That evening Esther did find favor in the eyes of King Xerxes and was chosen as the new queen. Not only does her story demonstrate the difference between a submissive and a rebellious spirit, but it also teaches women how to enter and change a man's world.

You see, ladies, you are living in a man's world. Although modern society is "liberated," men remain the primary controllers; that will never significantly change. So women must learn how to live and overcome in a man's world. That is why the story of Esther is so essential for women to understand.

Just as I (Jimmy) teach men that Jesus is their greatest example as a man and as "Bridegroom" for the Church, women need to know that Esther is the best example in the Bible of a woman being able to be strong and submissive at the same time. She met her husband's needs and was everything God created her to be.

Wives, in order to be successful in your relationship with your husband, you must realize that no matter how popular dishonoring men is today among women—it never works. In fact, it will do more damage to your relationship with your husband than any other one thing. Men are the same in one area: They all need honor. (We didn't say they *want* honor. We said they *need* it.) In fact, honor is a man's foremost need.

Just as Esther endeared herself to her harsh, heathen husband by her godly behavior, you can do the same. Esther didn't succeed because she was special; she succeeded because she was obedient. We don't know the status of the relationship between you and your husband today, and of course, we don't even know what your husband is like. But we do know this. Every man is essentially the same as far as his basic needs are concerned, and the power of God's Word is great enough to change any of them.

A man's four basic needs are honor, sex, kindred fellowship, and domestic support. With the story of Queen Esther as a backdrop, the remainder of this chapter will list and describe these four major needs and explain how a wife can meet them.

Honor

Honor is a man's greatest need. That is why Paul wrote to women in Ephesus, "submit to your husbands as to the Lord" (Eph. 5:22, *NIV*). The standard of a wife's behavior in marriage is to treat her husband as she would treat Jesus. How would you talk to Jesus? How would you serve Jesus? How would you disagree with Jesus? These are the types of questions a woman needs to constantly ask herself regarding her behavior toward her husband.

While many women might not admit it, they feel like saying something like this, "Well, my husband doesn't act like Jesus, so he doesn't deserve being treated like Him!" Although no man can measure up to Jesus (and some men even less so than others), a woman must understand that the Bible does not qualify this admonition. In other words, Ephesians 5:22 does not say, "Wives, submit to your husbands only if they behave themselves and do not get on your nerves."

Another Scripture without qualifications to which you can relate is Ephesians 6:2, in which children are told to honor their mothers and fathers, repeating one of the 10 commandments (see Deut. 5:16). How would you like it if your child acted disrespectfully toward you and, when you corrected him, said, "I don't have to obey or honor you, because you are not a good mother (or father)"? The Bible didn't instruct us to honor our parents only if they are honorable, but to honor them no matter who they are or how they act. Surely, as a parent, you are glad God didn't put a certain standard on parents' behavior before they are to be honored. If He had, all parents would be in trouble many times, because none of us is free of times when our behavior falls below the standard that would *deserve* honor.

The same is true of husbands. Paul knew there wouldn't be a perfect husband, so he gave an unqualified admonition for women to honor them, which was in line with God's prophetic words to Eve in the Garden of Eden.

Someone may say, "But my husband abuses me" or "I have a friend whose husband is physically and emotionally abusive. Should she honor him?"

First of all, a woman shouldn't subject herself or her children to an abusive man. This is sometimes a dangerous statement to make, because some women call anything that curbs their desires or wills "abuse." However, the types of behavior that are real abuse and should not be tolerated are these:

1. Any type of emotional, sexual or physical abuse that God has not given a wife grace to endure. In other words, something she simply cannot undergo without suffering significant personal harm.

2. Anything that is causing real damage to her and/or her children, especially when there is an unwillingness by the husband to take responsibility for his actions and take serious steps to change.

One of the greatest sins a man can commit against God is to abuse a woman or child. An abusive man needs to be confronted and challenged about his behavior. In fact, in many cases, he needs to be prosecuted by the law. Unfortunately, there are certain types of enabling women who put up with men like this much too long and will not take steps to bring the abuse to an end.

If you are being abused, there is a way to deal with it in a sensible, godly manner. First, tell your husband you are not going to live with his destructive behavior. Affirm your love and commitment to him, but tell him you are serious. If he does not change, tell him you will have to move out for your own protection. In the case of a truly violent man, you may need to communicate this by letter or by a telephone call after you have moved out.

Second, find a safe or neutral place to live. Whether it is a shelter for battered women or the home of a friend or relative, find some place to stay that protects you and your children from your husband's abuse.

Third, go to your pastor or a Christian counselor for help. Tell him or her about your life and the abuse you are experiencing. Let that person minister to you and give you guidance through your situation. Also, if your husband is sincere about dealing with his problem, this is where he needs to go for help. You need a godly third party to help you work through this situation and keep your husband accountable. If he will not seek pastoral or professional help, it is a bad sign for the future of your marriage.

Finally, pray for God's intervention and miracle power to be released in your situation. Don't give up or give in until you see a change. Notice that we never once told you to dishonor or divorce your husband, because you can respond to his abuse without dishonoring him. As you do, God will honor you as He defends you and works in the heart of your abusive husband.

At this point, some reader may well say, "I mostly agree. But what if my husband never changes? Am I supposed to live separated and single for the rest of my life?"

In 1 Corinthians 7, Paul gave some gracious guidelines for spouses who have been rejected through abuse. At some point, divorce may be an option if your abusive spouse never changes, but only after you follow these guidelines or something close to the spirit of them.

First, don't do anything for at least two years. Give God that much time to work. It may be hard, but you need that much time to heal and pray anyway. Don't listen to people telling you, "Divorce the jerk." They may mean well, but they are not representing you, your husband or God well.

Second, continue to pray for your husband. Communicate to him as best as you can your love for him and your desire to work things out, but only if he will get help. Don't compromise. If he is sincere, he will do what it takes.

Finally, if your husband still has not changed after two years, don't file for divorce until you have prayed and received approval and peace from God in your heart. We know of one situation in which God gave a woman grace for many years to wait for her abusive husband. He eventually was saved, totally reformed, and their marriage was restored. Whatever your particular circumstances, God will always give you the right answer, as well as the grace and strength to go with it.

To fulfill the admonition to honor your husband, consider these suggestions for honoring him in powerful and practical ways.

1. Allow Him to Fail

Any woman is willing to honor a man who never fails, but there is no such man. Almost any woman is willing to honor a man when he succeeds or is doing well. What separates a mature wife from the rest is how she responds when her husband fails. This is the test of true honor. Every husband is bound to fail or do wrong things many times during his life, so if a wife dishonors him at those times, she is certain to have a dishonored and wounded husband.

I (Jimmy) will never forget the time I asked a distinguished older couple in our church to share their testimony about marriage one Sunday morning. I asked them because, after more than 30 years of marriage, they still were madly in love. He treated her like a queen, and she treated him like a king. I couldn't wait for them to share their testimony because I wanted everyone present to benefit from it.

The woman began by saying something that almost knocked me out of my seat. With her loving, sacrificial, distinguished husband standing next to her, she told how, at the beginning of their marriage, he was such a lousy husband!

She said, "When we first married, my husband didn't know how to manage money. In addition, we were broke, and he never spent any time at home with me. He worked all of the time. He was insensitive to my needs and never prayed or led us spiritually."

Those were not her only negative comments about her husband; however, as she spoke, he smiled and stood proudly by her side. I could hardly believe it!

Then, as she concluded her remarks, this godly woman said something every woman needs to hear.

"When my husband and I began to have all of our trouble early in our marriage, I knew I had a choice to make. I could nag him and try to change him, or I could even leave him. But in my heart, I knew none of those things were right.

"So I finally decided to let him fail and let God correct him as I honored and loved him. After a period of time of praying for him and letting him fail, I saw God begin to change my husband right before my eyes. Today, I have a righteous husband who loves me and meets my needs.

Ladies, I didn't find this man the way he is today, and I didn't make him this way by nagging or demanding. I let him fail, as I prayed for him and treated him with honor."

What a powerful testimony! One will seldom, if ever, make progress by dishonoring others or trying to force them to change. It will only be by praying for them and treating them better than they deserve.

Of course, you can express your disagreement to your husband at any time and about anything. You are not supposed to be a robot or a doormat. But when you tell him how you feel, do it in an honoring manner and then leave it with him, as you pray for him diligently. The only other option is to try to force him to change through nagging or manipulation. Hopefully, you have realized that you may seem to win a few battles that way, but you always lose the war with those methods.

Let your husband fail. We promise you, if you will honor him even when he knows he should not be honored, God will use it in a powerful way to deepen your husband's love for you as well as to deal with his heart.

2. Honor Him Where You Want Him to Be, Not Where He Is

Proverbs 31 describes the virtuous woman. She is a model woman, a good example of how a righteous wife and mother is to behave. Her husband is honored in the gates of the city because of her. In addition to all of the other accomplishments, she is credited with being at least partially responsible for her husband's position of honor.

Imagine a large, empty bottle with a cork lying in the bottom. This is a picture of a bad husband. Like the cork in the bottom, the husband is resting at a point much lower than he should. But what if you put water in the bottle? That would make the cork rise. The cork will always rise to the highest level of the water. In the same way, your husband will rise to the level of your praise and honor.

This is why Paul wrote in Ephesians 5:22 the words "as unto the Lord." Your husband may not act like Jesus, but if you will give him the kind of respect and honor you would give Jesus, he will rise to that level. It is like pouring water into his empty bottle of honor. It is the surest means possible to get the cork to rise. Also, because you are the one filling it up, your husband is going to be drawn to you, as you are meeting his deepest need—to be honored.

The best way to get your husband's attention is by honor. The best way to change your husband is by honor. The best way to get your husband to desire you and spend time with you is by honor. Because it is his deepest need, it is your most powerful asset. Providing honor for your husband is just as critical for him as his making you feel special and secure in his love is to you.

3. Cover His Faults and Reflect His Strengths

Although you must be able to privately communicate your concerns, hurts and needs to your husband in an honoring way, you must cover his faults everywhere else: before your children, to your parents and friends, to his friends and associates, and so forth. Do not expose his weaknesses. Let him know he can trust you totally to honor him and cover his faults.

If there is a situation of abuse or other serious concerns you need to discuss with someone, go to your pastor or a Christian counselor whom you can trust. But don't go to a friend or parent to uncover problems with your husband. Unless your friends and family are very mature and discreet, doing so will cause problems.

Sex

As most women realize, sex is a powerful force in a man's life! As a wife, you are God's only legitimate resource for satisfying your husband's needs. This puts you in a very important place. Most women realize the intense nature of a man's sexual drive, but many women do not respect that. Many women don't want to meet their husband's need for sex as often as he needs it.

So they refuse, or call their husbands "perverts" because they want sex too much. A wife needs to understand two things about the destructiveness of this attitude and behavior:

1. When a wife rejects her husband's sexual needs, she is rejecting the man, because his need for sex is an essential part of

his makeup. Therefore, you cannot reject the sexual part of your husband and not have rejection affect the rest of his being.

2. When you refuse to meet your husband's sexual needs in a proper fashion, it leaves him vulnerable to temptation outside the marriage.

Although affairs are unjustifiable sin and devastating to a marriage, a woman should understand that the main reason most men have affairs is for exciting sex. Women are drawn to affairs because they find a man who is attentive to them and makes them feel special, while most men are drawn into affairs for a lot less noble reasons. They simply want a good, exciting sexual experience.

Of course, there are some men who have a great sex life at home but still have affairs. However, most men are not this way. When their sexual needs are met at home, they are content to remain faithful. On the other hand, affairs are not justified because a man's wife does not give him satisfying sex. Nothing justifies immorality or unfaithfulness.

To understand how a wife can aggressively meet her husband's need for sex, consider these suggestions.

1. Understand the Strength and Importance of the Male Appetite for Sex

Don't underestimate it or reject it. In addition to understanding a man's need for sex, it is very important that you communicate to your husband that you understand and accept it.

Rather than making her husband beg for sex or feel guilty for his need, it is healthy for a wife to approach him and say something like, "Honey, I know you need sex, and I just want you to know I am committed to meeting that need. If you'll simply communicate what you want and when you want it, I'll do everything I can to fulfill your desire."

When a wife does this for her husband, it creates a powerful bond of love and trust between them. Likewise, a husband should be just as committed to meeting his wife's sexual needs, as well as her other needs. Such an attitude by both partners makes for a dream marriage.

Just one word of clarification: Sometimes a husband may ask his wife to do something sexually that is sin or that would violate her conscience. *A man does not have the authority to make his wife sin,* nor should he ask his wife to do something that violates her conscience. But when you must refuse your husband, do it in a sensitive, godly way.

Say something like, "Honey, I'm sorry, but I just can't do that. Isn't there something else I can do instead?"

2. Understand the Visual and Physical Nature of a Man's Sexual Appetite

Men are a lot different from women in the ways they become sexually aroused. Whereas women are mostly non-visual and get sexually excited gradually by romance, soft touching and atmosphere, men get sexually excited much faster, mostly through sight and touch.

This is the reason men are drawn to pornography and pictures of half-clad women. Although it is sinful and damaging to a man and a marriage, it illustrates the visual nature of a man's sexual appetite. In fact, there is an entire lingerie industry that thrives on the visual appetite of men.

Although many women understand a man's visual sexual stimulation, there are a couple of common problems most women have in this area.

The first problem is *comparison.* Would it surprise you to know that, according to one report, more than 90 percent of the fashion models in the industry suffer from low self-esteem? These beautiful models often feel they are really not that attractive, and one of the major reasons is that they compare themselves with other models.

Women's behavior in comparing themselves to other women often is unhealthy. As a woman walks by, the group will scan her constantly from head to toe while exchanging sarcastic remarks about her appearance. One can watch a group of women looking at other women and the observers will often pick the others apart—or if another woman is very attractive, pick themselves apart.

The problem with comparison is that it basically is self-rejecting, which also is an indirect accusation of God. Whenever we covet or criticize something someone else has, we normally end up being resentful or insecure. The best thing is to accept the way God made *you* and do the best you can with what you have. Anytime you put too much emphasis on looks, it is dangerous. The same thing can be said about putting too little emphasis on looks, as well.

Although many women have the problem of comparison with their clothes on, the problems get worse with their clothes off. While their husbands are trying to disrobe their wives so that they can look at them, many wives are trying to cover up so their husbands cannot see them. Why? That is because most women don't like their own bodies.

Few women are happy with their natural sizes or the shapes of their breasts, and even fewer women like their hips and legs. Age and pregnancy magnify the problem.

Ladies, relax! Stop being intimidated and belittled by a perverted world that is trying to get all women to look like models for a diet-drink commercial. Be yourself. Be the best you can be. Look the best you can for your husband in the bedroom and out of the bedroom, because he needs you to look your best. A husband should do the same for his wife.

However, wives need to understand how strong a man's visual stimulation is, look their best for their husbands at all times, and not be ashamed to be naked while their husbands enjoy looking at them in the bedroom.

The second problem women have in understanding a man's need for visual stimulation is their basic feeling that nakedness is wrong, and perhaps, even "dirty." Women usually have a much stronger natural sense of physical modesty. It is more difficult for a woman to be openly naked. I (Jimmy) remember the first time Karen found out I took showers in an open shower at the YMCA with all the other men. She freaked out and didn't believe we did not each have a private little stall with a shower curtain.

A woman's sense of natural modesty is God's way of protecting women and society at large; but when shyness or modesty is taken into the marriage bed, it is damaging. In other words, be modest everywhere except when you are alone with your husband. Then give him the visual satisfaction he needs. Even if you cannot understand what there is about your body that turns him on, rest assured that it really does.

One brief story illustrates this point. During a marriage seminar one time, I (Jimmy) was making this point about a man's need for visual stimulation. I was going to politely suggest that women wear sexy nightgowns and bedwear rather than flannel gowns.

I started to say, "Ladies, there is a place for flannel gowns but you shouldn't wear them too often," but I only got the first part of the sentence out. I said, "Ladies, there is a place for flannel gowns," and one man in the middle of the room shouted, "Yeah! The fireplace."

The room erupted with laughter, and it took several minutes to restore order and resume the seminar. That man's remark was typical of how most men feel about visual sexual stimulation.

3. Be Creative and Sensitive

While a woman should not have to jump through hoops and learn a new sex trick every week to satisfy her husband, she should make regular efforts to be creative and aggressive. When our children were still living at home, we tried to have a day or two of special time together at least once a month. We would drive to a nearby town and rent a motel room, or send the children to their grandparents' overnight.

We tried to do this fairly often, because we found early in our marriage that it is hard to be totally free and comfortable about prolonged sex when children are in the house or when there are other distractions. Although you can and should enjoy normal, regular sex under these conditions, there are times when a wife needs unrestricted romance and a husband needs prolonged, creative sex. These times can be enjoyed at home or away, but the key to enjoying such pleasurable events is to plan them and make them happen.

Just as a man should aggressively romance his wife, a woman should aggressively pursue her husband sexually. In fact, if your husband knows some exciting sex is at the end of the line, he will become much more romantic at the beginning.

Be sensitive to your husband. Don't make him beg for sex. Even during your menstrual cycle when you cannot have intercourse, there still are creative ways to satisfy his needs, if you will only be sensitive and available.

Kindred Fellowship

I (Jimmy) have told Karen a million times that there is no one in the world I would rather be with than her. The reason I want to be with her is because I like her, and I enjoy doing things with her. There were times in our marriage when we didn't get along and I wanted to get away from her, but those times are gone.

When a couple does not want to be together, it is an unhealthy sign for their marriage. The more a couple is physically separated, the worse it is. Certainly each spouse can have friends with which to enjoy certain interests. There are proper times for being apart. But if a couple is relating properly, they should be best friends to each other and desire to be together. If both spouses have all of the same interests, that is great. However, if you find your interests being very different from one another's, some compromise will be necessary. Here are two suggestions:

1. Make an Effort to Be Involved with Your Husband in the Things He Enjoys

I (Jimmy) was elated when Karen decided to learn to golf. I loved to golf with her, but she always said she did not want to go. Now, it is such a good time for us to be together, and it is so much fun. It also meant a lot to me that she would make a sacrifice to enjoy what I en-joyed so much.

For some of you women readers, it may not be golf your husband enjoys, but hunting, fishing, bowling, or a number of other things. While you do not have to like it or do everything he does, become interested and involved as much as you can in the things he enjoys. This is a powerful way to deepen your friendship, fun and intimacy together.

2. Do Not Mother Your Husband

Some women become so wrapped up in the identity of motherhood while their children are growing up that they cannot separate their children from their husbands. As a result, they end up mothering everyone in the house.

Your husband does not need for you to be his mother. He needs for you to be his lover, friend and helpmate. Be careful in the way you dress and act that you do not become dull or overly domesticated. Stay exciting and interesting, and reserve some time for pleasure and fun with your husband.

Domestic Support

There is an old saying, "A man's home is his castle." In many ways, this is true. A man's home is the place he goes to find honor and fulfillment. As long as his needs are met at home, it remains his preferred place to be. But when a man's home is no longer honoring or fulfilling to him, he will be tempted to turn his heart and attention away from it.

I realize that while many women are working outside the home now, it is still true that most women are more domestic than men. But a husband should not encourage or support a decision for his wife to work unless he is willing to take his part in domestic responsibilities. Nevertheless, the ideal situation still is for a woman to be able to devote full time to her home.

Understanding that most women are very concerned about their home and don't need a lecture from us, we want to make this simple point: A woman should make her home a place her husband loves to be. When a home is clean, orderly and decorated as nicely as possible, the atmosphere is more enjoyable.

By doing the best you can with your housework, meal preparation, and so forth, your home will provide an atmosphere for peace and harmony for you and your family.

We hope you have read something in this chapter that gives you a better understanding of your husband's major needs and encourages you to meet those needs in an aggressive manner. More than anything, however, we hope your husband will be as committed to meeting your needs as you are to meeting his in a sensitive and aggressive way.

As you commit yourself to being the best wife you can be, we pray God will grant you the marriage you have always dreamed about.

WHEN YOU ARE BUILDING ALONE

Janice was an attractive, 26-year-old woman with two children. As she introduced herself and we became acquainted, I (Jimmy) was impressed with her kindness and sincerity. Although she was in my office because of marriage problems, I soon sensed she was a willing and healthy builder in her relationship with her husband.

After we talked briefly about her and about some general topics, I changed the direction of the conversation by asking Janice why she needed counseling. With an obvious change of tone and enthusiasm, Janice related the story of her crumbling marriage.

"My husband, Ted, is seeing another woman," Janice said in a matter-of-fact way.

"He comes home to change his clothes and eat, but then he goes back to his girlfriend's house to sleep and spend the rest of his time. Although I have confronted Ted many times, he will not talk about it. He treats me as if I do not exist. I am here today because I cannot go on like this any longer. If something does not change, I am going to have to do something to protect myself and my children."

As Janice concluded her story, I felt she was being truthful about her husband and about her unwillingness to continue in such a marriage. While she displayed a good, loving heart, it was obvious she had endured some major storms in an unstable marriage. As a result, she was seeking counsel to see if there was any hope for her marriage or at least for herself.

Today, there are tens of thousands of bad marriages like Janice's that are unstable and unsatisfying because one spouse is unwilling to contribute or actually is doing something to destroy what the other spouse is trying to build. I have counseled many hurting people—the majority being women—who are victimized by a marriage partner who is either non-constructive or destructive in their relationship.

While these situations create a unique set of problems for the spouse who is sincerely trying to build the marriage, there are biblical answers offering real and powerful solutions. No matter where you are in your marriage today, there is a biblical way to confront any problem. Rather than remaining a helpless victim, you can aggressively deal with your marriage problems in a manner guaranteed to bring results.

To illustrate this, let us return to the story of Janice and Ted. After listening to her and asking some basic questions, I said, "Janice, are you willing to fight for your relationship with Ted? I mean, if I could tell you something to do today that would save your marriage, would you be willing to do it?"

Janice quickly responded, "Surely. I'll do anything. Although I really am hurting right now, I still love Ted, and I don't want to break up my marriage. Certainly, I'm willing."

Pleased with her answer and attitude, I began to give Janice biblical counsel to help her confront Ted and their failing relationship.

"Janice," I said, "if you were like Mary and Martha of Bethany, and Jesus was coming to your home after a hard day of ministry, how would you respond to Him when He came in the house tonight?"

She thought a few minutes, and then slowly answered, "Yeah, I think I know what you mean. Well, if Jesus were coming to my home tonight, I would love and serve Him as much as I could. You know, if it were Jesus, I guess I would do my very best to please Him."

"Good," I responded, "you've got the idea. Now, let me ask you another question, What time do you expect Ted home today?"

Janice said, "He usually comes in after work to eat and change clothes around 6 P.M."

"Janice," I continued, "the Bible says that Ted is Christ's representative in your home. Although I understand Ted is doing a poor job of representing Jesus, he nevertheless occupies a very important position. Therefore, you need to treat Ted in the same manner and the same attitude as you would treat Jesus."

As I spoke, her countenance dropped. After a short silence, she said, "Jimmy, do you understand what I told you about Ted? He's sleeping with another woman. He hasn't given me the time of day in months. And you want me to treat him like Jesus?"

Fully sympathizing with Janice's feelings and legitimate frustration concerning Ted, I said, "Janice, I understand everything you told me about Ted. I know he is an ungodly, insensitive man. But Ted is not here today asking for my counsel—you are.

"Therefore, my responsibility as a biblical counselor is to tell you what the Bible advises you to do. By the way, Janice, I'm not asking you to participate in sin or condone sin in Ted. I am advising that, in spite of Ted's present condition and situation, you treat him as you would treat Jesus. Do it as unto the Lord."

Sensing her obvious reservations about the counsel I was giving, I decided to take a different train of thought for a few minutes.

"Janice, let's say you don't take my advice to treat Ted like Jesus. What are your other options? As far as I can see, here are the options available to you. First, you can continue to live as you are now. However, you've already told me that you can't take that any longer. Second, you could threaten Ted. Tonight, when he comes home, you could yell and scream at him and threaten divorce. However, I don't believe that would be your best option to save your marriage, because Ted might very well take you at your word and leave you."

Quickly, she said, "I have yelled and screamed at Ted and threatened to divorce him, but he only called me a name and told me to go ahead and see if he cared."

So I said, "Well, divorce is an option. But I believe your presence today in my office indicates that you don't want to do that."

"You are right," she replied.

"Well, Janice, I know prayer is powerful, and I know you have been praying for Ted and your marriage."

"I surely have," she exclaimed.

"That's great," I said, "and I am sure that is one of the main reasons your marriage has lasted this long. However, as great and powerful as prayer is, it cannot replace obedience. In other words, Janice, God's

Word tells us to be witnesses and to share the gospel. So, although we pray for lost souls, the world will not be saved until we go out and witness. We must follow up faith-filled prayer with faith-filled action for the cycle to be completed."

I continued, "Janice, I realize you are the righteous partner in this marriage who is being victimized by an unrighteous partner. I also realize you have prayed and done everything you have known to do. But I am telling you something today that very possibly could save your marriage. In fact, if you will go home today and begin to treat Ted as you would Jesus, I promise you, it will get his attention."

She summarized my instructions, "So what you are telling me to do when Ted comes in tonight is to love and care for him as if he were Jesus."

"That is right," I replied, "and you need to continue to do it every day from now on."

She said, "I can see what you're telling me is right. It's just going to be hard to treat Ted that way when he has treated me so badly. What makes it worse is to think about his being with his girlfriend later tonight—but I know this is right."

Then she asked me another question that I had anticipated. "Jimmy, what if it doesn't work? What if I treat Ted as I would Jesus for a long period of time, and he never changes?"

"Janice," I responded, "I can't predict the future, but I can tell you what I believe and what my experience has been. First, God honors those who obey Him and put faith in His Word. If you will do what is right, I absolutely believe God will honor your obedience. Second, my counseling experience with many women and men who have been in similar situations has been that when they treated their unrighteous spouses with love and honor, one of two things happened: Either the spouse responded positively to the love and example and repented, or the unrighteous spouse became so provoked or convicted by the behavior of the righteous spouse that he or she left. Either way, Janice, the problem is resolved by righteous behavior."

At this point, I could tell she was in agreement with the strategy I had outlined. However, before she made a commitment one way or the other, I added, "Just because you treat Ted as you would treat Jesus doesn't mean you can't openly and honestly confront him about your feelings and frustrations. It simply means you do it in love and with respect.

"As you love him and serve him aggressively, that gives you a platform from which to speak with honor but also with honesty about your needs and hurts. In other words, don't be a doormat or a passive target for abuse. Nor should you be hostile or return sin for sin. As you love Ted aggressively, confront him honestly about his behavior."

Janice nodded her head with approval and said, "I understand, and I believe I can do that."

"Great," I replied, "I want you to go home and try your best for an entire week to love Ted as you would Jesus. Then come back and tell me what happened."

With a cautious smile on her face, she said, "Okay, I'll do my best and come back next week."

We concluded the session with prayer, and she went home to face her tough assignment. Several times during that week, I thought about Janice, wondering how she was doing. I anxiously waited for our next session to hear the results.

When her appointment time arrived, she came into my office looking as nice as before, but much more joyful.

After a brief greeting, I asked her the big question, "Well, how did it go?"

Beaming a big smile, she responded, "Well, I've surely got his attention," and I said, "Give me the details!"

She related her week-long experience this way. "When I left your office last week, I thought all that day about how I would treat Jesus if He were coming to my home that evening. I finally decided that I would cook Him a big meal and serve Him all evening, doing whatever He wanted me to do. So I did this for Ted the first evening. I got dressed up as nicely as I could, cooked his favorite meal, and from the time he came in the door until he left to go to his girlfriend's house, I served him and loved him as much as I could."

I then asked, "What was Ted's response?"

Janice said, "On the first evening, Ted just kept looking at me funny and saying things to himself under his breath. I couldn't really tell what he was thinking, but I knew I had his attention. So I kept it up all week."

"Every night, when he came home, I would greet him warmly, looking my very best with a hot meal on the table. I had the paper ready for him by his favorite chair and the house cleaned up. By the second evening, Ted had begun to say a few things to me in a civil way but nothing substantial. However, for me, it was a big improvement.

"On the third evening, Ted was reading the paper after supper, and I was sitting with him in the living room. As we sat there he lowered the paper from in front of his face and said, 'What's going on? What are you doing?'

"I really didn't know how to respond, but I said, 'I'm just treating you like I'm supposed to. You are my husband, and I love you. I'm sorry I haven't treated you like this before. I've made mistakes, and I hope you will forgive me. From now on, I'm going to treat you with honor and serve you as I should.'"

My curiosity was piqued, and I asked, "Then what did he say?"

She responded, "He mumbled something under his breath and put the paper back in front of his face. But for the first time in months, he spent the night at home. He still wouldn't sleep with me, but at least, he was in the house. In fact, he only went to his girlfriend's house once after that evening. I've definitely got his attention. But what do I do now?"

After commending Janice for the faith and courage it had taken to do what she had that week, I told her to continue the same course the next week. I also told her to watch for an opportunity to ask Ted to come and see me. I told her if he asked her again what she was doing or why, to tell him that she was talking to a man at her church who was telling her that she had not been treating her husband as she should.

I told her that she should say, "He is helping me learn to love you and meet your needs. By the way, he would like to meet you next week."

But I cautioned her to wait for the right opportunity to tell him I wanted to talk to him. I hoped that Ted would be curious to meet a man who had been telling his wife to treat him like a king, in spite of his ungodly lifestyle.

The next week, Janice brought Ted back with her. As she bounced into my office, she was smiling so widely that it looked as if it might hurt her! Ted shyly followed.

"Well, hello, Ted. It's very good to meet you," I said.

He answered, "Hi," glumly and sat down on the couch by Janice but as far away from her as possible.

"I'm so glad you could come to see me today," I said, as I sat down in a chair facing them.

"Sure," Ted said, in the same tone as before.

"Well, Ted," I continued, "I am sure Janice has told you we have been talking about your marital situation."

"Yeah," he said, "she told me you have been talking to her, and you want to talk to me." This time, he had a little more energy in his voice.

"That's right, Ted. I wanted to talk to you today about your marriage and to see how you think it could be improved from your perspective."

At that point, Ted began to shift around on the couch, as he said, "I guess you know I've been messing around on Janice. I mean, I have a girlfriend I've been kind of living with for a long time."

"Yes, I was aware of this," I said directly. "By the way, Ted, what is the present condition of that relationship?"

"Well," Ted responded, "I don't know. Although we have a sexual relationship, I really don't love this other woman. And she has been putting a lot of pressure on me lately to leave Janice and marry her. But I really don't want to marry her. However, my relationship with her has been better than my relationship with Janice. I haven't known what to do, although I knew I had to do something soon. But in the past week or so, I've been thinking that I probably need to break off that relationship and try to work things out with Janice."

"That's great," I told Ted, as I watched Janice wiping her eyes with a tissue. "I believe you're on the right track. So, are you ready today to make a commitment to your marriage with Janice?"

I knew I was putting him on the spot, but I also could tell Ted was very impressed with Janice's new attitude toward him.

"Yes," he said, "I'm ready."

Janice reached over and grabbed Ted's hand. Although he didn't make a physical response to her gesture, tears began welling up in his eyes. In my office that day, Ted received Jesus Christ as the Lord of his life by praying the sinner's prayer and committing his life to Christ.

I led both of them in a time of personal repentance and forgiveness to each other. By the time they left my office, they were walking hand in hand. They came back the next week, and we talked more about their marriage and the problems they were having. I also spoke to Ted about his new commitment to Christ and his need for fellowship.

Week after week, Ted and Janice came to my office. Although there were serious problems to overcome, and some times were better than others, both were willing to do their parts. In fact, over a period of months, I developed a close relationship with them, especially with Ted. I couldn't believe how much he loved the Lord and what a great personality he had!

Sin had robbed this precious couple of the life God had meant for them to have. Now, with Ted as the spiritual leader of the home, God has rebuilt their marriage. Today, they actively attend and serve the church. They have a model marriage and family, and Ted is a strong leader.

All of this miracle story began with a woman who was willing to righteously build alone in faith, being God's partner to redeem what was being destroyed by the devil and sin. While all stories don't end up as happily as this one, many of them do when the couple responds to problems in a biblical way. Even when a marriage is not restored as God wants it to be, godly behavior protects the righteous party from needless damage and from being pulled into a "sin-for-sin, hurt-for-hurt" cycle of destruction.

Whether or not you are building your marriage alone, consider the general principles discussed in the following chapter. They are applicable to any person in any situation. As you apply these principles, God will greatly bless you and work with you to save your marriage.

Not only are these principles powerful to conquer Satan's strongholds and schemes in your marriage, but they will improve your personal life as well. These four principles are for the spouse who is building a marriage without the proper support and cooperation of the other partner.

Four Principles for Building Alone

1. Complete Submission

The first principle is *complete submission* to God. This powerful principle that will defeat the devil in our lives is revealed in the book of James.

> Submit yourselves, then, to God. Resist the devil, and he will flee from you (Jas. 4:7, *NIV*).

Before we can make progress in overcoming anything in life, we must learn that submission to God is the most important issue that determines success or failure. According to James, if we submit to God and then resist the devil, we will win.

The problem with submitting to God is that humility is required, the kind of humility that admits, "I am weak and ignorant, and I cannot succeed without God."

This is completely opposite to the natural attitude of many people who say, "I can handle this situation. I have a plan figured out to deal with it!"

This kind of arrogance and independence leaves an open door for Satan's destruction in lives and marriages. The only safe place to be is under God's protective covering, and the only way to get there is to submit to Him completely.

Consider what James wrote immediately before this principle:

> But he gives us more grace. That is why Scripture says: God opposes the proud but gives grace to the humble (v. 6, *NIV*).

If we want God to give us grace and help in what we are going through, we must humbly submit to Him and do things His way. If we will not, it is a sign of pride and independence and *"God opposes the proud."*

While going through a difficult time in marriage, one of the most natural tendencies is to defend *yourself.* When you have been hurt and rejected by someone close to you, it causes serious injury to your sense of self-esteem and security. To compensate and protect from further damage, often a person will put on a proud, tough exterior to deal with the situation.

Although this may be the natural, human thing to do in society, it will not solve the Christian's problem. In fact, it is guaranteed to complicate matters. Jesus taught us while He was on Earth how to deal with enemies and people who mistreat us.

In Luke 6, we read where Jesus commands us to love our enemies, pray for those who mistreat us, and to do for others what we would want them to do for us—even if they are against us. Not only are these teachings true because they come from Jesus, but they also are true because they work!

When you become proud and defensive toward your spouse, you will begin to react to his or her behavior in a sin-for-sin cycle of destruction. Although you may think your behavior is justified because of your spouse's behavior and because he or she "started it," that is not true. Who started it does not matter. What matters is solving the problem. Unrighteous behavior never solves problems, but righteous behavior does.

Recall what James 4:6 teaches about God giving grace to the humble. This means that people in a problem marriage must submit themselves to God and deal with their situation as God directs. He then will powerfully work in and for them to overcome the problem. I (Jimmy) have witnessed this many times as a victimized spouse decides to righteously confront a problem marriage. Not only have I seen many marriages healed in a seemingly miraculous way, but I have also seen God provide grace and strength to the righteous spouse.

Isaiah 55:8 tells us that God's thoughts are not our thoughts and His ways are not our ways. In other words, God sees from a heavenly, all-knowing perspective, so our best advice will come from Him. The way to obtain this advice is by humbly submitting your mind and will to Him.

As you daily seek Him for answers, as well as praying and petitioning Him about your problems, you not only will realize His faithfulness but will also experience the grace and peace that accompany humility. Before you do anything else, submit yourself completely to God. This single act will change you from a co-destroyer of your marriage into a tool in God's hand to save and restore the broken walls of your relationship.

Remember, natural tendencies will lead into destruction, while God will lead into green pastures and beside still waters (see Ps. 23). Although you may feel you are going through the valley of the shadow of death at this time, *do not fear;* He is with you. Submit to Him and rest in His power.

2. Willingness to Suffer

The second principle for building alone is a *willingness to suffer.* We realize that isn't a pleasant thought, but we must sometimes suffer in life. While we hope this suffering will not be meaningless or unnecessarily prolonged, it is inevitable that each of us will suffer in some way. The book of 1 Peter gives us some instructions for enduring these times of suffering.

> But how is it to your credit if you receive a beating for doing wrong and endure it? But if you suffer for doing good and you endure it, this is commendable before God. To this you were called, because Christ suffered for you, leaving you an example, that you should follow in his steps. "He committed no sin, and no deceit was found in his mouth." When they hurled their insults at him, he did not retaliate; when he suffered, he made no threats. Instead, he entrusted himself to him who judges justly. He himself bore our sins in his body on the tree, so that we might die to sins and live for righteousness; by his wounds you have been healed. For you were like sheep going astray, but

now you have returned to the Shepherd and Overseer of your souls. Wives, in the same way be submissive to your husbands so that, if any of them do not believe the word, they may be won over without words by the behavior of their wives, when they see the purity and reverence of your lives (2:20–3:2, *NIV*).

Just as Jesus suffered for us, we must be willing to suffer for others. We must respond to the hardship and abuse others direct toward us without retaliation or revenge and without sin. By the example of Jesus, we are instructed not to threaten those who mistreat us. Instead, we are to be righteous examples to them as we entrust ourselves to God.

I believe it is interesting that right at the end of Peter's discourse on suffering, he addresses the issue of wives in a problem marriage. The majority of those I (Jimmy) deal with who are in unequally yoked marriages in which one spouse is building alone are women. They typically are more sensitive to the conditions of their marriages and much more willing to seek help. Therefore, Peter's natural connection of the issue of righteous suffering with the issue of women in marriage still is appropriate today.

While every principle being discussed in this chapter is applicable to a man building alone in his marriage, the majority of people in this situation are wives struggling with problem husbands. Karen once was one of these women. I was an ungodly, insensitive man. My behavior caused her to suffer a tremendous amount of emotional pain. However, her prayers and righteous behavior were instrumental in God's being able to transform our marriage.

We don't expect and we don't believe that God expects, anyone to become a helpless target of abuse in marriage, as we have written before in this book. Since we dealt with this subject in-depth earlier, we're not going to take the space here to go over it again. However, we do want you to understand the suffering we are talking about does not include significant or extreme damage to yourself or to your children. It does, however, mean dedicating yourself to endure emotional, financial, spiritual and domestic hardships that may be caused directly by your spouse.

Someone may say, "No! I'm sorry. I just won't put up with my spouse any longer. I'm leaving, and I'm going to go find someone who won't put me through all of this pain."

Although we can understand why many people would not want to endure the pain of suffering through the problems in a marriage, here are some things to think about before making such a decision:

- First, even if you leave the marriage, you are going to suffer. Not only is there the emotional agony, but also there are financial loss, the pain and hardship of any children who are involved, and many other things that will simply not disappear overnight. When you leave the marriage, you take with you a trail of constant reminders and responsibilities whether you like it or not. So why not suffer righteously for the marriage and confront the problems?

- Second, when you met your spouse, you didn't think he or she was going to be the problem you now see. So what makes you think you would be able to make a better decision next time? Over and over again we have seen people jump from one problem marriage to another problem marriage, fully believing they were solving their problems with new spouses—only to find out they had only exchanged problems.

    A good marriage is like a good diamond: Most of the time you have to knock off a lot of carbon to see its full beauty. However, once you have beheld the unique beauty underneath the dark earth, you know it has all been worth it.

- Third, many people have the misconception that if they find the right person, they will have positive feelings all of the time. Because of this wrong thinking, many people feel they've made a mistake when they face problems in their marriage. They are tempted to give up and live in defeat or else go back out into the world and try to find "the right one." That is nonsense!

Every marriage is going to experience problems. No married couple will have positive feelings about one another all of the time. The pathway to the marriage you want is not some soap-opera, romance-novel mentality. It is a committed, hard-working relationship where you do what is right and have faith to believe God will supply the proper results.

Make up your mind to follow Jesus' example and suffer righteously for your marriage. Remember, when you were lost in sin, Jesus suffered for you. If it was not for His righteous suffering, the world would be in a hopeless mess today. However, because of Jesus' pure, sacrificial love, we have a means for salvation and restoration.

Jesus is the model for all of those suffering in bad relationships today. Follow Him and look to Him daily, and He will lead you through the problem into victory.

3. Vision

The third principle is *vision*. Proverbs 29:18 says, "Where there is no vision, the people are unrestrained, but happy is he who keeps the law."

What do you want your marriage to become? How would your spouse behave if he or she were righteous? Before you can be successful, you need to know what success looks like. If you don't know what you want, it will be an accident if you get it.

Before a great building is built, the architect has a plan. Before a work of art is created, the artist knows in his mind what he wants to produce. Before a great song is recorded, a songwriter has first heard it playing in his mind. Anything good or great that happens in this life will usually happen as part of a plan, not by accident.

This is one of the powerful truths of Proverbs 29:18. We are instructed to set our eyes on a plan in order that our actions and attitudes can be directed in the direction of that plan. If you do not have a plan, your behavior will be *unrestrained*.

A good way to understand this is to think about a horse grazing in a pasture. When he doesn't have a purpose or plan for his life, he wanders around the pasture at random. Now, think about a horse with a plow behind him. As he plows, the farmer guides him in a straight path. As he moves, his action is productive and predictable. Also, the horse wears blinders over his eyes to keep his attention focused directly in front of him.

In the same way, we need to have a plan for our lives. This plan begins as one seeks God and asks Him what His will is for his life. God usually will give an inner impression in one's mind, an insight concerning His will. These impressions are important, but they also must be in agreement with God's Word. In fact, much of His individual visions for our lives will come directly from the Bible. He told us in His Word what kind of marriage He wants us to have.

Although He fills in the gaps in the general principles with personal revelation for our individual lives, the bulk of what He desires for us is found in His Word. Therefore, it is essential that we read and study the Bible to find His will for us.

Once we have prayed for God's will and studied His Word diligently to understand His desires for us, we must then act and pray in a proper manner designed to reach those goals. For example, if God's Word says we should have righteous children, how does He instruct us in achieving that goal? His Word is full of wisdom and insight for parents desiring to raise righteous children. If we will do what God's Word says we should, righteous children will be the result.

The same is true of any other area in our lives. As we pray and seek God, He will give us insight and vision for where we need to go. And if we will act and pray in obedience as God's Word is leading us, we will get there.

Do you have a plan for your life? Do you know what you need to do to confront the problems and challenges of your life and marriage?

If not, the first thing you must do is seek God for the plan and for the answers. Remember, when you do not know where you are going, it will be a miracle if you get there! Using God's Word as your ultimate authority and source for truth, seek His will on what you should be doing, and work every day to get there, one step at a time.

4. Positive Support

The fourth principle in building alone is *positive support*. It seems as if everywhere you look today, a support group is springing up for individuals, couples or families needing help. It's wonderful! When we are going through difficult times, we need someone to pray with us and encourage us. We also need someone to be accountable to in order not to do dumb things or be left to ourselves.

We hope you have a pastor and godly friends who can and will give you the support you need. Whether we admit it or not, all of us require this type of emotional and practical undergirding, especially in the difficult hours of our lives. If you do not have someone to talk with and pray with concerning your marriage difficulties and/or other problem areas, begin to pray for such a person and begin to seek out someone like that.

The best place to look is a Bible-believing church. Look for a pastor, counselor, support group and/or godly individual to whom you can talk and with whom you can pray regularly concerning your situation. Be sure the counsel given you is biblical. You don't need a lot of opinions. You need godly counsel and encouragement.

In seeking such encouragement, carefully consider this advice:

- Be careful with whom you share the details of your life and marriage. It is especially tempting for women to tell intimate details to family members and friends. Unless they are very mature and godly people, you are making a mistake. If you go to more than two or three people with your problems, you also are making a mistake. Find godly, mature people and tell them your problems and feelings. As you pray with them and talk to them, ask them to pray for you regularly and keep you accountable by honest confrontation and advice.

- Don't be discouraged or influenced by unrighteous people who encourage you to do the wrong thing or persecute you for doing the right thing. Follow God and seek the encouragement you need from people who are godly. If you do this, you will be able to withstand the vast amount of ungodly advice and influence from people in the world. You will find it difficult to withstand the pressure to sin if you do not seek God and encouragement from godly people.

If you are in a marriage that you are building alone, we hope you have found help and encouragement in this chapter. Although there are many questions that may not have been answered or issues that we did not discuss, we hope you will find your answers in one of the other chapters in this book. If not, we are sure that God will lead you to the answers you need as you seek Him earnestly.

We pray God's richest blessings on you as you endeavor to find God's perfect will for your life. Today, as you righteously build alone, we pray you soon will be building a dream marriage together with your spouse.

FIVE ESSENTIAL SKILLS FOR MAXIMUM PLEASURE

Sweet and Sour Pleasure

Some of the most rewarding experiences in my (Jimmy's) life have occurred during the period of time I spent preparing couples for their marriages. I was able to counsel with each couple getting married in our church, spending an hour a week with them for five to six weeks prior to their weddings.

The policy of our church is that we will not conduct a wedding ceremony unless the couple has completed our marriage preparation course. Consequently, of the hundreds of couples who have completed the course, a very small percentage of them have divorced or had serious marriage problems.

In fact, I have personally counseled and conducted wedding ceremonies for many couples, almost all of whom were a part of our congregation. Out of that number, I know of only a few divorces. That is not a perfect record, of course, but it's much better than the average.

If there is any one subject people need to be informed about, it is marriage. This one relationship has the power to make many people miserable or ecstatic; therefore, they need correct information and serious preparation. Also, marriage is a complex institution of spiritual, physical, financial, social, domestic and mental requirements. This complexity requires couples to be committed to preparing themselves in every area.

A large part of the problem in marriages today is simply a lack of adequate preparation before marriage. Couples either don't know they *should* prepare themselves or they don't know where to get help. It is a tragedy that we have so many educational programs available for so many subjects today, and yet few of them teach people the skills necessary for marriage. For the lack of preparation, then, many couples end up caught hopelessly in the throes of a bad marriage.

In addition to teaching premarriage couples much of the information in this book, we also give them specific instructions in five important areas of marriage. We call these "the pleasure areas." They are sex, communication, children, finances and in-laws. For almost every couple, the main reason the two people have decided to marry is one of the above.

To prepare premarriage couples in these areas, I have used a helpful form called a Marriage Expectation Inventory. This lengthy form asks each engaged partner what his or her expectations are for marriage, primarily in the pleasure areas above. Both are asked to fill the form out separately without discussing their answers and return the forms the next week for comparison in the presence of a counselor.

Most couples to whom I gave this form returned it the next week, shaking their heads, and saying things such as, "Boy, these questions were tough. I've never thought about these things very much before."

Most engaged couples never give marriage a lot of deep thought. Of course, they talk about where to live and the general desires and dreams they have, but that is not enough. Marriage is the most important endeavor in life, with the exception of one's personal relationship to Jesus. Therefore, shallow knowledge and a few casual conversations about the future are a prescription for failure for a couple in love.

In addition to responding to the inventory form with a sense of confusion and frustration, many couples were in significant disagreement about critical issues in their upcoming life together without even realizing it. As we compared one couple's completed forms regarding their expectations concerning children, the woman had expressed her desire to have only two children, while her fiancé had written that he wanted six or eight!

She quickly responded, "What? No way!"

Many other couples wrote down totally contradictory answers related to careers, where they would go to church, how they would spend their money, their sexual expectations, and so forth. The time they spent preparing for marriage was lifesaving.

In fact, of all the couples counseled, about 15 percent decided against marriage, having realized they were not as compatible as they thought. For those who did complete the counseling, the effort they expended to prepare themselves properly still is paying dividends today.

Although God designed money, children, sex, communication and in-laws to all be rich and rewarding aspects of marriage, for many people these areas have become a minefield of hurt and disappointment. Excited about getting married and attracted to marriage by the potential for fulfillment and pleasure, millions of couples each year say "I do," hoping to find what they are looking for on the other side of the wedding ceremony. However, because our society is largely untaught about the skills of married life, the very areas that attract couples into marriage are the ones most couples list on their divorce petitions as reasons they want out. What could and should have been a lifetime of pleasure turned out to be a painful experience. So, like insects seduced into a Venus flytrap, couples seek the sweet taste of the pleasures marriage offers only to find out in a matter of a few months or years that they are trapped in a destructive relationship.

But the good news is this: *There is a better way.*

Before specifically addressing the skills required in the five pleasure areas of marriage, I want to teach you how to keep your marriage pleasurable and successful for the rest of your lives together. To do this, I want to remind you of one of Jesus' most important parables, the parable of the sower, in Mark 4.

As Jesus was teaching a large crowd one day, He wanted to impress upon them what was required to be productive and successful disciples. Many people were coming to Jesus and committing themselves to Him, but Jesus knew most of them were unaware of the commitment they were making and of the price of success.

Therefore, Jesus told a parable to teach the three qualities necessary for pleasure and success in the kingdom of God. These same three qualities are all essential ingredients for long-term pleasure and success in marriage. Read the parable as it was told by Jesus:

Listen! A farmer went out to sow his seed. As he was scattering the seed, some fell along the path, and the birds came and ate it up. Some fell on rocky places, where it did not have much soil. It sprang up quickly, because the soil was shallow. But when the sun came up, the plants were scorched, and they withered because they had no root. Other seed fell among thorns, which grew up and choked the plants, so that they did not bear grain. Still other seed fell on good soil. It came up, grew and produced a crop, multiplying thirty, sixty, or even a hundred times. Then Jesus said, "He who has ears to hear, let him hear" (Mark 4:3-9, *NIV*).

According to Jesus' parable, there are three qualities that prevent long-term success just as they make all soil unfit for cultivation and productivity. They are described as stony ground, thorny ground, and shallow ground. So if you find yourself being represented by a certain type of bad soil, you can know that your relationship with Jesus and your spouse will not be as pleasurable or as successful as it should be.

On the other hand, Jesus described the good soil that had none of the negative qualities preventing long-term fruitfulness. So the good soil could bear anywhere from thirtyfold to a hundredfold. Not only in your relationship with Jesus but also in your marriage, you must be good soil bringing forth the good fruit while avoiding at all costs the negative qualities that prevent that fruitful, long-term relationship.

To help you do this, take a closer look at the three qualities necessary for long-term success in marriage.

Three Foundations for Permanent Success and Pleasure in Marriage

Number One: Knowledge—"The Hard Soil"

The first kind of soil Jesus identified as unproductive was the *hard soil* beside the road. As the seed fell on this hard soil, the birds of the air immediately would come and take the seed away. Because the soil was hard, the seed was whisked away easily and without any opportunity to take root.

Hosea 4:6 records, "My people are destroyed for a lack of knowledge" (*NIV*). Whenever we enter into marriage without a soft heart seeking to know God's Word, we are sitting ducks for Satan's deception. Not only can he easily steal truth from a hardened heart, but he also can easily deceive the ignorant mind. Much of the foolishness and sin the world so readily accepts today was introduced because of a lack of knowledge and acceptance of God's Word.

Concerning the importance of our knowledge of God's Word, Jesus said in Matthew 4:4:

Man does not live on bread alone, but on every word that comes from the mouth of God (*NIV*).

If God's Word did not say anything about children, sex, communication, finances and family, perhaps all of us would have an excuse for failure. However, God's Word is full of practical information telling us how to conduct ourselves in every area of life.

The first thing each one of us needs to do in life is to seek God diligently for His truth and grace. Jesus made us this promise in Matthew 6:33:

Seek first his kingdom and his righteousness, and all these things will be given to you as well (*NIV*).

Every essential for successful living is waiting for us, if we only will seek God first.

While I (Jimmy) was doing marriage preparation counseling, I had many couples beg me to make an exception and marry them without counseling. Before I knew better, I made some exceptions and agreed to marry them if they would agree to take the counseling sessions afterward. I soon found that was a big mistake.

First of all, after they were married, they seldom came for counseling. Second, in almost every case where I made an exception, the couple ended up divorcing or having major problems within one or two years. I learned very quickly never again to cater to couples who refuse to slow down enough to prepare themselves properly.

In marriage counseling, I have never had a problem helping a couple who were willing to learn. As I gave instruction to a couple and gave them books to read and assignments to do between our sessions, I never once have had a problem with those who really studied and applied themselves. However, in every single case of a failed marriage, being too proud or too lazy to learn was the major contributor.

As Jesus taught the parable of the sower, He first emphasized the importance of having an open, teachable spirit. The good soil is plowed up and ready to accept the seed. Year after year, good soil becomes more broken and soft. This is the picture of a good heart.

In addition, not only do we need to listen to what God's Word says to us before we marry, but for the rest of our lives, we need to have open hearts toward Him as we seek Him for the seed of life.

When the birds come to steal the seed from the good soil, they cannot find it because it is working within the soil and will soon begin to burst forth with life. Do not allow yourself to become comfortable with anything less than full knowledge of everything God's Word has to say. Your life and marriage depend upon knowing His Word fully. Consider what the following two powerful Scriptures teach:

> Jesus said, "If you hold to my teaching, you are really my disciples. Then you will know the truth, and the truth will set you free" (John 8:31-32, *NIV*).

> Wisdom calls aloud in the street, she raises her voice in the public squares; at the head of the noisy streets she cries out, in the gateways of the city she makes her speech: How long will you simple ones love your simple ways? How long will mockers delight in mockery and fools hate knowledge? If you had responded to my rebuke, I would have poured out my heart to you and made my thoughts known to you. But since you rejected me when I called and no one gave heed when I stretched out my hand, since you ignored all my advice and would not accept my rebuke, I in turn will laugh at your disaster; I will mock when calamity overtakes you, when calamity overtakes you like

a storm, when disaster sweeps over you like a whirlwind, when distress and trouble overwhelm you. Then they will call to me but I will not answer; they will look for me but will not find me. Since they hated knowledge and did not choose to fear the Lord, since they would not accept my advice and spurned my rebuke, they will eat the fruit of their ways and be filled with the fruit of their schemes. For the waywardness of the simple will kill them, and the complacency of fools will destroy them; but whoever listens to me will live in safety and be at ease, without fear of harm (Prov. 1:20-33, *NIV*).

Number Two: Commitment—"The Shallow Soil"

The second type of soil Jesus referred to as incompatible with long-term fruitfulness was the *shallow soil*. This kind of soil will accept a seed and allow it to grow for a period of time. However, because it is shallow, the seed cannot send roots down far enough to become stable and to find the moisture and nutrients it needs. Therefore, when the sun begins to beat down upon the young plant, the shallow soil cannot sustain it.

One of the most troubling aspects of divorce is that people who get divorced once stood together years prior to their separation and vowed "for better or for worse, for richer or poorer, in sickness and in health, to love and to cherish, till death do us part." They made a lifelong covenant with one another to be faithful no matter what came along. (That is why marriage vows include the possibility of bad times.)

These commitments made to one another are supposed to give the couple security. In the past, no matter what happened, both parties were committed. Today, that simply is not the case. Many people who marry today are not totally committed.

By the way, I'm not trying to make everyone who is divorced feel guilty, because I know many people are innocent victims of divorce. Although they were willing to stay and work things out, their spouses were not. If you are in this category, please don't take what I'm saying personally. However, if you are a person who makes lifelong commitments lightly and then considers or threatens divorce every time problems come along, I am talking to you.

Although God is willing to forgive all sins, nevertheless, we must recognize the serious nature of breaking marriage vows. God told us in Malachi 2:16 that He hates divorce. Why does He hate it? Because it represents unfaithfulness, and God is a faithful God. When He tells us He will never leave us or forsake us, that is exactly what He means. Wherever we are and whatever we are doing, He is with us. Sometimes we may wish He was not—but He is.

Married couples must wisely accept the fact that divorce is not an option and acquire the depth of character and convictions necessary to endure times of difficulty and tribulation. Every marriage is certain to have tough times. Although there is no glory in simply suffering through life, there is tremendous benefit in being faithful in bad times and learning from problems and failures.

This is one of the main things that build a strong and successful marriage. Furthermore, whenever we bail out in the hard times of planting and working the fields of marriage, we never experience the joy of reaping the promised benefits associated with harvesting.

In my office, I have a picture of a large sailboat sailing on a troubled ocean. I specifically chose this picture because it reminds me of a powerful saying I once heard: "A calm sea never produced a good sailor."

During the difficult times of ministry, I often look at that picture to remind myself to persevere. As I have endured seasons of difficulty and discouragement, I have always found that these times work a depth of character in my life that nothing else can accomplish. Also, after having endured hard times, I am encouraged that I can do it again with God's help.

Likewise, there is great strength and security brought into a marriage when two people refuse to give up. Remember, a strong marriage is not produced from a fairy-tale existence. It is produced by two people committed to working and sacrificing throughout their lives to make their marriage all it can be.

Marriage is like the old story about breakfast. The question is asked, "Who is more committed to providing your breakfast, the chicken who laid the eggs or the pig who provided the bacon?" The obvious answer is the pig, because the chicken was merely involved, while the pig was totally committed! Do not be merely involved in marriage. Be totally committed! From this foundation, you can be assured of permanence and success.

Number Three: Discipline—"The Thorny Soil"
The third type of unproductive soil that Jesus mentioned was *thorny soil*, soft and deep enough for seed to grow, but too crowded. Rather than working to establish a good, clean environment in which to cultivate seed, the thorny-soil person lives life at random, allowing whatever comes along to attach itself either to him or around him.

As it relates to marriage, we must build the proper disciplines into our relationships and refuse to allow those influences that are harmful or unnecessary to grow up around us. For example, the discipline of a personal relationship with God is the most important ingredient to a successful marriage, but it requires effort to achieve it. We also must learn to pursue each other and to meet each other's needs, but this also takes discipline.

Finances, children, church involvement, keeping priorities straight, and maintaining personal health all require discipline. Whenever we work at keeping our lives healthy, the result will be lasting pleasure and success. However, when we do not discipline ourselves to build and maintain the proper order in our lives, the result will be a deteriorating lifestyle overcome by a weed patch of undealt-with problems, uncrucified sins, and unmet needs. What a needless way to lose the satisfaction of a once-pleasurable marriage.

If you are just now getting married, work every day to build the right disciplines in your relationship. If you have been married awhile and realize your love life has become choked by unhealthy attitudes and habits, repent of your error and begin today to discipline yourself properly.

Remember, the athlete who wins the prize doesn't win simply because he enjoys the sport. He wins because he has disciplined himself to do those things that will cause him to succeed. In the same manner, your marriage will not succeed simply because you thought it was a good idea that worked in the beginning. It will only succeed in the long run as you build into your life the proper disciplines that lead to success.

Knowledge of God's Word, commitment to the relationship, and daily personal discipline are the three foundations essential for the protection and permanence of the blessings God desires to bestow upon us in marriage. It is foolish to build a house without a foundation. It is equally foolish to expect marriages to remain permanently satisfying without the proper foundation.

God designed marriage to be a union that would produce incredible pleasure and benefits. He did not design these blessings to be temporary. He meant them to last for the rest of our lives. In fact, God's plan intends the blessings of marriage to grow in intensity throughout our lives. But, in order for this to happen, we must be like good soil: ready to be taught, deep in character, and disciplined for success.

We hope you will make the proper decisions to prepare your heart for lasting success in marriage. As you do, the next five chapters are offered to help you gain some basic knowledge in the five pleasure areas of marriage. We hope you will be enlightened and encouraged as you read on.

SKILLS FOR COMMUNICATION

During two visits to the Republic of Panama, I (Jimmy) drove many times over the Bridge of the Americas. It stretches over the Panama Canal and connects South America with North America. To say the least, that is an important structure to land travel.

In the same way, *communication* is just as important to a marriage. Communication acts as the bridge that connects the lives of two persons, making free access to the other person's heart and mind possible. Communication is not just important, but essential, to a marriage. Most people can benefit from improved communication skills; therefore, in this chapter, we want to share some basic truths and principles that should enlarge your ability to communicate.[1]

Before discussing the five keys to proper communication in marriage, we want to lay some groundwork. To begin with, we need to realize the incredible power of words. According to the Bible, the universe and everything in it was created by God's spoken words. In like manner, much of the private world surrounding each of us has been created by words—our own or those spoken over us by others—which we believed.

Proverbs 18:20-21 explains this truth:

From the fruit of his mouth a man's stomach is filled; with the harvest from his lips he is satisfied. The tongue has the power of life and death, and those who love it will eat its fruit (*NIV*).

Words possess incredible power—power to wound or heal, to destroy or build up. We must discipline ourselves to use words that build up, strengthen, encourage and heal. The opposite occurs when we succumb to the common temptation to wage warfare on our spouse because of frustrations or hurts.

When you realize you have launched verbal missiles, repent and ask for forgiveness. I (Jimmy) had to do this with Karen. Early in our marriage, I verbally abused her with cutting, sarcastic and belittling words. After Karen forgave me, she told me that nothing I had ever done in our marriage had hurt her as deeply as the harsh words I had spoken to her.

On a television interview one day, famous comedian Jonathan Winters was speaking openly about his abusive childhood. As he seriously recounted how his father had beaten him severely and abused him in other ways, he made a comment I will never forget. He told the interviewer he would gladly take a physical beating over a verbal one anytime. The scars of verbal abuse that he suffered from his father were much worse than the physical scars. That is something for all of us to think about.

Not only must we understand the incredible power in words, but we must also understand that one day we will give an account to God for every single word we speak. In Matthew 12:36-37, Jesus said this concerning the future judgment:

> But I tell you that men will have to give account on the day of judgment for every careless word they have spoken. For by your words you will be acquitted, and by your words you will be condemned (*NIV*).

If you have spoken words you know are unclean or harmful, or you continue speaking them, you must repent to God and ask His forgiveness. When you do, He will forgive you as the atoning blood of Jesus erases your sin. In other words, if you will sincerely repent from the sins of your mouth, you will not have to stand in judgment for them on the last day.

If you do not become responsible and accountable to God for the words you speak, on the last day you will be in for a rude awakening and an eternal consequence for your disobedience by your tongue. Additionally, in this life, you will reap the bitter harvest of the seeds your sinful mouth has sown. The answer is to repent to God, your spouse, your children, and anyone else you have sinned against with your spoken words. Then begin to carefully express positive and healthy words toward them.

Next, you need to understand how essential communication is in bonding your marriage. Regardless of how long you have known each other or how good your marriage is otherwise, you simply cannot become intimate as a couple without proper communication.

I have known many couples married 40 years or longer, yet they still don't know each other well and remain distant in their relationship. You see, it doesn't matter if you share a house, children, bedroom, checkbook, or many other things if you are not sharing your thoughts and feelings through proper communication.

Communication is *the* most important vehicle for our marriage relationships to establish spiritual, emotional, mental and practical oneness. No wonder Satan constantly attempts to accuse us to one another, tempting us to sin with our mouths and to withdraw from each other verbally.

He realizes that if he can poison or prohibit our words, he easily can control and destroy our relationships. Don't allow this to happen. Commit yourself now to speak honest and loving words to your spouse daily to build and maintain a strong bridge of communication.

The third basic need for good communication is understanding and accepting the differences between men and women. Proper communication in a marriage can occur only when the needs and differences of each spouse are understood and respected.

For example, for a man to communicate properly to his wife, he must understand her need for deep, detailed communication, as we discussed in the chapter on husbands meeting their wives' needs. A woman does not want headline answers; she needs the details, the full story.

When a man does not understand a woman's need for patient, detailed information, he will often resent her need to know. In fact, many men feel their wives are interrogating them or mistrusting them because of their desire for information. Instead, men must understand that God created women with this need.

The strength and intimacy of the marriage relationship is fully dependent upon the man's willingness to freely communicate. Remember this, men: Your wife's need for open communication is as important to her as is your need for sex. To turn off the flow of your words to her has the same impact upon her as when your sexual needs are turned off.

Men must learn to accept and appreciate how important their words are to their wives. From early in the morning until late in the evening, day in and day out, the words men speak to their wives create the world they must live in. If this is a safe, loving world of abundant provision, wives will flourish and respond to men accordingly. However, if this atmosphere is harsh and unfulfilling, husbands must realize the danger this environment produces for their wives and, consequently, their relationships with them.

Also, just as men must understand and accept the differences in their wives, there also are some differences wives must understand and accept in their husbands. Men are emotionally different from women. How and where they communicate are different. Men are emotionally modest and physically immodest. Although a man doesn't mind revealing his body as much as a woman, he is much more careful about uncovering his soul.

Women are the opposite. A woman is physically modest and emotionally immodest. She is much more self-conscious about her body, and about where and how she reveals it. The same woman who is so modest about her body will stand at a checkout counter and tell a perfect stranger some of the more intimate details of her life. It can be quite amazing to a man to hear a group of women talk. Although women see such conversation as healthy and normal, it is quite uncomfortable and unnatural for most men.

Because a woman is physically modest, she needs a protected atmosphere to be able to enjoy sex, a safe and protected environment to be able to open up and share her body. But most men can enjoy sex almost anywhere, no matter who is around.

In this same way, because men are emotionally modest, they need a protected environment in which to open up emotionally and begin to talk. Men feel frustrated and violated when they are expected to spill their guts with other people around or when they have just walked in the door from work.

What helped communication between Karen and me was my commitment to open up and talk to her and her agreement to allow me to determine the right time and place.

Ladies, if you are in the habit of telling family and friends everything that goes on in your marriage and/or all the things your husband says and does, don't expect your husband to open up. Men feel frightened and violated to think their wives betray them by sharing the details of their lives with someone else.

While it is appropriate to share certain things about your life and marriage, you must carefully communicate to your husband that he can trust you. Remember, if you violate his emotional modesty and safety, it has the same effect as if he showed his buddies at work naked pictures of you and explained the details of your sex life.

To summarize, we all need to realize the incredible power of our words. We must also understand it is impossible to build a strong marriage without regular, healthy communication flowing in both directions. Finally, we need to remember when communicating that our spouses are different and how to accommodate these differences.

When you understand those three things, you will be well on your way to healthy and pleasurable communication. Remember however, just because you are talking does not mean you are communicating!

As you commit yourself to building a strong bond of communication in your marriage, the following five keys will help you succeed.

Five Vital Keys to Communication in Marriage

Number One: Mutual Concern—"Caring"

Have you ever talked to someone who would not look you in the eye or who was obviously distracted? It's a frustrating experience to say the least. Whether a person will not look you in the eye, speak to you kindly, or something else, it isn't difficult to tell when someone does not care about you.

If it is a checker at the grocery store or someone you casually meet, that attitude on the other's part is only a minor inconvenience or annoyance. However, when it is your spouse, it becomes very painful.

For proper communication to take place in marriage, we must be careful to show each other that we really care. This process begins as we affirm within ourselves the value and esteem we have for our spouses. It continues as we regularly tell them how important they are to us and how much we care about them. But the crowning glory of our demonstrations of how much we care comes from the overall communication of our lives.

Consider carefully each of these seven daily components of your life that can most effectively communicate to your spouse your genuine love and concern:

1. Eye contact
2. Affection and body language
3. Countenance, the look on your face
4. Voice level and tone
5. Frequency of contact
6. Attitude toward serving and pleasing
7. Sensitivity to inner needs, hurts and desires

When these seven components are being demonstrated in a positive, consistent manner, spouses know we care about them, making it much easier for them to open up and communicate with us. However, when these seven components are absent—or present in a negative, inconsistent manner—we are demonstrating a lack of real caring to our spouses and putting up a barrier to open and honest communication.

With every area of our hearts and lives, we must daily communicate to our spouses the fact that we care about them. Also, remember that caring does not require strong emotions. The core of genuine, Christlike concern is to make a willful decision to appreciate and support another individual.

Once we have made this choice and acted it out in real ways, positive feelings almost always will follow. This is only one of the blessings of a marriage built on willful obedience to God.

Number Two: Intellectual Devotion—"Listening"
There is a difference between hearing and listening. Hearing is a physiological function of the ear. Listening is an intellectual devotion to

what the ear is picking up. In fact, it is possible to hear something without really listening to it. An example is a person who lives next to a busy highway. Although the noise is quite annoying at first, after a period of time, that person learns to tune out the noise from the highway and listen to other things.

In the same manner, it is possible to hear what someone is saying to us without really listening. Although we may be looking at the person, smiling, and saying, "Uh-huh" regularly as we nod our heads in agreement, it is possible to do all these things while thinking about something else.

It is like the old saying, "The lights are on, but no one is home."

Whenever our spouses are speaking to us, we should listen carefully. Many times, people are communicating things beyond the words they are saying. We can only understand fully what is being said when we are genuinely listening. Also, if we don't listen to our spouses, they will soon know it. If this becomes a regular occurrence, they will learn to save their words for someone who will listen.

If there is some reason you cannot concentrate on what your spouse is saying at the moment, you need to be honest and deal with it, because you cannot deprive your spouse of regular communication. You must learn to deal with distractions and problems regularly and properly so that you can tune in clearly to what your spouse is saying.

To help you listen and to show your spouse that you are listening, it often is helpful to ask questions about what is being said. Don't interrupt too often, but ask questions on something you would like to have more information about or make brief comments appropriate to what is being said.

It is equally important to look at the person who is talking to you. Wandering eyes soon lead to a wandering mind. You don't need to stare. In fact, if you do, your spouse will probably feel uncomfortable. However, as you listen, make sure your spouse is the center of your attention.

The distractions of television, a newspaper, or other things can be very damaging to communication. Surely, all of us talk around the house while we are doing other things. However, regularly, we must have devoted, protected times of good conversation in which we are not competing with anyone or anything else.

Karen and I still do this, either early in the mornings when we walk together or late in the evenings when things begin to slow down. Those two times of the day give us a basis for excellent communication. After more than 30 years of marriage, we still need it and enjoy it.

Once your spouse has finished saying something, giving a response is another essential way of communicating that you have tuned in to what has been said. You do not have to totally understand or explain everything your spouse has said, but you need to let him or her know that you have heard everything that was said.

If there is an appropriate response, give it. Sometimes your spouse needs to hear you respond with what you think about something he or she has said. Other times, you simply need to say something that conveys the knowledge that you have understood. Whichever is needed, you must be sensitive enough to your spouse to communicate that you want to hear what he or she has to say.

Harsh, critical words or a blank, distant stare at the end of something freshly spoken quickly erects a wall between a couple who is trying to communicate.

Number Three: Verbal Affirmation—"Praise"

Psalm 100:4 says, "Enter his gates with thanksgiving and his courts with praise; give thanks to him and praise his name" (*NIV*).

According to the Bible, we enter God's gates with *thanksgiving*, and we enter His courts with *praise*. Our words of affirmation and praise for God usher us into His presence. God loves to be in the presence of praise; so, when He finds someone willing to praise Him, He surrounds that person with His presence and love.

This same truth applies to all people who, because they have been created in the image of God, also love to be praised and thanked. Praise is the key that unlocks the heart of any person. Try it with a child sometime. Begin to praise him and see what happens. In an atmosphere of affirmation, a child prospers and opens up. However, criticize the same child constantly and see what happens. The child, who so greatly blossomed in the presence of praise, will become embittered and emotionally closed in.

If we are not careful, we tend to forget our blessings and focus instead on our problems and all the things we do not have. That is why the discipline of praise and thanksgiving is so important. Concerning this truth, Psalm 50:23 says:

> He who sacrifices thank offerings honors me, and he prepares the way so that I may show him the salvation of God (*NIV*).

What a powerful Scripture! Even if we don't feel like it, if we bring a sacrifice of thanksgiving to God, we are preparing the way for Him to do great things in our lives.

The same is true of marriage. If we are not careful, we will soon forget our spouses' good points and the reasons we love them. As soon as this happens, we inevitably begin to focus on the negative issues of our marriages and on all of our spouses' bad points. Then a tone of complaint and discontentment is set within our homes, and bad things will begin to happen.

We must discipline ourselves to thank and praise our spouses. Even if we do not feel like it, and the only thing they do correctly is tie their shoes, we need to remember it, focus on it, and let our spouses know that we think they are the greatest shoe tie-ers in the world. By so doing, we are paving the way for God to do great things in our marriages.

Number Four: Loving Confrontation—"Speaking the truth in love"
Concerning the Church growing up to be mature and one in Christ, Paul wrote these words to the church at Ephesus:

> Instead, speaking the truth in love, we will in all things grow up into him who is the Head, that is, Christ (Eph. 4:15, *NIV*).

Another Scripture from Proverbs reinforces the same truth:

> Do not let kindness and truth leave you; bind them around your neck, write them on the tablet of your heart. So you will find favor and good repute in the sight of God and man (3:3-4).

In marriage, there will be many occasions when we must confront our spouses on something they have done that we do not like. This can range from a slight concern to a deep offense. Because these times are inevitable, we need to learn the skills required for a healthy confrontation. Some of the greatest damage to marriages occurs during a time of confrontation when a couple is trying to resolve a dispute. The problem is not the *confrontation*; it is the *method* used to confront.

The Bible gives us some wise words to help us avoid damaging one another in confrontations and to allow the opportunity to regularly air grievances and concerns. The first thing to learn in confrontation is to balance truth with love.

Anytime we are confronting our spouses, as Proverbs 3:3 says, we need to tie truth and love around our necks. *Truth by itself is dangerous.* Some pride themselves on how truthful they are. Many times, however, these same people brutally butcher others with their harshness and lack of sensitivity. Therefore, truth must never travel alone.

Likewise, love by itself is useless. Without truth beside it, love is just a spineless, meaningless blubbering of goodwill. Some people would never speak truth that would be helpful to other people or keep them from harm but, at the same time, pride themselves on how loving and non-judgmental they are.

Real love must contain truth. Patting someone on the back while he or she is on the way to hell is not God's definition of love. Likewise, getting in that person's face and screaming, "You are going to hell, buster," is not love either! Love is walking up to someone, putting your arm around him or her, and graciously speaking the truth with genuine concern and affirmation for that person.

Any marriage with an imbalance of truth or love is unhealthy. The greater the balance of these two virtues, the healthier the marriage.

Once we commit to confront one another in a loving and truthful way, we need to learn the importance of proper timing. Consider what Ephesians 4:26-27 says:

> In your anger, do not sin. Do not let the sun go down while you
> are still angry, and do not give the devil a foothold (*NIV*).

Often, the reason spouses have such volatile clashes is because they do not deal with issues in a timely manner. As frustrations and offenses build up, it is like building up a large heap of debris, trash and garbage. Then, when it does come to a head, it is like throwing gunpowder into the pile. Everything explodes at once. The longer you wait to discuss problems and concerns, the more you ensure a big blowup somewhere down the road.

Also, the longer you wait to talk things out, the more opportunity the devil has to accuse you to each other and to introduce unhealthy feelings and thoughts into the relationship. Be committed to talking things out daily in a truthful and loving way.

Another important practice in addressing problems with spouses is to begin confrontation with affirmation. In other words, confrontation should begin something like this: "Honey, I really love you, and I am glad we're married. I'm more committed today to our relationship than ever before. Also, I'm proud of you, and I see so many good and positive things in your life. However, we need to talk about one thing . . ."

Confrontation initiated in this manner makes what you have to say much more acceptable and non-threatening to your spouse. The opposite of this approach begins confrontation with insults or threats, immediately placing the spouse in a defensive posture against the confrontation.

Another thing to remember when confronting spouses is to not tell them what they were or are thinking or feeling and not to blame them for your feelings.

For example, it is destructive confrontation when one spouse says something like this to the other: "Yesterday when you were leaving the house, I said, 'Goodbye,' and you just walked out the door without saying a word. I knew you were paying me back for what I did the night before. Well, when you retaliated, I *really* began to resent you!"

Although we do know what our spouses say and do, we may not really know what their feelings or thoughts are unless they tell us. When we try to interpret what they meant or felt, many times we will be 100 percent wrong.

We should not try to impose on them our opinions as to what they are thinking or feeling. If we do, that normally causes resentment. Just because your spouse did something that created anger within you, it was not necessarily the *spouse* that caused the anger.

Sometimes anger and other emotions rise up because we misunderstood what our spouses meant, did or said. Other times, our emotions erupt because of immaturity on our part or simply out of human nature. To blame one's spouse, as people tend to do many times, is unfair.

Regardless of what has happened, here is an example of the proper way to confront a spouse. After genuine affirmation, you should say something like this: "Honey, when you left the house this morning, I said, 'Goodbye,' and I didn't hear you respond. I'm wondering if there is something wrong between us that we need to discuss, because I'm feeling a little hurt and insecure. Is everything okay?"

This approach doesn't accuse or blame. It simply states what you are thinking and feeling in order for the two of you to talk things out. Obviously, if your spouse does something bizarre or wrong, then tells you nothing is wrong and he or she does not want to talk about it, you still must pursue the matter. However, you must be careful not to try to dominate, manipulate or intimidate your spouse into saying what you want to hear.

Most people don't like confrontation. In fact, a lot of people would rather do almost anything than confront someone.

I have heard many people say, "I'll do anything in the world to keep peace rather than confronting."

The problem is that you *cannot* have lasting peace without confrontation. Don't keep sweeping hurts or resentments under the rug in your relationship, or one day, like gunpowder ignited by the fuse of anger, there will be a huge explosion. Commit yourself every day to dealing with problems and issues in a loving and truthful manner. The result will be a peaceful and pleasurable relationship.

Number Five: Intimate Discussion—"Openness"
The climax of all communication in marriage is the special time we share in intimate discussion. While a lot of communication and many conversations are essential in marriage, the highlights of marital communication are the special times of deeply personal, intimate conversation.

As you establish a protective atmosphere in which open communication can flow, you should cherish and seek special times to share your innermost thoughts, feelings and dreams. In these intimate times, share with your spouse the deep, positive expressions of your heart about how much you love him or her.

This may occur as you two sit alone in a special moment, or even in the afterglow of sex, but do not take these special times for granted. And do not hide your inner self from your spouse. The more you open up, becoming honest and vulnerable, the more you truly will know each other, and the deeper your intimacy and love for one another will be.

We hope you have been helped by what you have read in this chapter about communication. We also hope you will begin to put these principles and truths into practice. Regardless of how much we read or understand about communication, experience is what makes it meaningful. We pray you will develop a deeply rewarding communication aspect to your marriage.

Note

1. There are some excellent Christian books on the market that cover the subject of communication in depth. We encourage you to buy and read as many of these books as possible. Some of our favorite authors on this subject are H. Norman Wright, Gary Smalley, John Trent, and James Dobson. All of these men have written really insightful material to help us learn to communicate with one another.

Skills for Financial Success

I (Jimmy) will never forget how shocked I was when I first heard the statistic that about 50 percent of all couples filing for divorce list financial problems as the leading cause. Although I cannot vouch for the accuracy of that statistic, I can say from my own experience as pastor and marriage counselor that a great number of marriages do fail because of financial pressures and difficulties.

Money and material blessings are meant by God to be a source of blessing and security, but for many couples, finances are a curse and a cause for fighting and insecurity in their relationships. Regardless of your financial situation, you need to respect the powerful influence finances have on your marriage.

To help you succeed financially and to avoid or overcome many of the dangers of finances in marriage, in this chapter, we will explain seven biblical principles for financial success.

Principle Number One: Ownership

Psalm 24:1 states, "The earth is the Lord's and all it contains, the world, and those who dwell in it."

The first fact we must acknowledge before we can truly succeed with our finances is, *We own nothing, and God owns everything.*

The first step we must take on the road to financial freedom and security is to repent to God for taking possession of the things in our lives and neglecting to recognize His ownership and authority over them.

Next, we must completely submit everything we have to God and be obedient in handling our finances and making financial decisions.

That is where most of us go wrong. Believing money and things really belong to us, we make decisions without praying or consulting the Word of God. The result is financial instability at best and often financial disaster somewhere down the line.

To avoid this result, we should surrender everything we have to God. When we surrender all and then do with it as God directs, there is no reason to fear. God is not going to allow His own belongings or decisions to be brought down. However, if we have not given everything we have to God and made decisions in obedience to Him, our fears are well based, because God never promised us security or blessing apart from complete submission to Him.

God has promised us tremendous blessings and rewards when we submit everything to Him and then become stewards over what He trusts to us in obedience to Him. According to Jesus' parable of the talents in Matthew 25, the rewards are great when we accept our Master's money as His stewards and do His will.

However, the parable also teaches the eternal results of rejecting our accountability to God. Though the world worships money, the Christian man or woman must not. Rather, we should be stewards of our money as obedient servants of God. When we do, not only will we live in security and peace of mind, but we also will live in the prosperity and blessing God promises.

Principle Number Two: Stewardship

Malachi 3:8-12 states:

> "Will a man rob God? Yet you rob me. But you ask, 'How do we rob you?' In tithes and offerings. You are under a curse—the whole nation of you—because you are robbing me. Bring the whole tithe into the storehouse, that there may be food in my house. Test me in this," says the Lord Almighty, "and see if I will not throw open the floodgates of heaven and pour out so much blessing you will not have room enough for it. I will prevent pests from devouring your crops, and the vines in your fields

will not cast their fruit," says the Lord Almighty. "Then all the nations will call you blessed, for yours will be a delightful land," says the Lord Almighty (*NIV*).

I (Jimmy) will never forget the time early in our marriage when Karen asked if she could give $40 to the church. At that time, she was not working; and I was making less than $800 a month to provide for our family.

I broke into a cold sweat just thinking about giving money away. We were barely making it at the time. I had the attitude that it was bad enough if you had to go to church; but when you started having to pay for it, you really were a fanatic. Nevertheless, against what I thought was right at the time, I allowed Karen to give the money. Even with my bad attitude, unbelief and fear, I could tell immediately a difference in our financial situation after she gave to the Lord. Although we didn't have any more income, we could sense God's blessing on our finances. So we gave again and again and again. The more we gave, the more we could sense God's blessings on our finances.

God directs us to test Him with our finances and let Him reveal His power and faithfulness by opening the windows of heaven and pouring out a blessing until it overflows. He also promises that He will rebuke the devourer for us if we will give Him the first and best of our finances.

While it does not make sense to our carnal minds that giving away money will mean more, it is true. The only way you totally will understand this truth is to *test* it. Once you do, God's Word promises results.

When we give the first tenth (the tithe) of our income to God, we are affirming that He owns everything. Tithing also communicates faith in God. In addition, without the tithe, the local church—part of God's Body on Earth—becomes weak and unable to function properly. Therefore, God commands us to give Him the first and best of what He has given us.

In addition to everything else tithing does, it communicates to God our recognition that all blessings come from Him. It is a powerful way to say, "Thank You, God." As we do this, God responds with more blessings.

Related to the issue of giving, some preach the "false" prosperity message, telling people to give to God and He will make them rich. This simply is not true. The truth is that if you give to God according to how He blesses you and specifically directs you, God continually will bless you and prosper you.

By the way, the correct definition of "prosperity" is "having enough to do God's will for your life."

Do not give simply to get rich or to manipulate a Scriptural promise. Give because you love God and appreciate His blessings. But you also can give expecting to see results, because He is faithful.

Karen and I now give about 20 percent of our income to the local church and Christian ministries. It is my personal conviction that the first 10 percent of everything we receive should go to the local church. After that, we should give to the poor and make offerings to the church for special projects.

We also can give to missions works or Christian ministries. If you do this presently, you know the joy and blessing giving brings. If you are not giving as you should, do not try to follow Karen's and my example or that of anyone else. Seek God for your own situation as you honor and obey His Word. As you do, you will begin to see Him work powerfully in your finances.

Principle Number Three: Leadership

Proverbs 11:14 states, "Where there is no guidance, the people fall."

Financial counselors tell us they have never counseled a couple who have a budget and are facing major financial problems. By budgeting, major problems are avoided. The type of financial planning that involves sitting down and seriously considering demands matched against income should be initiated by the husband, with assistance and support from the wife.

When we exercise proper leadership in making financial decisions, peace of mind and an acute sense of direction are noticeably present. Without a solid plan and direction for our finances, we make decisions based on personal whims and our hearts' desires.

If we do not encounter immediate problems, we continue today as we did yesterday. However, the day is sure to come when we stare reality in the face, having to assume responsibility for problems that stem from mismanagement of finances.

For couples who desire to start a budget and a plan for the future, *The Family Financial Workbook* by Larry Burkett is an excellent resource.[1] I personally have used this workbook and believe it is an invaluable tool for developing a family budget.

You need to understand that having a budget does not mean you should become legalistic with your finances. In fact, the process of developing a budget is as important as the budget itself. Once you have established a budget, you have a valuable tool to help you attain good money management skills.

Another area of leadership in finances is *estate planning.* We encourage every couple to seek counsel from a Christian lawyer, accountant, or estate planner to help plan for your future. It is important to have up-to-date wills, proper amounts of life insurance and retirement funds, as well as a savings plan for education and other family needs.

All of these things require good planning, a characteristic of a wise leader. If you lack the skills required to do these things yourself, then seek the advice and counsel of those Christians who do.

And please, husbands, do not make the mistake of not completely informing your wife about the details of your finances and estate. Not only does your wife need to participate in these decisions, but the unpleasant reality is that she probably will outlive you.

As a church, we have helped many distraught widows sift through financial and personal records following the deaths of their husbands. The husbands' deaths were tragic enough; but, in many cases, the wives knew very little—if anything at all—about the estate, which only added unwanted and unnecessary grief.

We recommend an excellent resource tool for women entitled *The Widow's Handbook* by Charlotte Foehner and Carol Cozart.[2] Unlike the title indicates, the best time for a woman to read this book is while her husband is still alive to help her plan for future events. However, even if that is not possible, this book is a great source of help for widows.

Sit down with your spouse and talk about these matters. As a husband, be responsible to make sure your wife is well informed and in agreement about your complete financial position. Most of us do not like thinking about these things, but we must be mature in our thinking and prepare for the uncertainties of life such as being disabled, as well us the certainty of death.

Long-term financial success requires planning and discipline. Do not put it off. Begin right now to get your financial house in order. If you will, your marriage will greatly benefit, and it will keep getting better, as you obey God and He continues to bless you.

Principle Number Four: Contentment

First Timothy 6:8-10 states:

> But if we have food and clothing, we will be content with that. People who want to get rich fall into temptation and a trap and into many foolish and harmful desires that plunge men into ruin and destruction. For the love of money is a root of all kinds of evil. Some people, eager for money, have wandered from the faith and pierced themselves with many griefs (*NIV*).

Being content does not mean you cannot have dreams and desires for greater things. It simply means that you are thankful for what you have and are willing to wait for God's provision and timing to get more. True contentment means that you will be thankful if you never have more than food and covering.

Discontentment is a destructive force that drives us to get more and to get it now. To make matters worse, advertisers today are experts in inciting us to be discontented with what we have and to lure us to possess their products, even if we have to go into debt to do it.

Many couples are in financial bondage today because they either are ungrateful for what they have or are trying to keep up with society (or possibly some family member or friends) who look down on them if they do not conform. While none of us wants to be totally out of step with those around us, we must be committed to a lifestyle of contentment, no matter how wealthy or how poor we are.

Contentment means that we regularly give thanks to God for the blessings in our life and are able to rest and be at peace with what we now have. Contentment also means we are able to come to God and truly submit our desires for more to Him with a thankful attitude. When we can do these things, we know we are safe from the dangers of greed and discontentment. The degree to which we cannot or will not submit our desires to God is the same degree to which our financial welfare is in danger.

As 1 Timothy 6:10 explains, loving money is a root of all sorts of evil, and it will always usher pain and suffering into our lives. Do not allow the deceitfulness of riches to hold you in bondage. Love God and use money as He directs.

Throughout our life, Karen and I have known many rich people and many poor people. Repeatedly, we have seen this vivid truth in their lives—the amount of money people have is not what makes them happy. Only knowing Jesus and being in His will can make one happy.

Principle Number Five: Faithfulness

Proverbs 28:20 states, "A faithful man will be richly blessed, but one eager to get rich will not go unpunished" (*NIV*).

Some people are sitting ducks for con artists selling get-rich-quick schemes.

"Give me ten thousand dollars, and I will make a hundred thousand in thirty days," many people are promised. Con artists know that greed is their number one tool. If they can incite enough greed in people, they can manipulate them to do just about anything.

The truth is that very few people ever will get rich overnight. For the vast majority of us, faithfully working and wisely planning over many years will be how we establish financial security. About the way to get rich, one financial expert said, "Spend less than you make, and do it for a long time."

Faithfulness is God's way. Day in and day out do what is right, and it will result in success. Just like the fat person who wants to lose in 3 weeks the weight they have gained over 30 years, many of us keep believing in quick methods for financial prosperity. However, just as diets don't work like that, fly-by-night financial schemes don't either.

The answer is to discipline ourselves to live correctly every day. Faithful, proper exercise will bring strength. Faithful, proper eating will bring a trim waistline. In the same manner, faithful, proper stewarding of our finances year in and year out will bring security and success.

Don't gamble on quick solutions to your desires or problems. Be faithful as you obey God's Word daily. Not only will you get what you are looking for, but when you get it, you will have it for the rest of your life.

Principle Number Six: Freedom

Proverbs 22:26 states, "Do not be a man who strikes hands in pledge or puts up security for debts" (*NIV*).

There are three basic issues related to freedom in finances all of us need to carefully consider. The first is *debt*. Although we don't believe it is a sin to borrow money, more and more we realize that too much debt is bondage. Most people probably have to borrow money to buy a home or a car; however, a Christian's goal in life should be to pay cash for everything, especially non-appreciating items.

When I (Jimmy) was younger, I thought borrowing money to get what I wanted right then was worth it as long as I could make the payments. Now I know better. Having experienced the pressure and bondage of debt in my life, I have decided it's just not worth it. With the exception of my house, I pay cash for everything I get. If I need something and cannot afford it, I wait until I can afford it. Doing things this way means I don't have things I want or need as quickly as I desire, but it also means I don't live with the pressure of debt or the high interest rates that come with it. I'm able to live in peace, well within my means.

If you are presently in debt, make a plan to get out and stick by it. As you pay off your existing debt, begin to save as much as you can in order that you can pay cash in the future for the things you need. I know that this may be very difficult right now for some people, but it is going to be even more difficult for you if you do not. Also, your marriage will be greatly affected by a wise or unwise decision.

The second issue of financial freedom has to do with *business partnerships*. After having been involved in one myself, as well as being exposed to many other partnership situations, I can say without hesitation that they can be dangerous. Unless a partnership allows one person to be in control and sets protective parameters from the very beginning, it will probably end up unsuccessfully. In fact, many innocent people have lost a lot of money through partnerships. Like a marriage resulting in divorce, an unsuccessful partnership can be very painful and financially devastating.

The third issue related to financial freedom has to do with being a *co-signer on someone else's debt*. The Bible is very clear in stating that we are not to co-sign debts for others. This is wise advice from God for protection of our money and relationships.

Co-signing makes one a co-debtor who is just as responsible for the debt as the borrower. Rather than co-signing, either give a financial gift or let a lending institution take care of the situation without your involvement.

Principle Number Seven: Selflessness

Jesus said to His disciples in Matthew 16:24, "If anyone would come after me, he must deny himself and take up his cross and follow me" (*NIV*).

Selfishness poses a dangerous threat to the well-being of any marriage. For example, when one or both partners compete for or unduly control the family's financial resources to make sure they have what they want first, then bitterness, resentment and financial instability, or even chaos, are inevitable.

Lasting financial security and success begin with a mutual attitude of selflessness. In other words, even if it means not being able to get what you want, you must be willing to deny yourself for the welfare of your marriage and family. That kind of attitude is Christlike. Therefore, God honors it as He blesses those who are willing to lay down their lives for Him and each other.

We believe these seven principles will lead you to lasting pleasure and success in your family's finances. Although you may not be an expert, begin today to apply yourself and obey God's principles for financial success.[3] If you will, God will bless you, and you will begin to experience the life-long pleasure that obedience and discipline bring.

Notes

1. Larry Burkett, *The Family Financial Workbook* (Chicago: Moody Press, Revised Edition, 1990).
2. Charlotte Foehner and Carol Cozart, *The Widow's Handbook* (Golden, CO: Fulcrum, Inc., 1988).
3. There are many excellent Christian books available to give you a better understanding of your finances. In fact, there are so many excellent resources on this subject, there is no reason for any of us to fail or keep on failing. Some of our favorite authors on finances are Larry Burkett, Charles Givens, Pat Robertson, and Ron Blue. We encourage you to buy and read some of these authors' materials.

Skills for Successful Parenting

We have a son and a daughter, Brent and Julie, and they are both wonderful children. They are both grown and happily married, so it is difficult to think of them as children anymore. Today, and throughout the years of child rearing, they have been a delight to us.

Through the process of raising our children, we have learned a lot about being parents. Although we have done some important things right, we also know we have made some mistakes. In this chapter, we will discuss some important biblical foundations for parenting and disciplining children, as well as some things we have learned about how to be godly parents.

Our children are given by God as precious gifts to bring pleasure into our lives, but this will happen only if we are proper stewards over them. Next to our relationships with God and our spouses, our children should be the most important priorities in our lives. They require and deserve a lot of time, love and attention from both parents. When we give it to them, we invest wisely. They bless our lives and grow to be responsible adults of whom we can be proud. But when we fail to love our children and to meet their needs properly, they can become major problems and a threat to our marriages.

To understand the biblical basis for parenting and the skills required to rear children properly, one must understand the four major needs of a child that only God can completely satisfy. They are identity, security, purpose and acceptance.

These needs of your children are the same as yours, but there is one major difference. As adults, we are able to establish a personal relationship with Jesus and our spouses in order to find the deep, inner satisfaction that we need. However, although our children can accept Christ and love Him at a young age, during the first 18 years of their lives, having their needs met is largely dependent upon us. In fact, for our young children, we are like God to them. We are their protectors and providers. We are the lovers of their souls and their judges. Therefore, as parents, we must understand the critical roles we play in meeting our children's four deepest needs.

For meeting these needs, the goal should be to slowly wean them from our care and usher them into the arms of God. Whether we realize it or not, that is our real purpose as parents. We must realize that children's understanding of who God is and what He is like is most influenced by the characters of their parents and the parents' treatment of the children.

When parents demonstrate a balance of love and truth to a child throughout his or her young life and invest themselves faithfully in the development of that child, it will be easy for a child to understand and accept the Lord. But when a parent is absent, rejecting, cruel, abusive and/or weak, the child will not have his or her needs met and will have a more difficult time understanding and accepting God.

Consequently, the twofold purpose of each parent is to:

1. Usher the child into an understanding and acceptance of Jesus Christ as Lord and Savior, and
2. Meet the four basic needs of the child.

Parents can measure success by these two standards. In other words, when a child is grown and ready to leave home, the parents should be able to say two things: "We have done everything we could to reveal the love and nature of God to our child and to lead him or her to Jesus," and "We have met every major need in our child's life in a faithful and sacrificial manner." If parents can truthfully make those two statements, they have been godly parents.

In leading our children to the Lord, the best thing we can do is love God and live a life that is pleasing to Him. Children observe and learn more than they are taught by parents. They are much more influenced by who we are and what we do than by what we say or teach. Therefore, parents who try to legislate love for God or religious beliefs to their child (beliefs that they themselves are not willing to live out in front of the child) are not parenting properly or providing the role model their child needs.

Parents who live what they believe to the best of their abilities are doing the best possible thing to train their child or children properly. The parents' personal habits, attitudes, language, friends, church participation and marriage relationship all have a profound impact on a child. To reinforce this truth, think about how your parents' values, beliefs and behavior have impacted your life and understanding of God.

Throughout the lives of our children, as we endeavor to model and educate them into the love and acceptance of the Lord, we must likewise endeavor to meet four major needs.

How to Meet the Four Major Needs of a Child

Number One: Acceptance

From the very first moments of life, a child begins to sense the nature of his or her environment. Parents and pediatricians alike are learning the importance of providing a child with the proper environment from the moment of birth. The sensing of the nature of one's surroundings continues throughout his or her life.

Because of our deep need to be accepted, we feel safe and secure wherever we are. Acceptance enhances the sense of self-worth and belonging. When we experience rejection rather than acceptance, we feel insecure and detached, and a sense of aloneness and vulnerability is heightened. Consequently, parents must do everything possible to demonstrate love and acceptance to a child from the moment of birth. It is important for parents to communicate to their child in four major ways.

1. Physical Affection

Young and older children alike need to be touched and held by both parents. We never outgrow the need for such physical affection. When parents regularly touch and hold their children warmly, acceptance is communicated to them in a powerful way.

The opposite is true when affection is lacking. The less parents touch and hold their children, the more emotionally detached and rejected they are likely to feel.

2. Verbal Affirmation

All children need to be praised and complimented throughout their lives. They need to hear their parents say they love them every day. When children are placed in an atmosphere of praise and verbal affirmation, they bond to their parents and grow up believing in themselves. However, when there is an atmosphere of quietness or criticism, children will sense a lack of acceptance.

3. Availability

A lot is being said and written about spending quality time with children. Although we agree that the time we spend with our children should be quality time, we know that children also need large *quantities* of time around their parents, especially when they are younger. Parents who spend too much time at work, at church, with friends or doing other things leave their children feeling alone and unimportant.

Although we all need to live a balanced life with many interests, we must protect a healthy amount of time and energy to spend with our children. This lets them know we accept them and care for them.

4. Expression

There are two things every child needs from parents: a sense of belonging and a sense of identity and individual expression. A healthy person always has a balanced sense of who he or she is and to whom he or she belongs. An unhealthy person either feels a lack of belonging or a lack of identity. Therefore, as parents, we need to let our children know we respect their feelings, opinions and individuality. Although we must teach our children to obey us and to conform to certain standards, we must not overwhelm their individual identities with our own opinions or dominant personalities.

Parents who try to over-control a child's life or make that child into something *they* want him or her to be are harming the child. Although parents should lead a child in the right direction, they also should give the child room to be an individual and to make certain personal choices.

As a child gets older, his freedom must increase until finally one day that child is on his or her own, having a sense of personal identity and a sense of belonging to loving parents.

Number Two: Identity

All of us have a deep need to feel unique and significant. Parents begin to communicate this sense of identity to their children by letting them know how special they are. A child should not be compared to brothers or sisters or made to overly conform to the family system. Rather, a child should be allowed to express himself in an atmosphere of love and order.

I (Jimmy) remember one young man who was being emotionally crushed by his father, who pushed the son throughout his life to be a football player. When the young man resisted, the father browbeat him and tried to make him feel guilty. Although a parent sometimes needs to *make* a child do something the parent knows is best, care must be taken to try not to make a child live the parent's personal plan for his life.

The older children get, the more their feelings and opinions should dictate the direction of their lives. Children should not be given the freedom to self-destruct, but they should have the right to be who God made them to be and to find themselves within safe parameters and in His will.

Number Three: Security

A child's sense of security is derived chiefly from the stability of his or her parents' lives. Therefore, when a child senses strife in the home, he or she immediately will feel insecure. Whenever there is financial pressure, although the parents may not discuss it openly, a child will intuitively sense it and become insecure. Parents need to respect the natural sensitivity and emotional vulnerability of their children.

Even if parents know their disagreements are not going to end in divorce, the children do not need to hear them argue or fuss. They need to see their parents love and serve one another. Therefore, parents should be careful how they live their lives in every area.

With careful living by the parents, children will sense that they are safe, and their need for security will be met. Children also need patient instruction and communication concerning their fears and things they need to know about life in general.

The bottom line is this: Children feel secure when they are in an atmosphere of stability and love. Parents need to do everything possible to create this type of environment for their children. Setting parameters and disciplining them properly also makes them feel secure in the family environment of love.

Number Four: Purpose

Even when a child is young, he needs to be taught that God has a special purpose for his life. As we tell him he is special and unique to us and to God, we need also to let him know God created him for that special purpose that will be revealed someday.

As parents, we meet our children's basic need for purpose by giving them responsibilities around the house and with the family. Children need to learn to pick up their toys and keep their rooms clean. As they get older, parents should continue to give them increased duties and responsibilities, but this should be done in a balanced way.

Balancing responsibilities with the fun and activity children need requires sensitivity on the part of parents. Children should have time to be children, time for fun and friends, yet they should do their part of the chores around the house. This is a critical part of making them feel fulfilled and important.

We need also to encourage children to serve in church and in the community. Children need to be educated from the Bible about their spiritual giftings and how to use these gifts to help and serve others. From the time our children are young, we need to pray for them to find and fulfill their ministries for God.

No person ever will feel fulfilled or have a true purpose in life until he or she is fulfilling God's call on his or her life. Remember, we will not be judged only for the good and bad things we have done, but we also will be judged according to whether or not we have obeyed God's will for our lives.

When a child is taught to be productive and responsible, he is happier and feels he has purpose. However, when a child is allowed to be irresponsible or lazy and is never taught to obey God's will for his life or take responsibility in the family, church and community, he will be unfulfilled and unhappy.

Therefore, from the time children are young, parents need to give them responsibilities and instructions commensurate with their age and abilities.

The remainder of this chapter will provide instruction on child discipline, an issue many parents are intensely interested in but often do not know much about. To make things worse, there is a major school of thought at present that teaches parents not to spank and to disregard the authority of God's Word.

There Is No Excuse for Abuse

There are four important issues that need to be considered by every parent in addressing the matter of child discipline and spanking:

1. Abusing a Child Is Without Excuse

While we believe in spanking children, we absolutely do not condone child abuse. The way we distinguish between discipline and abuse is that abuse subjects a child to either physical, emotional or spiritual influences that are harmful and demonstrate something to him that is unlike God's nature. On the other hand, proper spanking does not damage a child. Rather, proper spanking protects a child and reveals to him the truth that God punishes those who disobey Him and His Word. Therefore, spanking is helpful to a child when it is done in a proper manner.

The difference between proper and improper spanking is illustrated by a scenario like this:

You have warned your son, who is old enough to understand your expectations, concerning something. You have told him that if he disobeys you in this matter, he will be spanked. Then he disobeys.

You should take him to a private area. Never yell or scream unless it is in an emergency, such as a warning of some kind. ("Watch out! A car is coming!") Also, you should never discipline your child in public unless it is an emergency. Rather, when he disobeys you, calmly lead him to his bedroom or a private place.

When you get there, say something like, "Johnny, Dad (Mom) told you not to ride your bike in the street, and I saw you out there just a minute ago. You could have been run over by a car. You disobeyed me. I want you to bend over the bed. I am going to have to spank you."

By this time, a child normally is crying, begging, bargaining and twisting around. The main thing the parent needs to do is keep a straight face and control his or her own emotions. With a paddle, wooden spoon or wooden rod (not your hand or a random instrument), swat the child on the bottom two or three times. You must hit him hard enough to cause discomfort but not hard enough to cause damage.

Once you have finished the spanking, put the child on your lap, or if he is older, sit him down beside you and hug him. As you hold him, tell him you love him and forgive him, but you do not want him to disobey you anymore.

Once you have said these things, pray for him.

When you have finished, say something like, "Johnny, Dad (Mom) loves you. You are a very good boy. Now, go out and have fun, but stay out of the street!"

This is the way we have spanked our children since they were very young. As we did, we never once abused our children, and they grew up secure, well-behaved, and happy. Without love and proper training, parents who abusively spank their children typically have waited until their emotions are out of control.

As an example, abusive parents warn a child over and over with something like, "Billy, you do that one more time, and you're going to get a whipping!"

Because the parent doesn't follow through, Billy learns not to respect what is said; and, unfortunately, the parents wait until Billy pushes them to the edge of their control before doing something. Then they do too much.

Listen, parents. When God tells you He is going to do something, He always does it. Therefore, when you don't follow through with what you tell your children, you are demonstrating unfaithfulness and dishonesty. This will cause major problems with your being able to get your child to respect and mind you. As your child gets older, he also will have a distorted image of God.

Another thing the abusive parent often does is flail a child physically and verbally. Hitting a child randomly all over his body with your hand or an instrument is unsafe and unhealthy. Also, yelling at a child, calling him names, and disciplining him in public damages a child emotionally.

Finally, do not lie to a child to instill fear into him. For example, when a child misbehaves or disobeys, do not tell him God is going to kill him, or that his arm will fall off. Speak truth lovingly to children and follow through with what you say. This way you can stay in control as you responsibly discipline your children.

2. The Anti-spanking Lobby

There has been an onslaught of teaching in the past 40 years instructing parents not to spank their children. These so-called experts in child-rearing methods teach that spanking causes children to resent and hate their parents and provokes them to adopt violent lifestyles. By not spanking children, their "natural" goodness will be expressed.

In addition to being in total disagreement with God's Word, there are many problems with the philosophy of these secular, and even sometimes Christian, "gurus" of child behavior. I want to list three of these problems, or three fallacies with this philosophy.

The first fallacy is that these humanistic "philosophies" constantly change, so they cannot be presenting absolute truth. For example, 50 years ago, doctors and experts began to discourage mothers from nursing their babies. Instead, mothers were encouraged to put them on formula, because it was healthier for the babies. About 20 years ago, suddenly that all changed. Mothers now are being encouraged to nurse their babies because it is healthier.

The second fallacy is that the theory of people who tell us not to spank our children does not match the Word of God. The Bible has much to contribute to the issue of parenting and child discipline. Read Proverbs 13:24; 22:6; 23:13; 29:15; Ephesians 6:1-4; and Hebrews 12:11.

The basis of almost all of the anti-spanking teaching today is humanism. This political and religious philosophy teaches that we do not have a sin nature. Rather, everyone, including you and your child, has inherent goodness inside. According to this philosophy, if you can just put your child in the correct environment, his "natural goodness" will come out. While we agree that children should be in a positive environment, the truth is, we all have sinful natures that must be corrected and held in check. Without the proper discipline and restraints, our children will self-destruct if left to themselves.

If children are inherently good, then why are they so naturally selfish and rebellious? From the day our children were born, we loved and cared for them. However, they never became "naturally" kind with their friends. We had to teach them. It was not "natural" for our children to obey us—we had to teach them. It was not "natural" for them to have good attitudes—we had to teach them. People are not naturally good; they are naturally sinful.

Isaiah 53:6 says:

We all, like sheep, have gone astray, each of us has turned to his own way; and the Lord has laid on him [Jesus] the iniquity of us all (*NIV*).

Not only are all people naturally prone to sin, but the only way goodness comes into our lives is when we follow Jesus. According to Galatians 5:22, goodness is a fruit of the Holy Spirit's presence in our lives. Without Him, we may be good compared to someone worse than us, but we are not truly good and certainly not good enough to be saved by *our* goodness—only by the grace of God.

The third fallacy anti-spanking teachers have is their reasoning that spanking causes a child to become violent. While we do agree that abuse will affect a child adversely, we do not agree that spanking makes children violent.

Actually, the truth is the opposite. Correct discipline teaches a child to respect others and to restrain his or her behavior. An excellent argument against the spanking-causes-violence school is this: If you get a ticket for speeding and have to pay a $50 fine, are the police teaching you to be a spendthrift with your money? Are they teaching you to spend?

After you pay the fine, do you think you will get an irresistible urge to start giving money away? Or perhaps you are going to get an irresistible urge to hit the mall and shop 'til you drop. Of course not!

You are fined for speeding to get your attention and restrain your behavior. This is the same reason why parents spank children.

3. Spanking Is Right but Not the Answer in Every Disciplinary Situation

While believing in spanking, one must be careful not to use one method as a cure-all for every problem. For example, sometimes a child's behavior is communicating an unmet need or a hurt. One needs to be sensitive to children to know when something wrong is going on inside them.

There are times, then, when another form of discipline may be more effective. I don't believe in grounding a child, because it punishes the parent along with the child. I do believe in withdrawal of certain privileges and in other creative ways teaching our children to behave.

On the one hand, we need to be careful that discipline does not damage the children or subject them to an ungodly influence. On the other hand, we must make sure our forms of discipline really get their attention and make them think twice next time. Therefore, using spanking as our main form of discipline, we should nevertheless be sensitive to our children and creative in our parenting.

4. Parents Must Be in Agreement with Their Plan for, and Patterns of, Discipline

When parents do not agree on how they discipline, or when one parent does not support the other one, there is an extremely harmful influence on children and on the marriage. Therefore, agreement should begin with a concerned and involved husband. Rather than leaving the discipline to the wife, the husband should aggressively think about, pray about, and involve himself in the discipline of the children.

Both the husband's and the wife's feelings and beliefs should be heard and respected, for they both bring an important and legitimate perspective to the discussion of discipline. Once both partners have expressed their feelings, an agreement must be reached and followed through consistently in disciplining the children. Neither parent should be the sole disciplinarian. Both should be. When one parent disciplines a child, the other parent should back that one up. If there is any concern or disagreement, it should be expressed privately.

It is unhealthy for a child to grow up in a home where the parents are in constant disagreement over the matter of discipline. It is also unhealthy when one parent becomes the lover and the other one becomes the disciplinarian. Even if it means compromise, parents must find a point of agreement and support each other.

Both parents should love and discipline their children. Again, the husband must take the lead in this but be sensitive to his wife. As he does, and as the couple faces the challenges of parenting in agreement together, they will be sure to succeed.

Although we realize there are specific details and ways to discipline or parent children that we have not covered, we do hope you have been helped and encouraged by this information. There are many good Christian books that go into detail answering questions for concerned parents.[1]

The main thing we need to do is put ultimate faith in God's Word. We need to seek as much help and support as we can from God and from godly people. We hope you will be blessed as a parent as you experience many years of joy and love with your spouse and children.

Note

1. Authors such as Dr. James Dobson and Dr. Grace Ketterman have written excellent books to help parents deal with almost any given age or situation. How blessed we are, in the twenty-first-century Church, to have not only God's Word but to have astute Christian experts to guide and help us in critical areas. If you have not already done so, visit a local Christian bookstore for books to educate and inspire you to be the parent God wants you to be.

Skills for Sexual Pleasure

Of all the forces that draw a man and woman together and provide pleasure in their lives, none can surpass sexual intimacy. Designed by God for both pleasure and procreation of the human race, sex is the universally spoken language of love.

However, since mankind's early history, sex also has been one of the most exploited of all our sinful weaknesses. This, combined with the fact that we live in such an immoral, deceived and seductive society, requires us to be informed and careful as we seek fulfillment in this important area of marriage.

To understand the nature and importance of sexual intimacy, we first must remember that it was God who created this delight in the first place. God wanted us to have pleasure. He also wanted a man and a woman to share a deeply personal area of their lives that would bond them together as it produced intimacy and mutual satisfaction. Therefore, God created sex.

Just as with everything else God has created, Satan has done everything he can to pervert it and use it to destroy us. For this reason, God has told us in His Word how we can fulfill our need for sex while avoiding the sensual destruction everywhere around us.

To understand how to fulfill sexual needs and desires in marriage, while avoiding those areas of sexual involvement God has prohibited in His Word, we first must be aware of what God has commanded us not to do. These are the seven sexual practices that God forbids:

1. Sex outside of marriage: adultery, fornication
2. Sex relations with a member of the same sex: homosexuality

3. Sex relations with a member of your family: incest
4. Sex relations with animals: bestiality
5. Sex fantasies or desires for someone other than your spouse, which amounts to adultery in God's sight; pornography of any kind, as well as mentally playing out lustful fancies for real or imaginary women or men
6. Sex that finds pleasure in pain or violence: rape, sado-masochism, brutality
7. Sex that involves body parts not designed by God for intercourse: sodomy, anal sex

Within the parameters God has placed on sex, we are free to enjoy sex with one another. God is not a prude, and sex is not dirty. It is a wonderful creation designed to give us pleasure. The reason He has commanded us not to do these certain things is not because He is trying to keep something good from us. It is because He knows destruction awaits those who practice these things. Therefore, in trusting God and accepting the restrictions He has placed upon our sexual practices, we can enthusiastically pursue sexual fun and fulfillment in marriage.

In counseling couples over the years and in teaching marriage seminars, including teaching on sex, I (Jimmy) have had many questions from couples about their sexual practices. For example, many couples have questions about oral sex or other issues that the Bible does not specifically address. As they ask me these questions, here is how I answer. First of all, no preacher or anyone else has the right to tell someone what is right or wrong if it is something the Bible does not address. Couples must decide those things for themselves. In making these decisions concerning sexual practices that are not specifically forbidden in Scripture, here are some important questions to consider:

1. Does this increase oneness and intimacy?
2. Is it mutually pleasurable or at least mutually agreed upon? (Spouses should not be forced to do anything against their wills.)
3. Is it hygienically and physically safe?

4. Can I do this with a clear conscience before God? (God is not a prude, and He is not embarrassed by sex. However, according to Scripture, if we cannot do something by faith, it is sin.)

5. Is this something I would want my children to practice in their marriages someday?

If a sexual practice can pass these questions favorably, then you should have no reluctance in enjoying it in marriage. However, if it cannot, you should continue to pray about it—or simply decide not to do it. Remember that the most important aspect of sex is not what it does for you personally. It is what it does between a couple and also to each partner's conscience before God.

For the remainder of this chapter, we are going to share some specific problems encountered in the practice of sex, both by the husband and by the wife, and also offer some suggestions that will help each partner to fulfill his or her spouse.[1]

While men typically have a strong appetite for sex and a need to fulfill this urge in marriage, they also have some major problems. The first is misinformation and deception.

As a young boy around eleven years of age, I (Jimmy) was introduced to pornography. A neighbor had access to *Playboy* magazines, and every month a group of us boys would gather to look at the new one. Some of the older boys even showed the younger how to masturbate. From then until I married, I regularly was exposed to locker-room talk in which guys swapped stories about their sexual exploits and also displayed more pornography. There was also what I saw and heard on television and other places.

As a result, when I was dating, I was looking for a girl who could live up to what I had seen and heard all of those years.

The problem was that I had been *lied to and misinformed* by the pornographers.

Pornography is not real! Although you may see a beautiful woman who has a great body, or a sexy movie with all of the things that turn you on, you *must* understand that it is not reality! Those beautiful young women in *Playboy* and the other men's magazines have not had children, and also, their photographs have been airbrushed so that any flaws are covered up.

Those girls get paid for posing. When they are finished, they go back home to reality. The same is true for porn stars. Although they may scratch, moan and groan on the screen, they are *acting a part*, a fantasy, for money.

Too many men are greatly influenced by the sex industry which is profit-motivated. It has no interest in telling the truth about sex in marriage. The only interest the industry has is *profits*. Anything that will make money will be shown. The sex industry has learned that sin is what sells their product best. It continues to lure men with a perverted and unhealthy product. When they take the bait, they are sure to be influenced by what they see.

As an example of the dangers of pornography, consider John's real-life story. John (not his real name) is a traveling salesman, who regularly stays in motels and hotels that show adult movies. About three years ago, he got into the habit of watching pornographic movies.

As he became sexually excited by what he saw during the week, he would come home and try to get his wife to do what he had seen in the movies. However, she was repulsed. His wife had been sexually responsive to him all during their marriage, yet he thought the new techniques he had learned from the movies could improve their sexual relationship.

As John's perverted fantasies of sexual fulfillment began to crumble, because of his wife's disgust and refusal to participate, he was faced with a dilemma: Would he sin by trying to force his wife's cooperation or perhaps even go outside his marriage for fulfillment of his fantasies through prostitution or adultery? Or would he see the error of his ways and get help?

Thankfully, John sought pastoral help, and both he and his marriage were healed. However, there are millions of other unhealed "Johns" still out there.

Although it is perfectly permissible to share sexual needs and desires with your spouse, the inspiration for those needs and desires should not come from pornography or locker-room lies. The products of today's sex industry cause men to use their wives rather than love them. They also drive men to selfishly satisfy their own lusts, rather than being selflessly led to meet a wife's needs.

To put it bluntly, most of the information about sex found in pornography began in the pit of hell, and that is the only place it belongs. Men, if you are involved in pornography, get out. It will destroy your life and your marriage. And if you have been trying to get your wife to match your "movie mistress's" performance, or to match those of your sinful fantasies, stop and turn your heart to God.

With your heart turned toward God, honestly share your sexual needs with your wife and express your desire to please her. Let her do what she is comfortable doing, as you aggressively serve her and seek to fulfill her needs. If you will, you will find lasting fulfillment in a practice that brings a lifetime of pleasure, not pain.

What You Don't Know *Can* Hurt You

Another problem many men have in the area of sex is ignorance of a woman's sexual makeup. The reason is that many men think women basically are just like men. Therefore, they want their wives to be turned on by looking at their naked bodies. They expect their wives to turn on and off as quickly as they do.

Also, they want their wives to have "mountaintop" experiences every time they make love. Sorry! Those expectations will not happen, because women are very different from men as it relates to sex.

Consider this list from an article published in a national magazine about "sex secrets women wish husbands knew":

1. Great sex, for a woman, begins with her life as a whole.
2. Many women find talk a turn-on.
3. Women, too, have performance anxiety.
4. Attention *after* sex can be vital to a woman's satisfaction.
5. Women need non-sexual touching and tenderness.[2]

Those sex secrets normally leave men cold, because they want women's sex secrets to be something like this:

1. Blow in my ear at a 45-degree angle.
2. Unbutton your shirt slowly, as I gaze upon your sculptured body.
3. Grab me passionately and throw me around the bedroom like a mad gymnast.
4. Stroke my body wildly with your rough, unclean hands.
5. Give me no notice of your interest in sex. I love it when you come home from work, ignore me all evening, then take me passionately right before you go to sleep.

Physically and emotionally, women respond to sex much differently than men. One person expressed it this way, "In the world of sex, men are microwave ovens, and women are crock pots." In other words, women cannot separate what happened this morning before breakfast from sex this evening. Everything in her life is a part of her sexual make-up. Men are completely different. After having a terrible day and knowing Armageddon is starting tomorrow morning, they can still think about sex. Although men are that way, they must understand and respect the differences in their wives. If they will, their wives will be much more sexually responsive.

A man should care for his wife and love her in non-sexual ways all day long. He also should be clean and well-groomed. During sex, he needs to slow down and be gentle with his wife, giving her time and attention before and after sex.

If he will do these things, he will find his wife to be much more interested, responsive and fulfilled. So, if you don't understand a woman's physical differences in sex, buy either of the books mentioned at the end of this chapter. Reading one of those could really help you to know how, when, why and where a woman is sexually aroused. However, the best information will come from your wife as you listen to her and seek to please her.

Women do have one thing in common with their husbands. Most of them don't understand how a man is designed sexually. Whereas women are romantic and emotional by nature, men are visual and physical. So just as a man should meet his wife's need for love and romance, a woman should meet her husband's visual and physical needs. A wife needs to reveal her body to her husband to allow full, satisfying body contact as a part of sex.

Because men typically have a stronger need for sex than women, sex is not just a preference or a pleasant event. It is a major need in his life. When a woman understands this truth, it is much easier for her to meet this need in her husband. As she does so in an aggressive and creative manner, she will be giving a great blessing to her husband and to their relationship.

If, as a woman, you do not understand the physical design of your husband and his needs and how he is aroused, please read some Christian books on the subject to help you. The more you know and understand, the more you will be able to meet your husband's needs.

There are two more major problems that many women deal with in enjoying and providing for their husbands sexually: (1) previous sexual and/or physical abuse, and (2) guilt.

Two Major Problems in Women's Sex Lives

Some studies indicate that as many as 50 percent of all women are sexually abused in some way before the age of 18. After counseling hundreds of women over the years, I (Jimmy) believe this statistic is very conservative. It is common to hear stories of sexual abuse by fathers, grandfathers, brothers, cousins, neighbors and strangers. Every story of abuse is tragic, and some are almost unbelievable.

When women have been sexually abused, they react in different ways. Some women feel dirty and guilty, so they begin a life of sexual promiscuity to deal with their inner feelings. Other women become frigid and sexually unresponsive, unable to disassociate their past tragedy with the overall subject of sex. For them, sex is a constant reminder of ugly scars in their lives.

Still other women block the memories of awful abuse out of their minds, refusing to deal with pain from the past. However, while their thoughts and feelings about sex may not be active in their conscious minds, past abuse prevents their functioning normally in the present.

Regardless of how a woman reacts to sexual abuse, she eventually must deal with her past in order to live successfully in the present and the future.

Drew and Pam (not their real names) were both 22 years old and had just graduated from college. They were a sharp young couple who could not wait to marry. After completing our marriage training classes, they were married immediately to begin their new life together.

After about two years, Pam called to say that they were having really serious problems and needed to come for counseling, which they did several days later.

When they came into my office, I could tell immediately that something was seriously wrong. They did not have the joy in their eyes that they had before.

Shortly after they arrived, I asked them directly, "What's going on?"

Drew began shaking his head and said, "I guess you need to ask Pam. She's the one with the problem."

As I turned toward Pam, I saw that she was already crying, but I said, "Pam, is there something wrong you need to talk about?"

Pam replied, "I don't know. I just don't know what is wrong with me. I just don't want Drew to touch me, and I don't know why," and she began crying so hard she couldn't speak.

As I comforted her, I looked inquisitively toward Drew.

Obviously upset and on the verge of tears himself, he said, "Jimmy, when we were dating, I could hardly keep Pam off of me. Although we waited until we were married to have sex, we were very passionate and really had to watch ourselves. But when we got married, and I tried to have sex with Pam, she would freeze up the minute I touched her or mentioned sex.

"For the past two years, I have basically lived without sex. The little sex I have had hasn't been worth it because of what I have had to go through to get it. Although I love Pam and I'm committed to our marriage, I'm tired of this, and I want to get it over with."

By the time Drew had finished his comments, Pam was more in control of herself, so I asked if Drew had presented an accurate picture of their relationship, and she said he had. Then I asked if there was a reason why she did not want him to touch her or have sex with her. She brokenly and quietly said no, as she began to cry again.

At this point, I already knew Pam must have been a victim of sexual abuse. Over and over, I had heard similar stories by women who had been abused telling of the painful effects on their marriages.

So I asked Pam directly, "Were you sexually abused as a child or young woman?"

She lowered her head and cried uncontrollably for at least 20 minutes. As she cried, Drew reached over with a painful look on his face and patted her on the back.

When she was able to regain her composure, I asked her the same question again, and she looked at me quietly and said yes.

I said, "Pam, can you tell us who it was?"

After looking at Drew and reaching over to grab his hand, Pam said, "I've never talked about this with anyone before. I'm terrified to talk about it now. I just don't know how to deal with it. It hurts so bad, and I know I've hurt Drew."

Interrupting her, I said, "Pam, it's okay. Many women like yourself have been abused. It is not your fault. God will heal you today, if you will get this out in the open and allow Him to work in your life."

Pam responded, "I really want to get this over with. I just don't know how to say it."

Looking back at Drew and then at me, she said, "Jimmy, my father sexually molested me regularly from the time I was 10 years old until I was a sophomore in high school." Turning to Drew, she said, "I'm sorry."

Drew began to cry as he reached over, hugged his wife, and said, "It's okay, baby. I'm sorry, too."

For several minutes Drew and Pam hugged and comforted each other. I could tell Drew was devastated by the news that his father-in-law had molested his sweet wife, but he was dealing with it in a mature way.

As the story developed, Pam related that her father would sneak into her bedroom at night and molest her. When she was 13, he had full intercourse with her and continued this until she was 16. Pam not only was dealing with feelings of shame and anger, but every time Drew touched her sexually, it reminded her of the incidents with her father, and those painful feelings would resurface.

When she regained her composure, I led Pam in a prayer of forgiveness of her father. That is the single most important act for a woman to be healed from abuse. Pam was persuaded that she was not guilty or dirty in God's eyes or in Drew's eyes.

Finally, I prayed *for* her and asked God to heal the scars in her mind and heart. I asked Him to do a miracle for Pam, erasing the pain of her past and creating within her a new and real desire for her husband.

As Pam and Drew left, I reminded them there would be challenges ahead, but to be faithful and to deal with them honestly. They followed this advice; now years later, they are doing well in their marriage.

If you are a woman reading this right now, there is a good chance you have been abused. If you have, forgive the person who abused you and pray for God to heal you and restore anything in your life destroyed by the abuse. As you do this (and continue to do it daily, if necessary), you will begin to experience genuine freedom in your life.

The second major problem with women and sex is guilt. In addition to having been molested or abused, if a woman has had premarital sex, an abortion or an affair, she will often be unable to enjoy sex as she should.

Although all of these sins are bad, none of them is unforgivable. Regardless of what you have done, the blood of Jesus is powerful enough to erase any sin when you repent. Therefore, if any of these past sins still weigh on your conscience, confess your sin to God, and turn away from it. As you do, put faith in the fact that you are forgiven and go on with your life enjoying sex with your spouse.

One more matter that is important for a woman to be able to enjoy sex is birth control.[3] It is important to find a safe and effective means of birth control on which both husband and wife can agree. Once you have done this, your ability to be intimate sexually without fear will be greatly enhanced.

Though there are many other facets to our marriage relationships, sex is still an important part of building and maintaining intimacy. We hope you and your spouse will both be fulfilled for the rest of your lives as you share this beautiful part of marriage together.

Notes

1. We recommend two Christian books on the subject of sex. Both are skillfully written by Christians and have a wealth of helpful information. The books are *The Act of Marriage* by Tim and Beverly LaHaye (Grand Rapids, MI: Zondervan Publishing Co., 1976) and *Intended for Pleasure* by Ed and Gaye Wheat (Old Tappan, NJ: Fleming H. Revell Co., 1977).

2. Kathleen McCoy, "5 Sex Secrets Women Wish Husbands Knew," *Reader's Digest*, January 1988.

3. Rather than going into detail on that subject here, let us encourage you to buy either of the two books mentioned earlier in this chapter and refer to the sections in them related to birth control. We do not personally feel as qualified in this area as the other authors are. Because this is such an important issue, we feel you need the best counsel possible.

Skills for In-Law Relations

One of the great blessings of marriage is the opportunity to extend your family. Through marriage, not only two individuals but also two families are linked together in a common bond. This special aspect of the marital union has tremendous potential for blessing our lives whenever we understand and are proper stewards over this expanded family relationship. However, when in-law and extended family relations are misunderstood or mishandled, few mistakes have greater potential to destroy a marriage.

In this chapter, we will discuss four principles for dealing with your parents and in-laws in marriage. These same principles also can enlighten those who are or may become in-laws on the proper role to play in a married child's life.

Included is an excellent resource entitled "Ten Commandments for Grandparents," which will help parents and grandparents to understand how they can be partners together to raise righteous and well-adjusted children.

Number One: The Principle of Honor

Many married couples get confused in their relationships with parents or in-laws because they don't understand the difference between authority and honor. God's Word says we always are to *honor* our parents. When we are living in their home, we also are under their *authority*, and we should obey them and treat them with respect.

Once we grow up and marry, we are to continue to treat them with honor and respect, but we must understand that they no longer have any authority over us. One exception to this rule might be when a married child or spouse is employed by a parent or in-law. In that situation, the parent has the authority any employer would have, but no more.

One of the most devastating problems in a marriage is for a parent or in-law to dominate or unduly influence the couple. Sometimes they do this by intimidating personalities, and other times, a parent will hold guilt or money over the heads of married adult children to gain influence with them.

Regardless of how parents or in-laws gain authority in a child's marriage, it is always wrong and damaging to a marriage, because it emasculates the man. Whether it is his own parent or an in-law parent, he immediately feels a lack of honor and significance as a man. And he should feel this way, because the God-ordained sovereignty of his home is being violated.

Parents should never try to exercise authority over their grown children, and children should never allow it. When parents control a child's marriage, a woman will lose respect for her husband and feel insecure.

As bad as it is when our own parents are controlling us after we are grown, it is even worse when it is our in-laws. Each husband and wife must understand the legitimate violation their spouses will experience if one of their parents is allowed to transgress the proper boundaries in their home and marriage.

When you get married, you must sever the ties of authority your parents have in your life. This doesn't mean you cannot take their advice or even seek their counsel. Rather, you are not *obligated* to do so or to follow their advice.

Once you are grown and/or married, your parents no longer have God-approved authority over you. You must understand this truth and make sure you act accordingly.

Again, let us say that regardless of your independence from your parents' authority, you should never dishonor your parents. Even if you must stand up to them and resist or correct something they are doing, you must treat them with dignity. You should not talk about them negatively or cut them down around each other, your children, or others.

You should pray regularly for them and let them know you love them in real, demonstrative ways. However, even as you do these things, you must never allow parents to violate the sacred boundaries of your marriage covenant.

Number Two: The Principle of Separation

Genesis 2:24 states, as we have read before in this book:

> For this reason a man will leave his father and mother and be united to his wife, and they will become one flesh (*NIV*).

When we get married, we must reprioritize our relationships with our parents. They can no longer occupy top position on our lists of priorities. For the sake of our marriages, we must make our spouses our first relationship commitment and top priority.

For this reprioritizing of life to take place properly, we must have a healthy separation from our parents and in-laws and be able to spend quality and quantity time with our spouses and children, alone. When we are able to separate properly from our parents, we are able to establish our own identities. We are also able to bond together as a married couple and as a family.

When parents and in-laws are around too much, it is unhealthy. Not only are we not able to develop our own identities, but also we will not bond properly with our spouses. Each spouse must make sure he or she is properly separated from his or her parents. People not willing to separate properly from their parents should not get married.

If you desire to live with, or submit to, your parents for the rest of your life, that is no sin. However, if you are married and unwilling to separate from your parents, it is a sin.

Even if neither spouse is bothered by the frequent presence or contact with parents and families, both husband and wife should understand that, nevertheless, it is unhealthy. Even if it does not bother you, it does bother God. He has a plan for your marriage, and although your parents are an important part of your lives, you must separate yourselves enough to be who God wants you to be.

Saying it another way, God designed the marriage relationship to grow in an atmosphere of separation. This is why He made women territorially minded. If it was up to men, many would live in a common building downtown. However, putting two women in the same house is different, because God built within women the need to separate and for each to have her own territory.

In deciding if your marriage is properly separated from your parents and in-laws, carefully consider the following four questions:

1. Do you or your spouse feel violated by the frequent presence or strong influence of your parents or in-laws?

2. Do you or your spouse spend a large amount of your free time talking to, or being with, your parents, in-laws or extended family, including brothers, sisters, cousins, and so forth?

3. Are most of your activities and close relationships with parents, in-laws or extended family?

4. Do you find it hard to make major personal or marital decisions without the approval of your parents, in-laws or extended family?

If you answered yes to any of these four questions, you really need to think seriously about what you are doing. If you answered yes to two or more questions, you need to take some immediate action for the sake of your marriage.

Although it may be difficult at first to make a change or to stand up to your parents or in-laws, everyone concerned will be better off in the long run if you take action now. Your parents and in-laws will respect you much more if you lovingly establish and maintain healthy parameters in your relationship with them.

In addressing this issue of separation, the subject of problem mothers-in-law usually arises. Although fathers-in-law have the same potential to make trouble, mothers-in-law seem more susceptible to becoming problems. We are not implying, by any means, that all women make problem in-laws.

Many mothers-in-law are a tremendous blessing to their married children and grandchildren, as are many fathers-in-law. However, some women have a more difficult time allowing their children to separate from them. When this happens, a problem relationship is sure to develop.

There are three elements that normally create a problem mother-in-law situation.

1. Mother-in-Law Lacks Other Fulfilling Relationships

The mother-in-law is single, widowed or lacks significant bonding and fulfillment in other areas of her life. If she has a good marriage, or is involved in activities and pursuits in life that keep her busy, she seldom is a problem to her married children. She is satisfied and fulfilled in other areas of her life. But, if she is bored and lacks fulfillment in other areas, her children often become a convenient way to fill this void.

2. Mother-in-Law's Identity Is Wrapped Up with Child's

The mother-in-law gains excessive security and identity through her children. When she turns her heart away from her husband to find excessive identity in her role as a mother, this is unhealthy. Not only can a strong marriage not develop when a man or a woman puts something else in the place of his or her spouse, but a healthy child cannot develop when his parent gains excessive identity or security through him.

A parent's use of a child to prop himself or herself up emotionally is called "triangling." Rather than God and the spouse providing necessary emotional strength, a parent turns to a child or children for emotional security. The problems with triangling a child (using our children to gain the fulfillment in life that we should seek elsewhere) are many.

First, when either parent uses a child to prop himself or herself up emotionally, *the child is being abused*. That is right: Children are not there for parents; parents are there for the children. So when a child becomes the fixer or stabilizer for a parent, the child cannot develop properly.

The second problem with triangling is that it perpetuates problems in the parents' lives. Rather than turning to God and their spouses to find inner fulfillment, instead, these types of parents will turn to their children. Therefore, the children are not free to lead normal lives, so they will never find fulfillment—and neither will the triangling parent.

The third problem with triangling occurs when a parent emotionally attaches to a child of the opposite sex. This is called cross-gender identification. A young boy needs a mother and father, but he needs more of his father, because he learns to be masculine and manly as he spends time around a man.

A father is a very important figure to a growing boy. If he does not have a father present in his home, the mother should make sure he spends as much time as possible around godly male influences. This is critical for his emotional and sexual development.

The same is true of a young girl. She needs a father and mother, but she needs more of her mother. The time she spends around a healthy, feminine mother is essential. She learns, as she observes her mother, how to be maternal and feminine, and how to behave with men. With this influence in her life, she is benefited greatly.

However, if a developing child is lacking strong identification with a member of the same sex, and especially with the same-sex parent, it is unhealthy. What makes this unhealthy situation even worse is a strong influence of the opposite sex stepping into this void and emotionally attaching to the child. Big problems are caused in a child when a parent does not attach to the same-sex child or if a parent overly attaches to a child of the opposite sex. The scenario just described is a leading contributor to homosexuality and sexual confusion today.

The fourth major problem with triangling a child is that the emotional attachment, which usually begins in childhood, often lasts for the rest of the child's life. Because she overly attached herself to her child as the child was growing up, the mother often feels devastated and insecure when her child leaves home. To compensate for this, many follow their children throughout life. While the love of the mother and her need for a relationship with her child is understandable, she must not be allowed to continue this unhealthy dependency.

The answer to a problem mother-in-law is not hateful words or harsh rejection. It simply is a matter of lovingly setting parameters and making sure she respects them. A problem mother-in-law needs to be told in so many words that she needs to pursue fulfillment with God, her husband and/or other areas of life. Although she needs to know you love her and there is an important place in your life for her, she also needs to know you will not take the place of God, her husband, her church, her friends, and other needed ingredients in her life.

Also, we hope every young mother has learned something as she has read this about mothers-in-law. Although you may be having problems with your husband, work them out, and don't allow yourself to triangle *your* child. Do not make your children your "fixers." Be a healthy mother to them and a loving partner to your husband.

One day, the children will leave home and probably get married themselves, and they will need to do so with your love and support and without your interference. This will only happen if you begin right now to make them a priority, but not your first priority. Seek God, your husband, and other interests in life. In so doing, you will be a healthy mother today and a good mother-in-law later in your child's life.

3. Mother-in-Law Is Adversarial with Child's Spouse

When a mother-in-law gains excessive identity through her child, she is threatened by anyone or anything competing with her for her child's love. Whether it is the husband's mother or the wife's mother, when she becomes jealous over the love she feels she is losing or has lost with her child, she usually will become competitive and hostile with her "rival."

She often will find fault with that person and will do things to get attention and affection from her child, even if it means doing something wrong or crazy. If this is occurring in your marriage, you must forgive your mother-in-law and understand that, in spite of her behavior, she is looking for love. Knowing this, you must nevertheless not allow her to do anything that would harm or divide your relationship. The answer is for the couple to present a loving and united front to her, while affirming your love for each other and enforcing proper boundaries.

Number Three: The Principle of Protection

In marriage, both spouses must be committed to protect their mates from their parents. Therefore, do not criticize your spouse to your parents and don't allow your parents to criticize your spouse to you. When parents begin to interfere in a relationship, lovingly confront them and refuse to permit them to do this.

When both partners protect each other from interference or criticism by parents, it builds an atmosphere of safety and trust in the relationship. However, when one or both spouses will not protect their mates from parents and family, damage is sure to result. Decide right now to honor your spouse and to insist on the same from your parents and family.

Even if it is an unpleasant task, lovingly confront your parents when they violate their rightful limits in your marriage, and do not let them succeed. Without dishonoring them, make it plain that you love them and need them in your life, but they must obey certain rules.

When a child asserts himself or herself properly in this kind of situation, it will usually result in a positive atmosphere of respect that protects and promotes a proper relationship with his or her parents from then on. In the rare cases when a parent refuses to respect the child's wishes, the child must lovingly defend his or her spouse and marriage, even if it means severing the relationship with the parents.

This same principle of protection also applies in your parents' relationships with your children. Your parents' time with your children is a privilege, not a right. So when they expose your child to influences of which you disapprove, they need to be confronted.

If they refuse to respect your wishes, do not let your children be around them without your direct supervision. As a parent, you must not be intimidated, for your children are God's precious and valuable gifts. Whoever they are left with should be someone who respects and supports your values.

To help parents and grandparents understand the importance of this point, here is a helpful resource.

Ten Commandments for Grandparents[1]

1. Thou shalt have no other duties before the care of thy grandchildren when they come to visit thee.

2. Thou shalt not set one grandchild above another lest thou showest favoritism, but let each share equally in thy affection and attention.

3. Thou shalt not bow down to thy grandchildren, letting them get the upper hand, for thy children are conscientious parents who must undo all the poor habits thou hast let thy grandchildren fall into. Rather, spoil them only a little, insomuch as the process is reversible and does not make them sick.

4. Thou shalt not take the name of the Lord thy God in vain, for it is oft said that "little pitchers have big ears," and the Lord will not hold him guiltless who sets a bad example for the younger generation.

5. Remember the Sabbath day to take thy grandchildren to church. Six days shalt thou play with thy grandchildren and take them to Disney World or swimming in the ocean, but the seventh day is the Sabbath of the Lord. In it thou shalt teach them to sing and love the Lord their God with their whole hearts, for in six days hast thou instructed them by precept and deed.

6. Honor the teaching of thy children, thy grandchildren's parents, that the days may be many in which thy grandchildren will be allowed to come and visit thee.

7. Thou shalt not ignore, discourage, nor otherwise neglect or belittle thy grandchildren.

8. Thou shalt not fail to make them feel like important individuals, worthy of thy love.

9. Thou shalt not bear witness of thy grandchildren's misbehavior, but try to solve these problems when they are with thee.

10. Thou shalt not take over nor criticize the discipline of thy grandchildren in the presence of thy children, thy grandchildren's parents, even if thou must bite thine own tongue to keep from doing so.

Number Four: The Principle of Friendship

One of the best ways to relate to your parents is to view them as precious friends. They are special people who committed themselves to you and to whom you are committed for the rest of your lives. They should be a priority to you, someone you spend time with on a regular basis to keep your friendship alive and fresh.

Just as you would deal with good friends if they did something to violate your home and marriage, deal with your parents in the same way. By so doing, you will establish the right spirit in the relationship and avoid an opportunity for wrongdoing on their part, just because they are family.

Concerning parents and in-laws living with you: In some cases, families have to live together for one reason or another; and, although it is not wrong, it normally is a dangerous situation. Unless you know God has told you to do it, and the right kind of relationship exists for it, generally it is not wise to try. However, there is one exception.

The exception to living with parents or in-laws is in the case of their old age or failing health. We owe it to our parents to help them and care for them in their golden years or during times of distress. Although these circumstances do not always mean they should live with you, when parents are in need of care because of sickness or old age, you should do everything possible to assist them.

This honors both your parents and your God. Remember, as your parents and your spouse's parents become older and in poorer health, be sensitive and supportive to them and to one another.

Parents and extended families are such a potential for blessing to a married couple. To experience the most out of your marriage and your broader family, we hope you will set the proper parameters while loving them in a Christlike manner. Remember, God designed marriage to operate in this loving but protected environment.

Note
1. Gloria Glenn, "Ten Commandments for Grandparents," *Pentecostal Evangel,* September 9, 1990.

CONCLUSION

While writing this book, we have wondered many times who would be reading it. Not knowing who you are or where you are right now, we hope you have been blessed by the information presented here. If you are a single person preparing for marriage, we hope you feel better prepared. If you are a divorced person still recovering from the trauma and heartache of the past, we hope you have been healed and encouraged.

Perhaps you are married and struggling with an area or areas of your relationship. If you are, we hope you are struggling less after reading this book. When the Lord healed our marriage, we told Him that we wanted to take the truths He had shown us and share them with others. What a wonderful opportunity writing this book has been to share in detail about the wonderful truths of God's Word.

In closing, we want to share three more things with you, the things I (Jimmy) always tell people as they complete my marriage seminars:

1. Expect Satan

In John 10, Jesus said the enemy only comes to steal, kill and destroy. When God has done something wonderful in our lives, you know the devil will do whatever he can to spoil it. As Peter wrote in 1 Peter 5, be on the alert for Satan's schemes against you and your marriage. Remember, if it was not precious to God, Satan would not attack it. Also remember that the One in you is greater than the one in the world (see 1 John 4:4).

2. Focus on Yourself

Sometimes when people attend my marriage seminars and really get a lot out of them, they will leave making statements like this: "Well, I sure enjoyed that, Peggy. Did you hear what he said about women submitting to their husbands?"

As you can guess, that is not what the information in this book is designed to do. Do not use this material to accuse your spouse, and please do not try to shove it down his or her throat. Pay attention to what God wants to do in your own life, and your spouse will become so curious he or she will read it from cover to cover to find out what is making life around your house so good now.

3. Persevere

On October 29, 1941, Sir Winston Churchill gave one of his shortest and most famous speeches. Here was the content of his message: "Never give in! Never give in! Never! Never! Never! In nothing great or small, large or petty—never give in, except to convictions of honor and good sense."

Those were wise words spoken by a courageous man. The Bible tells us the same thing. If we will keep doing what is right, regardless of what we see or of times of discouragement, God will honor us, and we will harvest the fruit of our labors. If we quit, we have not solved the problems; we have simply delayed or destroyed the harvest.

May God richly bless you!

Appendix I

As we wrote the first chapter about having a personal relationship with Jesus, we realized there might be some people reading this book who either would not know if they had this kind of relationship with Him or would realize that they did not and want to know how they could.

If you are one of these people, to help you have a personal relationship with Jesus, you must understand some basic truths about God and about yourself.

First, God loves you personally. He is with you right now. He also created you in your mother's womb, and He has a purpose for your life. God is not just "a great force in the universe"; He is the Creator of everything but yet a personal friend, who desires to relate to you individually.

Listen to what Jesus says concerning this truth in Revelation 3:20:

> Here I am! I stand at the door and knock. If anyone hears my voice and opens the door, I will come in and eat with him, and he with me (*NIV*).

In this Scripture, Jesus said He knocks on the door of our hearts, waiting to come in. He wants to be the Lord of your life, but He will not come in until you invite Him. Until you ask Jesus into your heart, you are lost and on your way to hell. And when Jesus does not live inside you, you lack the power to live as you should. Therefore, your only hope is to invite Jesus into your life.

We all are sinners in God's sight. We cannot earn His love by doing good things or lose His love by doing bad things. We can only accept His love by receiving Jesus Christ and living in obedience to His lordship. If you will confess your sins right now, God will forgive you. But when you have not received Jesus, your greatest sin is rebellion against God.

As you repent, invite Jesus to come into your life and submit totally to His lordship. Right where you are at this moment, you can know Jesus is in your life by repenting of your sins and inviting Him in. If you are ready to receive Jesus into your life right now, pray the following prayer or a similar one:

> *Lord Jesus, I am a sinner. I have sinned against You and against others. I deserve death and hell. I repent of my sins and renounce my sinful and rebellious lifestyle. I unconditionally surrender my life and every-thing in it to Your authority. I open the door of my heart to You now and invite You to come in. Fill my life, Jesus. Forgive me and cleanse me of my sins by the power of the blood You shed for me on the cross. Fill me now with Your Holy Spirit and give me the power to live for You. By faith, I receive Your forgiveness and Your presence in my life. Thank You for saving and forgiving me. In Jesus' name, amen.*

If you have sincerely prayed this prayer, you now are a child of God. It does not matter whether you feel anything or not. What matters is that you have done what God has said to do. In other words, you have now opened your heart to Him and received Him as your Lord. He said that if you would do that, He would come in. Jesus never lies. He is now in your life.

In order for you to be certain that you have done what is necessary to be saved, consider what the Bible says in Romans 10:9 about salvation:

> That if you confess with your mouth, "Jesus is Lord," and believe in your heart that God raised him from the dead, you will be saved (*NIV*).

According to this Scripture, you must pass a twofold test to know you are saved. First, have you confessed the lordship of Jesus? Have you personally, with your own mouth, confessed His lordship in your life and surrendered to His authority? If you have not, you must do this first before you can be saved.

Once you have confessed Jesus as your Lord, you must believe that God raised Jesus from the dead. In other words, you must believe that Jesus is God and God's Son. He is not like Buddha, Mohammed, and all of the other so-called saviors who are still in their tombs. He is the only true Savior and the only way to be saved. Do you believe this? If you do, and you have confessed Jesus as Lord, congratulations! You are a child of God and Jesus is living inside of you.

Remember, being saved and walking with God daily are done by faith. Ephesians 2:8-9 states this important truth:

> For it is by grace you have been saved, through faith—and this not from yourselves, it is the gift of God—not by works, so that no one can boast (*NIV*).

Our salvation is not because of how good we are or because we have some kind of physical proof that we are saved. Our salvation is because of the death of Jesus on the cross. He paid the penalty for our sins; and in doing so, He satisfied the anger of God toward us.

Therefore, because of Jesus, our sins can be taken away, and we can live in a peaceful, personal relationship with God. It does not matter who we are or what we have done. God has no favorite children. Everyone who accepts and follows Jesus by faith is equal in His sight.

As a new child of God, stand on your salvation and walk with Jesus every day by faith. He wants to have a personal relationship with you beginning right now. Pray to Him daily and seek to know Him through the Bible.

As you do, you will grow in faith and in your personal knowledge and love for Him. Also, refer to the next appendix for more information on how to grow in the Lord and deepen your personal walk with Him.

Appendix II

In the first chapter and throughout this book, we have mentioned the fact that only Jesus can meet our deepest needs. Here are some suggestions on how to practically seek Jesus each day and get everything you can out of your Christian walk. We are listing seven foundational stones for a lasting and fulfilling relationship with the Lord.

As we have walked with the Lord personally and have witnessed thousands of other Christians succeed and fail in their faith, we have noticed these seven qualities mark a solid and fulfilling personal relationship with Jesus.

1. Prayer

Take time each day to pray. We believe the best time to pray is in the mornings. If you need help in understanding how or why to pray, there are many valuable resources available at your local Christian bookstore.

2. Bible Reading

Read God's Word daily. You need a Bible translation that you can understand, of course. Personally, I (Jimmy) like the *New American Standard Bible*, the *New International Version*, and *The New King James Version*.[1] All are readable translations.

I use a daily Bible-reading plan called "The Victory Bible Reading Plan"[2] to tell me where to read every day. I like it for several reasons. First, I like it because I can read through the Bible in a year by reading about 20 minutes a day. Second, I like it because I do not have to find a place to read on my own. Third, by this plan I read in both the Old and New Testaments every day. I would highly recommend this plan to you.

Get this or some other plan to help you and encourage you to read and study the Bible. We have never known a strong Christian who did not pray and read the Bible regularly.

3. Be Constantly Filled with the Holy Spirit

Read what Jesus said about the Holy Spirit in John 14-16 and also in the first chapter of Acts. Jesus told His disciples it was better for them if He went away, because then He would send the Holy Spirit to be with us forever. Jesus said He would empower us, teach us, lead us, help us, comfort us, and remind us of Him. All of this powerful ministry of the Holy Spirit takes place as we seek Him and invite Him into our lives each day.

4. Fellowship

In order to walk with Jesus successfully for a long period of time, find a Bible-believing church that is excited about Jesus, and then get involved. Attend worship services regularly and become a part of a Sunday School class or a home Bible study group where you can build friendships and deeper relationships with people who love the Lord and who can encourage you in your faith.

5. Witnessing

One of the greatest ways to keep what God has given you is to give it away. Pray and look for opportunities to share your testimony about Christ with others. The more you talk about Jesus and share Him with others, the more real and exciting your relationship with Him will be. When you do not talk about Jesus or openly share what He has done and is doing in your life, you will soon begin to lose your enthusiasm as well as the freshness of your relationship with Him.

6. Serving

Without neglecting your personal relationship with God or your family, find a way to serve every week in your church or in some type of Christian ministry. You just cannot imagine what God will do in your life as you begin to use the blessings and gifts He has given you. Jesus never is as real as when we meet Him in the face of "one of the least of these" whom we are serving and loving for Him.

7. Giving

As we stated in the chapter on finances, God promises that He will open up the windows of heaven and pour out a blessing upon us when we give. Give at least the first 10 percent of your income to the Lord, and you will experience His daily presence and provision in your life.

Notes

1. *New American Standard Bible*, copyright © 1960, 1962, 1963, 1968, 1971, 1972, 1973, 1975, 1977 by The Lockman Foundation, La Habra, California; *The Holy Bible, New International Version*, copyright © 1978 by New York International Bible Society, published by The Zondervan Corporation, Grand Rapids, Michigan 49506; and, *The New King James Bible*, copyright © 1982 by Thomas Nelson Publishers, Nashville, Tennessee.

2. "The Victory Bible Reading Plan," Omega Ministries, P.O. Box 1788, Medford, Oregon 97501 (available online at www.the-cutting-edge.org).

ABOUT THE AUTHORS

Jimmy Evans is one of America's leading authorities on family and marriage relationships. He serves as president and co-founder with his wife, Karen, of MarriageToday™, a marriage ministry and national award-winning broadcast television program.

Jimmy's passion for marriage began out of the pain and near failure of his own marriage. As he and Karen both began to study and seek God's help to turn around their troubled relationship, they began to learn key biblical principles allowing God to heal them and build a strong and happy marriage. Realizing that there was a great need in the Church to help other couples who were struggling in their marriages, Jimmy began to counsel couples and lead small-group Bible studies in his and Karen's home. With an obvious anointing to minister to marriages, Jimmy's influence and desire continued to grow—moving from small-group leader to marriage counselor and, eventually, to Senior Pastor of Trinity Fellowship Church in Amarillo, Texas, a church he has pastored for more than 23 years.

During this time, a national marriage ministry was birthed, and the ministry of MarriageToday™ is now in its thirteenth year. Aired nationally to millions of homes each day, Jimmy and Karen share with viewers the practical, biblical truths to build a strong and happy marriage. The format of the *MarriageToday*™ television program is warm and welcoming to a wide range of viewers, and programming includes Jimmy's teachings as well as input from leading marriage and family experts from across the nation.

Jimmy has authored several books and created many seminars and resource materials to help build and strengthen marriages. Some of his more well-known works are *Our Secret Paradise, Freedom from Your Past, The Seven Secrets for Successful Families* and *Resolving Stress in Your Marriage*. He is a popular church and conference speaker.

*   *   *

Karen Evans is a native of Amarillo, Texas, and along with her husband, Jimmy, co-hosts the *MarriageToday*™ television program.

Karen has a passion for marriage and a strong desire to encourage and help couples learn to work through problems so that they can have a loving and fulfilling marriage and family. A committed volunteer for more than 20 years, Karen has served in many areas of ministry. Through Bethesda Outreach Center, Karen served the poor and needy of the west Texas Panhandle by assisting with food and clothing outreaches on a weekly basis. Karen has also ministered as a chaplain at Northwest Texas Hospital. Her love for people and her passion for prayer enabled her to be a strength and a comfort to the ill and to their families during times of stress and crisis.

Karen served in the role of Pastor of Prayer and Director of Women's ministries at their church for more than two years. She has been an active role model and has mentored many young women and helped them to develop Christian character, faith and values—living out the biblical exhortation in Titus 2 that the older women should teach the younger women in the things of God.

Jimmy and Karen have been married for more than 34 years, and they have two adult children and three granddaughters.

MarriageToday™
with Jimmy&Karen

Discover MarriageToday

MarriageToday, founded by Jimmy and Karen Evans, is called to establish, strengthen, save, and restore family and marriage relationships through a biblical message of healing, restoration, hope and encouragement.

We are committed to providing families with the teaching and tools they need to succeed through our TV broadcast, literature, resources, seminars and the Internet. And dedicated people are joining with us in our mission through prayer and giving. We are changing the future of our nation – one home at a time.

Find out more about MarriageToday at www.marriagetoday.org.

An Extraordinary Way to Partner –
An Amazing Resource for Your Marriage!

You are cordially invited to join a very special group of couples who value the teaching and encouragement that comes through MarriageToday, and who understand the power and importance of rebuilding and restoring marriage in America. They are MarriageToday's "Rock Solid Partners" – special people who appreciate the ministry of MarriageToday and want to see it continued and expanded.

What qualifies you as a Rock Solid Partner? A pledge of monthly suport to to help MarriageToday renew, restore, and repair marriages across America.

The benefits of becoming a Rock Solid Partner are numerous. One is a free subscription to the amazing monthly resource we call "Rock Solid Marriage." Each month you'll receive the audio CD with support materials created exclusively for our Rock Solid Partners.

To find out more about The Rock Solid Partners group and the exclusive Rock Solid Marriage resource call, write or click…

MarriageToday™
PO Box 59888, Dallas, TX 75229
1-800-868-8349 —www.marriagetoday.org

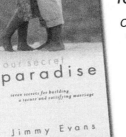